ISBN 978-1-5276-3747-4
PIBN 10877328

1 MONTH OF
FREE
READING

at

www.ForgottenBooks.com

By purchasing this book you are eligible for one month membership to ForgottenBooks.com, giving you unlimited access to our entire collection of over 700,000 titles via our web site and mobile apps.

To claim your free month visit:

www.forgottenbooks.com/free877328

English
Français
Deutsche
Italiano
Español
Português

www.forgottenbooks.com

Mythology Photography **Fiction**
Fishing Christianity **Art** Cooking
Essays Buddhism Freemasonry
Medicine **Biology** Music **Ancient
Egypt** Evolution Carpentry Physics
Dance Geology **Mathematics** Fitness
Shakespeare **Folklore** Yoga Marketing
Confidence Immortality Biographies
Poetry **Psychology** Witchcraft
Electronics Chemistry History **Law**
Accounting **Philosophy** Anthropology
Alchemy Drama Quantum Mechanics
Atheism Sexual Health **Ancient History**
Entrepreneurship Languages Sport
Paleontology Needlework Islam
Metaphysics Investment Archaeology
Parenting Statistics Criminology
Motivational

THE

ALBANY

REVIEW

WITH WHICH IS INCORPORATED

THE INDEPENDENT REVIEW

VOLUME I

APRIL—SEPTEMBER, 1907

LONDON
PUBLISHED BY JOHN LANE
THE BODLEY HEAD, VIGO STREET, W.
1907

RICHARD CLAY & SONS, LIMITED,
BREAD STREET HILL, E.C., AND
BUNGAY, SUFFOLK.

THE ALBANY REVIEW

VOLUME I. APRIL—SEPTEMBER, 1907

INDEX

(Names of Contributors are in Italics)

INDEX

P 231.

THE

ALBANY REVIEW

CURRENT EVENTS

IN January 1906 the nation determined, as never before, to set its house in order. In the spirit of that determination, the ALBANY REVIEW will put the condition of the people in the forefront of its political interests.

Social Reform There is a natural and commendable prejudice —which we share—against reformers who take themselves too seriously. But that does not affect the importance of social reform, which stands out, to those who think, as necessarily the most absorbing subject in politics. It has to do with men and women and children who surround us, whom we daily see, on whom we depend. It is the least abstract and the most human of problems, and those who treat it most adequately are those who keep themselves alive to its tragedy and humour. We are directly responsible for dealing with it, because we possess, in our common citizenship, the special means of doing so; so that it takes the shape, not only of an enthralling study, but of a primary duty which only wilful blindness can ignore. Legislation and personal philanthropy are alike needed. Both these aspects of social effort are represented below. Land reform—the most urgent question of the moment—is treated in a special article. Dr. McCleary, whose work in Battersea and Hampstead is well known, shows what has been and might be done by a system of health-visiting—a subject brought into prominence lately by the remarkable series of articles in the *Tribune* on "The Cry of the Children."

For the moment, however, attention is turned to imperial questions. The Colonial Conference will be rendered doubly interesting by the presence of **The Transvaal** General Botha. The grant of self-government to the Transvaal—one of the great events in our imperial history—is thoroughly in harmony with colonial feeling and with the best traditions of the Empire. Our Imperialists are indeed a peculiar people. They shout themselves hoarse over the acquisition of a new piece of territory or a great display of military force. But when we have accomplished a great act of justice and of faith—when we have established some real claim to that moral hegemony to which they appeal as justifying our expansion—when all the foreign press is astonished that we dare to keep our word, and is speaking of England in terms of generous admiration—they are as silent as if they were ashamed of themselves.

The Colonial Conference is a great opportunity for a Liberal Government. Liberalism—taking that word in its widest sense—has a theory of empire which **The Colonial Conference** corresponds with the actual facts of the British Empire as it is. Its leading principle, so far as the self-governing daughter-nations are concerned, is national independence, just as the leading principle of Unionism is imperial union. Both principles are needed; but it happens that the Colonies regard national independence as by far the most important of the two, not only as the basis of their own free development, but as the surest guarantee of permanent and cordial alliance with England. Thus on practically every question in which the Colonies are interested they must necessarily find the Liberals on their side. On all the important questions which will come up for discussion at the Conference—the constitution of an Imperial Council, the fiscal independence of each constituent nation of the Empire, the right of each to exclude aliens, the right of establishing national defence forces, military and naval, as opposed to the hated system of " tribute "—the Liberal inclination will be towards the complete freedom of each part, while the Unionist inclination will be towards central control. In fact, the sole question on which Liberal policy may come into conflict with Colonial ideas is that of the treatment of weaker races, whether indigenous or alien. It is to be hoped that it will be fully and frankly discussed. Liberals believe, to put it broadly, that white men are capable of self-government, and know what is politically best for themselves. They cannot accept the astounding doctrine so current among the thoughtless, which claims for small, white communities, *in the name of self-government*, absolute control over the destinies of unrepresented persons for whom the Imperial Government has made itself responsible !

It is likely enough that some of the Colonial Premiers —perhaps a majority of them—will put on record a resolution in favour of Fiscal Preference. But those

Preference and Immigration who suggest that this would make the unalterable attitude of the Mother Country appear invidious seem to have forgotten that the position at the Colonial Conference of 1902 was, after all, very much the same as in 1907. Sir Michael Hicks Beach was Chancellor of the Exchequer five years ago, and his views on the Fiscal question were precisely those held by Mr. Asquith now. Colonial statesmen are usually men of business, and we should suppose that the Conference will not devote much of its time to a discussion of the impossible. There is plenty of other work ready to its hand. It is inevitable, for instance, that the claim mentioned above, to prohibit the immigration of aliens, and in particular of Asiatics, will come up for consideration. Fortunately, the very delicate question of the treatment of Japanese subjects under this head is not complicated by any actual influx of Japanese into any part of the Empire. There is no such stream : there is not likely to be any. What the Government of the

3

Mikado asks for, in effect, is the courtesy due to a civilised nation. What our Colonies, or some of them, seek is a guarantee against being exposed to a possible, but not very probable, inflow of coolie labour.

An Imperial Zollverein being out of the question, some attention is likely to be bestowed on that old friend with a new face—a Council of the Empire. The Imperialist movement of the last two decades has had some concrete results, but has brought us no whit nearer the Federation for which Imperialists used to scheme a quarter of a century ago. Neither a Federal Legislature, nor any kind of Central Body with executive powers, is within the horizon of politics. On the other hand, there seems to be a general consensus of opinion that the periodical Conferences, of which this month's is the third, are not only unobjectionable, but are useful and likely to continue. That being so, various schemes are afoot for equipping the Conferences with information and increasing their utility. It is suggested, for example, that the Conferences should not cease to exist after each quadrennial meeting in London; but that the Conference about to meet should remain in permanent existence, its members being the representatives of the British and Indian Governments, and the Colonial Premiers, *ex officio*. As these gentlemen will be scattered about the four quarters of the globe, it is obvious that some central body in London, of a subordinate or ancillary character, will be necessary if this new departure in Imperial organisation is to be anything but a name. So it is suggested that a Commission of experts, with a kind of Bureau of Imperial Intelligence, should be set on foot in the metropolis, whose business it should be to inquire and consider into matters referred by the Premiers. By strictly confining the duties of this Commission and Bureau to the work of inquiry and confidential reporting, the advocates of this plan hope to avoid even the appearance of interfering with Colonial initiative and autonomy. However this may be, it is generally supposed that Mr. Deakin, Sir Joseph Ward, and Dr,

Jameson are more or less in favour of some such scheme; while Sir Wilfrid Laurier is acutely suspicious of setting up any sort of Central Imperial Council, however limited or safeguarded. The subject is one which all parties can afford to debate with patience and good temper, all the more because it is absolutely certain that the Mother Country will not exert the slightest pressure on the Colonies to induce them to commit themselves to this or any other scheme of organisation.

It is now practically settled that the Hague Conference will meet early in June, and as we write the programme is beginning to shape itself. Professor Martens has made his tour of the European capitals with a view to arranging the agenda, and he has discovered that the firm attitude of the British Government has made it impossible to exclude a discussion of the burden of armaments, and of international co-operation for simultaneous reduction. People who think more of the difficulties of diplomacy than the needs of democracy regard such a readjustment as impossible. The democracies do not; and, if they could express themselves, they would soon find a method, rough and ready though it might be, of securing relief. The significance of our Prime Minister's article in the *Nation* (whose appearance as a successor to the *Speaker* under Mr. Massingham's brilliant editorship we warmly welcome) is that he is the first European statesman to challenge the old-fashioned diplomacy, and to voice the great but inarticulate aspiration of the common people. In 1898, as he pointed out, this subject was the first on the programme ; and though no practical understanding was reached it was resolved that a further attempt should be made to solve the problem. Since then, in the Premier's words, "the weight of the burden has been enormously increased," and years have only strengthened the impression that the competitive multiplication of engines of war (growing more costly and destructive every year) is futile and self-defeating. "In regard to the struggle for sea-power, it was suspected (in 1898) that no limits could be set to the competition save by a process of economic exhaustion," unless an international understanding could be arrived at. At the present time there is a sort of understanding that if one power builds two battleships another power must build four or five and *vice versa.* It should be just as easy to arrange that if one power agrees to build only one the other should agree to build only two, and *vice versa.* It is not easy for Great Britain to initiate a discussion upon military expenditure because we are happily free from conscription. But on naval questions all nations look to us for a lead. This is fully recognised in Germany, where such important organs as the *Tageblatt* and the *Kölnischer Zeitung* have given a very favourable reception to Sir Henry Campbell Bannerman's article.

The personal narrative of Madame Savinkov, the first part of which we print below, throws a lurid light on the misery which a foiled and angry despotism can inflict. Such a story of the shattering of a single home gives a tremendous reality to the political struggle that we are watching in Russia. Whatever its ultimate fate, the central fact about the Second Duma is that it shows a majority of 356 against 102 in favour of responsible democratic government. This result, despite furious repression—elections held under martial law, manipulation of the register, proscription of the Constitutional Democrats, and the prohibition of any effective open propaganda—is a striking proof of the political capacity of the Russian people. The new Duma falls into three main groups, a weak Conservative Right in which the organisers of Jewish massacres, who call themselves the Union of Russian Men, predominate, a stronger Centre composed of aristocratic Polish Federalists and Russian Constitutional Democrats, and a very strong Left, which includes Labourists, Peasants, Social Revolutionaries, and Social Democrats. The elections developed an unhappy and meaningless conflict between the Liberal leaders and the Socialists, and M. Miliukoff laid great stress on the anxiety of the Constitutional Democrats to play the part of a genuine Centre. He even made some overtures to the Octobrists—the moderate Conservatives of the Right—

The Second Duma

which were however rebuffed. The Liberal rank and file, however, inclines to the Left, and at the same time the Left itself, with the exception of the doctrinaire Social Democrats, is anxious to work with them. The danger lies in the tactics of the extreme groups of Right and Left—the Social Democrats, who want above all else to bring the middle-class Liberals into contempt, and the violent reactionaries, who hope by provoking the Left to bring about the dissolution of the Duma. The question of tactics appears at the time of writing difficult in the extreme. The Court has given it to be understood that if the Second Duma, like the first, demands an amnesty for political prisoners and exiles, it will be immediately dissolved. M. Stolypin on his side has let it be understood that the same result will follow if the Duma opposes his ukases on the land question. Indeed, the whole official idea seems to be to get a microcosm of the Russian people together in a single building, and to terrorise it there, decorously and without bloodshed. It is of course quite possible that all this talk of dissolution is only vulgar bluff. Russian finances could hardly survive the shock of a second *coup d'état*.

Mr. Haldane's army scheme, which will be discussed in the next number of this Review by Major Seely, M.P., is a vigorous and courageous piece of re-
The New Army organisation. The army is at present organised in three lines: the Regulars, the Militia, and the Volunteers. The Militia play a difficult and demoralising part. They are a Home Army, but they supply drafts to the Regulars. The result is that their battalions are bled and disorganised. Mr. Haldane proposes to organise the army in two lines, consisting of the Field Force and a Territorial Army. The Field Force will number 160,000 officers and men organised in six divisions of infantry and four cavalry brigades. The Territorial Army will reach a total of 300,000 men, and it will be organised n fourteen cavalry brigades and fourteen divisions. The Yeomanry will form the cavalry of this army. The place

at present occupied by the Militia is filled ingeniously by an arrangement for a special contingent of 78,500 men, made up of men who are wanted for mobilisation, but do not need full training. All the objections that can be urged against the efficiency of this contingent can be urged against the efficiency of the Militia. On the other hand, unlike the Militia, the special contingent does not demoralise the Home Army, for it is kept quite distinct. Mr. Haldane proposes to put this new single Home Army under County Associations, which will look after the finance and business, try to work up local enthusiasm, and make provision for the supply of the county's quota of men. The conditions of service in this army are to be made a little stricter : eight days in camp will be accepted, but the whole army will go into embodied military training for six months on mobilisation in emergencies. It is anticipated that part of this Home Army will volunteer for foreign service. It has been suggested that it would be wise to arrange for some proportion at least to be excluded from such service. The general plan of the scheme is excellent, but we very much doubt whether, in the present state of the villages, there is much chance of raising any considerable force from the agricultural labourers. It is Land Reform, and Land Reform alone, that can give us a powerful army of free men.

The serious thing about the Progressive defeat in London is that it denotes the beginning of a class war. **Moderate London** There has always been a slumbering hostility between the working classes on the one hand and the great mass of the middle classes on the other, the latter feeling that the advance of municipal work and municipal efficiency is benefiting the former at their expense. The middle classes, including in that term those employed in business-offices of every kind, are far more numerous in a great commercial centre like London than in any of our manufacturing cities ; and they could at any time have made their power felt had they chosen to organise themselves. The unique feature of the late contest was that this hostility, always latent, was for the first time exploited, at vast expense, by a press and poster campaign such as London has never witnessed before, and, it may be hoped in the interests of decency, will never witness again. With a reforming Government in power, the last hope of all the anti-social interests was to procure a reactionary Council. Never before in England, on a scale approaching this, have companies and firms subscribed large sums to secure political objects. The contribution of the London and North-Western Railway to the London Municipal Society, which has been discussed in Parliament, is but a single instance. Such contributions are open to no other interpretation than a corrupt one. In the case of an individual it is always possible to argue that he subscribes to support his political convictions; but a company as such must clearly be—is, indeed, legally bound to be—guided solely by its material interests. The contest provides food for reflection in many ways. It shows that the cry of " No Socialism " is coming to rival that of "No Popery" in its appeal to the ignorance and panic of large sections of the people. Those who are afraid of any progress in a socialistic direction may be satisfied that there is not the least fear of its travelling too fast. It will always be liable in England to such violent checks as it has just experienced in London. Other causes were, of course, in operation. London is in an economical mood; and, having begun by putting in the Liberals as a protest against Tory taxes, it goes on to put in the Municipal Reformers as a protest against Progressive rates.

The performance of *Hedda Gabler* at the Court Theatre must rank among the important events of the month. It is seldom so remarkable a play is so remarkably given. Mrs. Patrick Campbell's acting of " Hedda " was not one hair's-breadth out. " Hedda," as a character, strikes us as at nce monstrous and familiar. She is a woman who conders herself *déplacée*, not merely by having married out of fast, fashionable set, and taken a humdrum bookish man, vith irritating little habits, for a husband; but one who

Ibsen at the Court Theatre

considers herself *déplacée* in the world itself. She is bored to death, like Madame Bovary—the marvel is that the psychology of Flaubert's famous novel is compressed into this astonishing play—but unlike Emma Bovary having experienced the delights of the children of leisure and pleasure she cherishes no illusions about them. "She has danced till she was tired." The whole of life appears to her mean and wretched, child-bearing a particularly odious humiliation, love a fraud, and even an illicit intrigue too "banal" to have any attraction. She prides herself on her boredom, lassitude and disgust, taking them for signs of an aristocratic spirit, which the experiences of vulgar souls can never satisfy. Living in a permanent condition of sulky conceit, her only pleasure lies in swaggering ; and since her circumstances are too narrow for display, she falls back on inflicting petty humiliations on those in her power, like her aunt Nora. It follows from this sullen arrogance that the one thing she cannot bear the thought of is—humiliation ; hence her dread of scandal, of being mixed up in anything shameful and sordid, like Lövborg's death ; hence the power of Judge Brack's threat to involve her in it ; hence her preference for suicide to remaining at his mercy; hence, too, the explanation of her never having yielded to the attraction of Lövborg or of any other man. Her ruling passion prevents her ever giving herself away. She could only marry a man she despised. This stupid, sullen conceit is like a wall dividing her from life ; she cannot throw herself into anything without dispelling her cherished illusion of superiority ; she is only safe in acting upon others from a superior height. She is envious and loves power; she therefore drags Lövborg down out of a kind of cold malignity, warmed by a little jealousy of Mrs. Elvsted, much as Iago's dispassionate hatred is just touched by a little lust for Desdemona. Like Iago, she is a kind of inarticulate playwright, too stupid to imagine, who gratifies at once a longing for power and a love of excitement by using human beings as puppets. This is the source of Hedda's impulse to make Lövborg drink, that she may see him "with vine-leaves in his hair," and to shoot himself, that she may know that "beautiful actions" are possible.

THE NEED OF THE MOMENT

THE Government is entering upon its period of testing and trial. The first year was of necessity a year of beginnings. Pledges given freely, if a little unwisely, by a party which was a rather forlorn minority in Parliament, and could scarcely believe that anything short of a miracle could restore it to a position of supremacy, had guaranteed the mortgage of the first session to very definite and specific proposals. A Cabinet formed out of ministers, some of whom had been ten years out of office, most of whom had never been in office at all, had a right to demand time in order to know its mind, to ensure smoothness of working, to gain some kind of control over a new House of Commons. The period, though one of feverish activity, has therefore been essentially a period of marking time. There has been no new step forward in social progress. One bill has extended the law of Compensation beyond its position of ten years ago. Another has restored the law of Trade Disputes to the position which it was supposed to hold until less than ten years ago. The Education Bill, made up of compromises, and becoming more and more complicated as the session passed, finally received its quietus from another place. The action of that " other place " has brought to the very forefront of public controversy a Constitutional question which must of necessity overshadow the general work of progress.

But to-day more serious students are considering the new Parliament with the interest which comes from hopefulness not unmingled with hesitation. What great advance in human well-being, in the condition of the masses of the people, or in the established strength and stability of the nation, is to be initiated by the Government of the greatest majority of any time in England's history ? Social reform has been in the air for many years. Leading politicians conclude their speeches with glowing periods concerning the welfare of the people. Many even boldly declare that this Parliament will be more conspicuous for social progress than any Parliament for a past century ; or that, if this social progress be not exhibited, the electors will be right to turn in disgust from a Liberalism which has become barren and sterile, unsuited to the condition of the time. A kind of ground-swell of the great storm of discontent which, under the name of Socialism, is troubling every country in Europe, has reached these islands. It is embodied in a Labour Party, protesting a similar demand for a life more independent and desirable and secure amongst those who gather at the basis of society, and bear the heaviest of its burdens. In a time of tranquillity and order, with the world at peace and an astonishing commercial prosperity, the first really democratic Government which England has seen, backed up by the strongest, most energetic and most loyal democratic majority that the House of Commons can expect to exhibit, is being offered such an opportunity for public service as few ever received in the past, or will ever receive again.

The land is the point at issue. Land legislation is the one thing needful. It is the line of least resistance, in that effort towards more equal distribution of opportunity which is the foundation of any Liberal policy.

In the country, direct access to the land must be provided for those who desire it, by means of compulsory powers of purchase, in the hands of both local and central authorities. A small holding must not be beyond the reach of any man who is willing and able to cultivate it. Rural housing must be dealt with on the lines laid down by the Select Committee of last year. In the towns, the rating of land values is needed, to secure to the community something more of the wealth that its industry has created. Each city must be able to control its own extension, and with the help of a centra department to provide for the housing of its citizens. Local authorities must be empowered to demand a declaration from each owner of the capital value of his land, and either to tax or to purchase it on that value. The whole of these questions are in essence one. The unfettered control of the land by private individuals is a far deeper source of social evil than the unfettered control of workmen by their employers. In less obvious ways, perhaps, but none the less really, it lies at the root of every one of our distresses and discontents. Land reform is the most effective method of dealing with large problems which are difficult to treat specifically in isolation—the problem of the unemployed, the problem of the slum, the problem of physical degeneration through sheer pressure of poverty. And the people are become increasingly alive to the truth. No one will deny it who has seen the way in which popular audiences respond to any sensible presentment of the facts. The unity and strength of the demand will be emphasised by the great demonstration of land reformers of every school which has been arranged for April 20, and which is to be addressed by the Prime Minister and Mr. Winston Churchill.

If the foremost place is here given to the country problem, it is not because the other aspects of land reform are to be regarded as unimportant. It is rather because land reform, supremely desirable as it is for the towns, has become for rural England a matter of life and death.

If the demand is not more definitely articulate, that is the fault of the crushing system which we perpetuate, in which hope has in part altogether died, and in part become an almost aimless desire for any kind of change. In the country districts the rural labourers twenty years ago believed that Government could do something for them. To-day they almost believe that Government can do nothing for them. They have been roused with difficulty, after the long period of acquiescence, once again to throw off the feudal tradition, to fling out of Parliament in scores of county divisions the representatives of the county families, to put in new men, poor men, some of them untried, many of them strangers with no local influences. They have been expecting some nearer prospect of securing the things which they desire. They have been wondering why the time is slipping by, with no attempts made to redeem the promises which were so freely given more than a year ago.

Faint-hearted supporters of the Government are alarmed at the reverse of the Brigg election, at the Progressive defeat in London, at anything and everything which gives an excuse for mild and comfortable courses of action. These things are signs, we are told, that we are going too fast. The explanation is of precisely the opposite kind. If they are signs of anything, they are signs that we are going too slow—that people are disappointed at the little that has been done in a year and a quarter of Liberal predominance, and are ready, in particular, to rally round a Tariff Reformer like Sir Berkeley Sheffield, who puts land reform in the front of his programme.

In rural England we have enjoyed to the full that "idle habit," as a great writer has called it, "which has grown upon us of owning the state of things to be bad, yet doing nothing to remedy it."

Europe has passed through, or is passing through, similar transitions, and has found or is finding its remedies. The nations are there revealed as so fundamentally determined to encourage an independent, free population upon the soil, as to devote time, intelligence, large expenditure towards this one aim. Our colonies have been experiencing similar trials ; and from the menace of the commencement of similar changes in Australia and New Zealand has come far-reaching legislation, designed to encourage the small and independent proprietor or leaseholder upon the land. We alone stand helpless, as if enchanted, wringing our hands over a change which we acknowledge to be disastrous, but which we can find neither energy nor intelligence adequately to combat; although it would seem that here more than in most of the difficult problems which have always troubled mankind or are the product of modern civilisation, there is at least a reasonable chance of finding a solution.

Only in England, weighted with feudal traditions, with so much of its country used (in famous phrase) as the pleasure ground of the rich, instead of as the treasure house of the nation, no similar effort has been as yet attempted. Yet in England also the land hunger has been sufficiently manifest, and the possibility of increased material welfare through its satisfaction. This has been demonstrated in dozens of tiny experiments scattered through the countryside. Up and down the country, and in many cases through the operation (as it seems) of hazard or caprice, villages which have been more fortunate than their neighbours have been given direct access to the soil in small parcels ; on terms other than those of day labourers, working for inadequate wage in the service of others. In these there has been shown the gradual transformation from a community of landless serfs into a community of free men.

The land hunger is not dead in England. Those who so fluently proclaim such a doctrine have not taken the trouble to penetrate below the outer surface of apathy and decay. The people will never come back, so the cry runs, from the fascination of the city life, the cheap music hall, the lighted streets, the insistent presence of the crowd, into the austere life in the vast and empty spaces which make up the deserted countryside of England. That is a generalisation upon *à priori* principle which may or may not be disproved in actual experiment. It is far more an expression of the experience of a cultured and pleasant society at the summit of the urban hierarchy, than any authentic voice speaking from the depths of its abysses.

But however this may be, there are certain obvious facts which no one can deny. The recent report of most careful investigation issued by the Board of Agriculture as a summary of its correspondence from all parts of England, shows that while the demand for allotments is practically satisfied, there is from north and south and east and west a pressing cry for the small holding through which the allotment worker may pass up the ladder of independence. Not indeed on all land, but in districts surprisingly at first sight unsuited, it has been shown in actual fact, where the effort has been tried, that the country population are able to respond to the opportunities offered ; to establish economic security on the soil, to pay their regular rent, to increase in population, to adapt themselves to the necessities of the new agriculture.

From the report of a Conservative Small Holdings Committee, deflected along Liberal and democratic lines, in common with the report of the Select Committee on Rural Housing, which describes in the slum village districts even more appalling conditions of affairs than in the slum areas of the city, there could be fashioned such a large and generous measure of social progress as would ensure a policy not inadequate to the hopes which have been created by the return of this great reforming majority, or to the responsibility which the people have given into its hand.

Here is the line of most successful action in the region of social values. Here also is the line of least resistance in the region of political change. The country districts have come back to Liberalism. Country Liberalism works under enormous difficulties. The pressure of the whole social machine is directed against it. Feudalism, even in the amiable, good-natured form in which it exists at present in the rural districts, can show its teeth when offended. The exercise of its influence was strikingly shown in the last general election, when almost all the Constituencies which had gone Liberal in the bye-elections, swung back into their old position ; and the evidence of the reason for this return to their old allegiance, amid a whole nation which was declaring for the other side, is full of suggestion and surmise.

Vital or not to social stability, agrarian reform is certainly vital to the existence of the party of progress. If it be neglected in the interest of other campaigns, whether against the power of the Upper Chamber, or in favour of measures which only affect the great towns, Liberalism perishes in the countryside—perishes unhonoured and unsung, because it failed to understand the hour of its great opportunity, and was blind to the needs of the time.

And land reform, in its widest scope, including town and country alike, is the true method of challenging the power of the Upper House. All sections of the progressive forces are here united. Town and country are agreed. The most passionate plea for a land policy comes from those in the cities who realise the great possibilities of a home market for the town products which would be given by a revived agriculture established in modest comfort upon the soil. Labour men and Liberals are here united. It is a Labour leader like Mr. Keir Hardie who is most insistent upon the demand for a drastic and far-reaching land policy, as being the most immediate method by which Labour can be directly aided in legislation. Collectivist Liberals and Radical thinkers, divided on many points of municipal development, are united in a policy of land reform; in which the former can approve of progress towards the control by the community over the land in its development; and the latter can welcome that creation of independence, freedom from trammels, and economic liberty, which has been their watchword for more than a century.

There is a grave division approaching in the future between the interests of the middle classes and those of the working classes, which is supposed by many to offer a direct line of cleavage which will shatter the forces of progress into two warring sections. But the middle class in the country can be gathered in entirely upon the side of reform. It is not only the labourer, not perhaps chiefly the labourer, who is found to attempt working upon the land when land is available. It is the many varied occupiers in the village, the small tradesman and the children of the small tradesman, the village blacksmith, the village carpenter, who, as experience proves, are prepared to embark upon the enterprise. And this enterprise when it succeeds, as is revealed in experiment to-day, is bringing prosperity to the middle classes of the village as much as to the working man.

And, above all, this policy offers possibilities of two equally welcome alternatives. Either it will become realised in action, in which case a definite social advance is established by a Liberal Government; or it will exhibit a House of Lords, largely a house of landlords, not, as they at present assert, defending the interests of the people, but solely concerned with maintaining their present feudal traditions and monopoly. If in a large measure of land and housing reform —the two are inseparable—the House of Lords mutilates or rejects such schemes, the nation would be fighting that assembly upon definitely-chosen ground, far more suitable than Temperance, Irish, or Education reform when the appeal comes to the people as a whole. If the Lords refuse the combat on such lines, then the bill will become law ; and the Liberal Government, instead of wasting another session in " ploughing the sands " of sterile deliberation, will be exhibiting to the whole people its capacities for understanding something of the vital needs of this country, and of ensuring that those vital needs shall not go unsatisfied.

There is another point to note, of no small moment to the present Government. They have done nothing this year for the unemployed. The President of the Local Government Board, when challenged in the debate on the Address, argued at length upon the futility of any direct method of dealing with the evil. He declared his conviction that in the provision of small holdings, and especially in the adequate housing of the people in the villages, there would be found means towards a solution. What will be thought of the good faith of his plea, if the session closes without bringing these means within sight ?

A sad commentary on Mr. Burns' argument is supplied by the building trade, which is at the present moment suffering more from unemployment, and showing less power of recovery, than any other. In consequence England presents the astonishing contrast, worthy of the satire of Carlyle, of the trade at one end standing idle because there is no demand for its services; and at the other end, Government Commissions reporting that half the houses in many of the districts of rural England, in their insanitary decay, are a menace to the health of the community and the future of the race.

By an unfortunate coincidence, which might perhaps have been foreseen, but which is now too late to mend, the campaign against the Lords seems about to be opened concurrently with the offer to the people of proposals in the very two directions where legislation is most difficult, and the force of resistance most marked. Temperance reform has always been necessary ; but it has also always been only able to advance by slow, rather difficult, stages. It excites division among temperance reformers. It excites very little interest outside the ranks of temperance reformers. Ireland, again, cannot be neglected, and Irish legislation is a standing dish, whatever party is in power. But the British people, unhappily, take no interest in Ireland except when Ireland is on the verge of revolution. When, as now, the whole nation is orderly and peaceably expectant, and in part orderly because expectant, the great mass of the English electors inquire in tired accents: " Why can't you leave it alone ? " Ireland cannot be left alone. Perhaps Temperance cannot. But taken together they fail to provide the lever or stimulus of a national hope and a national enthusiasm.

In addition to these, however, there is the promise in the King's speech of legislation dealing with small holdings, the valuation of land, and the housing of the working classes. Mr. Balfour's first criticism of that speech was to taunt the Government with the remote place occupied by these measures upon the programme of coming legislation. The first of the official amendments to the Address regretted the abandonment of social reform in the interests of constitutional change and the attack on the House of Lords. It is surely not too late for the Liberal party definitely to accept the challenge thus lightly laid down. If the Opposition demand this social reform, let them have this social reform ; and see how much they like it. No tiny half measures are of the slightest use. Tinkering at a big question merely produces the same volume of opposition as a larger measure, while at the same time it fails to command anything like the full possibilities of enthusiasm and support. The Liberal party has not only to carry a reform which in some small and secluded fashion may be productive of good. It has to reveal itself as a party interested in the social welfare of the people, understanding the large demand which in the name of human progress is being made by the twentieth century for the social welfare of the people ; realising, that is to say, the changing conditions of the world, and showing itself adequate to those changing conditions.

This country is emphatically in a period of transition. The old cries of the age just gone by, if they have ceased to trouble, have ceased also to allure. The new spirit of a people for the first time endowed with some measure of education, for the first time understanding something of the differences between extreme poverty and extreme wealth, and for the first time resolutely set upon a more desirable life for themselves and their children than any they have known in the past, is knocking at the doors of all political parties. The remedy is there if men will take the trouble to study the facts:—experience in this country, experience in other countries, the testimony embedded (perhaps entombed) in Government publications, the changing conditions of agriculture and rural life. No large social reform, indeed, can be easily achieved. If the thing could be effected by the passage of a bill after a few hours' discussion, or by consideration, as it were, between afternoon tea and dinner time, by those who take a languid interest in the subject, the thing would have been done long ago. It is a change which can only be effected by the collective wisdom of the community, utilising every force at its command ; realising that this thing is a matter of life and death ; determined that, despite any kind of opposition, this thing shall come to pass.

It is not hopeless; it is not impossible. The elements are there which can make the new life in England as effectually as they have made the new life in other less favoured countries outside its borders. Let those who will directly work the land have direct access to the land. Let a central government undertake, through organisation and expenditure, to furnish such independent holders with education, and by such assistance in organised industry as a central authority can give. Let the nation, through the local authorities, and through its own Central Department, stimulate the work of building in which private enterprise has failed in the villages. Let the Government, in a word, initiate these large and beneficent social changes this year. They would set in motion forces whose capacity for energy and desirable life few at the present time are able to realise. They would earn the gratitude of those who, in the coming time, when they contrast their own conditions with the testimony of to-day's indignities and oppressions, will rejoice in the benefits which have been won for the enriching of the life of the nation, and the common welfare of its people.

THE LAND QUESTION IN A COUNTRY PARISH

MY object in this paper is simply to describe the economic conditions of a single country parish, here in England, and from the consideration of these conditions to draw some inferences towards our future policy with regard to the Land. In modern life—in every department of it, one may say—bedrock facts are so veiled over by complex and adventitious growths that it is difficult to see the proper and original outline of any problem with which we are dealing ; and so it certainly is in this matter of the land question. Any one glancing at a country village, say in the neighbourhood of London, probably sees a mass of villas, people hurrying to a railway station, motor-cars, and so forth ; but as to where the agricultural workers are, what they are doing, how they live, what their relations may be to the land and the land-owners—these things are obscure, not easily seen, and difficult to get information about. And yet these are the things, one may say, which are most vital, most important.

The parish which I have in mind to describe is a rather large and straggling parish in a rural district, with a small population, some 500 souls, almost entirely agricultural in character, consisting of farmers, farm-labourers, woodmen and so forth, with a few miners and small artisans—on the whole a pretty hard-working industrious lot. Fortunately, one may say, there is hardly anything resembling a villa in the whole parish ; there is no resident squire, and the business man is conspicuous by his absence. The place therefore forms a good example for the study of the agricultural land question. The farms are not over-large, being mostly between 50 and 100 acres in extent. There is just the land, and the population living mainly by the cultivation of it. This population, as I have hinted, is not lacking in industry ; it is fairly healthy and well-grown ; there is no severe poverty ; and (probably owing to the absence of the parasite classes) it is better off than most of our agricultural populations. Yet it is poor, one may almost say very poor. Probably of the hundred families in the parish, the *average* income is not much over £60 a year ; and many, of course, can by no means reach even that standard.

Let us consider some of the financial and other conditions which lead to this state of affairs. In the first place, I find that the inhabitants have to pay in actual rent to their landlords about £2,500 a year. In fact, the gross estimated rental of the parish is about £3,250, but as there are quite a few small freeholders the amount actually paid in rent is reduced to £2,500. Nearly the whole of this goes off out of the parish and never comes back again. The Duke and most of the other landlords are absentees. This forms at once, as is obvious, a severe tax on the inhabitants. One way or another the hundred families out of what they produce from the land have to pay £2,500 a year into alien hands—or averaging it, £25 per family ! and this, if their average income is now only £60, is certainly a heavy burden. No doubt it will be said, " Here we see the advantage of having resident squires. The money would then return to the parish." But would it ? Would it return to those who produced it ? No, it would not. The spoliation of the toilers would only be disguised, not remedied. In fact, let us suppose (a quite ordinary case) that the parish in question were owned by a single resident squire, and that the £2,500 were paid to him in rent. That rent would only go to support a small population of servants and dependents in the place. One or two small shops might be opened ; but to the farmer and farm-worker no advantage would accrue. There might be a slightly increased sale of milk and eggs ; but this again would be countervailed by many disadvantages. "Sport" over all the farm-lands would become a chronic nuisance ; the standard and cost of living, dress, etc., would be raised ; and the feeble and idiotic life of the "gentry," combined with their efforts to patronise and intimidate, would go far to corrupt the population generally. In this parish then, of which I am speaking, the people may be truly thankful that they have not any resident squires. All the same the tax of £25 per family is levied upon them to support such squires in some place or other, and is a permanent burden upon their lives.

Less than a hundred years ago there were in this parish extensive common lands. In fact, of the 4,600 acres of which the parish consists, 2,650, or considerably more than half, were commons. They were chiefly moors and woods ; but were, needless to say, very valuable to cottagers and small farmers. Here was pasture for horses, cows, sheep, pigs, geese ; here in the woods was firewood to be got, and bracken for bedding ; on the moors, rabbits, bilberries, turf for fuel, etc. In 1820 these commons were enclosed ; and this is another thing that has helped to cripple the lives of the inhabitants. As is well known, during all that period systematic enclosure of the common lands of Great Britain was going on. In a landlord House of Parliament it was easy enough to get bills passed. Any stick will do to beat a dog with ; and it was easy to say that these lands being common lands were not so well cultivated as they might be ; and that *therefore* the existing landlords ought to share them up. The logic might not be very convincing, but it served its purpose. The landlords appropriated the common lands ; and during the 120 years from 1760 to 1880, *ten millions of acres* in Great Britain were thus enclosed.

In 1820 the turn of this particular parish came, and its 2,650 acres of commons "went in." I used to know an old man of the locality who remembered when they "went in." He used to speak of the occurrence as one might speak of a sinister and fatal event of Nature—a landslide or an earth-quake. There was no idea that it could have been prevented. The common simply went in ! The country folk witnessed the proceeding with dismay ; but terrorised by their land-lords, and with no voice in Parliament, they were helpless.

It may be interesting to see some of the details of the operation. In the Enclosure Award Book, still kept in the parish, there remains a full account. The Duke of Rutland, as Lord of the Manor, as Impropriator for Tithes, as Pro-prietor, and so forth, got the lion's share, nearly 2,000 acres. The remaining 650 acres went to the other land-lords. Certain manorial and tithe rights were remitted as a kind of compensation, and the thing was done. In the Award Book the Duke's share is given as follows—

		Acres	Roods
1.	"As Impropriator for Tithes of corn, grain and hay ; and in lieu of and full compensation for all manner of Tithes both great and small " .	1381	3
2.	"As Lord of the Manor," and in compensation for certain manorial rights, "and for his consent to the said enclosure "	108	2
3.	"For Chief Rents" amounting in the whole to £14	28	2
4.	"For enfranchisement of Copy-holds "	11	3
5.	"As Proprietor "	18	2
6.	"By sale to defray the expenses of the Act "	449	1
		1998	1

Thus we find, in exchange for the ducal tithes, nearly a third of the whole area of the parish handed over—most of it certainly not the best lands, but lands having con-siderable value as woods and moors. We find some acres adjudged to the Duke in consideration of his kind "con-sent" to the transaction. And most wonderful of all, nearly 450 acres surrendered by the parish to defray the expenses of getting the Act through Parliament ! And now to-day in the said parish there is not a little field or corner left—absolutely not a solitary acre out of all the vast domain which was once for the people's use—on which the village boys can play their game of cricket ! Indeed most valuable tracts were enclosed quite in the centre of the village itself—as for instance a piece which is still called " The Common," though it is no longer common, and many bits on which little cottages had been erected by quite small folk. It would be a very desirable thing that the Enclosure Award Books in other parishes should be investigated, and the corresponding facts with regard to the ancient commons brought to light generally over the country.

A third thing which cripples the agricultural interest very considerably is the incidence of the rates. The farmer's dread of the rates has become almost proverbial. And it is by no means unnatural or unreasonable. For there is probably no class whose estimated rental is so large, compared with their actual net income, as the farmer class. A farmer whose farm, after deducting all expenses of rent, rates, manure, wages, etc. yields him a clear profit of no more than £100 a year for his household use is quite probably paying £70 a year in rent. But a superior artisan or small professional man who is making £150 a year will very likely be only paying £20 in rent. It is obvious that any slight increase in the rates will fall much more heavily on the first man than on the second. The rates therefore are a serious matter to the farmer—and though the late Government did something to alleviate the farmer's share, considerably more ought to be done—especially in the way of shifting the incidence, and distributing the burden more fairly.[1]

As an instance of this latter point, let me again refer to the parish in question. We have seen that some 2,600 acres of common lands passed over to the landlords in 1820, ostensibly for the public advantage and benefit. Of these, at least 1,500 acres of moorland, held by the duke, are rated on an estimated rental of 2s. 6d. per acre. The general

---

[1] I am not here discussing the question of how far a rise of rates falls upon the landlord ; for though this may ultimately and in the far distance be so, it is clear that the farmer primarily feels the pinch, and not till he is nearly ruined is there any chance of his getting a corresponding abatement of rent.

farm-lands of the parish are rated on an estimated rental of 14s. or 15s. per acre on the average. Thus the moorlands are assessed at about one-sixth of the value of the farm-lands. This is perhaps excessively low ; but the matter might pass, if it were not for a somewhat strange fact—namely, that a few years ago when some twenty acres of these very moorlands were wanted for a matter of great public advantage and benefit, that is, for the formation of a reservoir, the ducal estate could not part with them under £50 an acre ; and a little later when an extension of acreage was required, the District Council had to pay as much as £200 per acre ! Now here is something very seriously out of joint. Either the moorlands are worth a capital value of £50 to £200 an acre, in which case they ought to be assessed from 30s. to £6, instead of at 2s. 6d.; or else if the rating at 2s. 6d. is really just and fair, surely it is monstrous that the public having to carry through a most important and necessary improvement should be "held up" and made to pay a ruinous price, simply because the land cannot be obtained elsewhere. The conclusion is, let such lands be rated in accordance with the capital value set upon them by their owners, and we shall have a much fairer and more equitable distribution of the public burden.

And this matter of the moors leads to the consideration of a fourth cause which cripples the land cultivator terribly in this country. I mean Sport. The nuisance and detriment that this is to the farmer has become so great, that unless strict measures are soon taken, widespread ruin will ensue. In many subtle ways this acts. With the enormous growth of wealthy and luxurious classes during the last fifty years, the tendency to turn the country districts into a mere playground has been most marked. The very meaning of the word Sport has changed. The careful working of covers by the occasional sportsman has been replaced by clumsy *battues*, with wild shouts and shrieks of "drivers," and huge slaughter of birds, half tame and specially bred for the purpose. Mobs of people, anxious to appear fashionable, and rigged out by their tailors in befitting costume, are formed into shooting parties. Rich men, wanting to get into Society, hire moors and woods, regardless of expense, regardless of animal slaughter, regardless of agricultural interests, as long as they get an opportunity to invite their friends.[1]   In Devonshire to-day the farms in many parts are simply eaten up by rabbits, because the landlords in order to provide plenty of shooting, insist on spinneys and copses and hedgerows and waste bits being retained in their wild state for purposes of cover !   On the northern moors the rabbits similarly devastate the farms along the moor-edges—not because the rabbits are preserved, for the shooting is mainly of grouse and pheasants, but because, the moors being uncared for except in this way, the rabbits are allowed to multiply without check.   They are the gamekeeper's perquisite.   Yet if the farmer who has a farm adjoining the moor carries a gun to protect himself against their invasions, it is conveyed to him (if a tenant of the same landlord) that he had better not do so, lest he should be suspected of shooting the grouse !   Thus is he paralysed from his own defence. In the parish of which I am speaking there are lands along the moor-edges which used to grow oats and other crops, but which now on account of the rabbit-nuisance are quite uncultivable in that way, and only yield the barest pasture.

In and about 1850, when wheat more than once reached £5 a quarter, the farmers and landlords were doing a roaring trade.   Rents were high, but the land could afford it. Farmers were anxious to increase the size of their holdings, and landlords were not averse to this, as it saved them trouble.   And so set in that tendency to roll small holdings into big ones which continued, with baneful effect, during all the second half of the century.   Sport at the same time came in to increase the action.   It was easier to pacify the few than the many over that matter.   It was simpler to hunt a pack of hounds over two or three large farms than across a network of small holdings.   Besides, the New Rich,

---

[1] The financing of these affairs is funny.   A large moor will let for the grouse season for £3,000, say on the condition of grouse being bagged up to, but not beyond, 2,400 brace.   Mid-week parties hurry in by rail and motor, stay for two or perhaps three nights and hurry off again, to be succeeded by other parties the following weeks.   The whole thing is conducted in the most mechanical way, with " drives," " batteries " and so forth.   And when the expenses are added up, including men employed, guests entertained, and rent paid, they certainly do not fall far short of the proverbial guinea a bird !

as well as the elder gentry, wanted widespread parks, and not a democratic rabble of cottagers at their very doors. And so the game went on. Soon prices of farmstuff fell heavily. But it is easier to get rents up than to get them down again. The alleviations of rent which *have* taken place since 1854 have been only painfully gained and grudgingly yielded. Wheat which was at 100 shillings a quarter then is at 30 shillings now ! And though other farmstuffs have not fallen in like degree, yet during all that period of declining prices, the British farmer has been pinched and pined all over the country. The landlord has been on top of him ; and with holdings often much too large for his need, and a yearly balance too small, he has employed far less labour and tillage than he ought to have done ; his land has lost heart ; and he has lost heart—till he has become to-day probably the least enterprising and least up-to-date of all the agriculturists of Western Europe.[1]

Such are some at least of the causes which have contributed to the decay of agriculture in this country ; and their consideration may indicate the directions in which to seek for a cure.

What is needed, first and foremost, is very obviously security of tenure, under such conditions as shall give both farmer and cottager a powerful interest in the land and its improvement. It is often said, and supposed, that the countryman now-a-days does not care about the land and the rural life, and is longing to exchange it for town life. I do not find this so. I find that he is compelled into town life by the hard conditions which prevail in the country—but not that he *wants* to leave the latter. Indeed, I am amazed at the tenacity with which he clings to the land, despite the long hours and the heavy toil ; nor can one witness without wonder and admiration the really genuine interest which he feels in its proper treatment, quite apart from any advantage or disadvantage to himself. It is common to find a farm-labourer expressing satisfaction or disgust at the good or bad tillage of a field with which he is in no way connected ; or to see a small farmer's son working early and late, perhaps

---

[1] There are many farms of 500 or 600 acres in Gloucestershire only employing five or six hands—or one man to a hundred acres !

up to the age of thirty, with no wages but a mere pittance in the way of pocket-money, and only a remote prospect of inheriting at some future date his share of the farm-stock and savings, and yet taking a whole-hearted interest in the work not really different from that which an artist may feel. There is some splendid material here—in these classes neglected by the nation, and overlaid by a tawdry and cheap-jack civilisation.

I say it is clear that they must be given a secure and liberal tenure of the land, and be free once for all from the caprice of the private landlord with his insolences of politica intimidation and sport, and his overbearance in parochial affairs. The absolute speechlessness of our rural workers to-day on all matters of public interest is clearly, to any one who knows them, due to their mortal dread lest their words should reach the powers above. It has become an ingrained habit. And it has led of course to a real paralysis of their thinking capacity and their enterprise. But place these men in a position where the fruits of their toil will be secure, where improvements can be made, in cottage or farm, with a sense of ownership, and where their vote and voice in the councils of the parish will not be dependent on squire or parson; and the world will be astonished at the result.

There are two main directions in which to go in the matter of secure tenure. One is the creation of more small freeholds; the other is the throwing of lands into the hands of public authorities, and the creation of permanent tenures under them. Though the latter embodies the best general principle, I do not think that forms a reason for ruling out freeholds altogether. In all these matters variety is better than uniformity; and a certain number of freeholds would probably be desirable. In the same way with regard to public ownership, if anything like nationalisation of the land is effected, I think it should decidedly be on the same principle of variety—creating not only State and Municipal ownership, but ownership by County Councils, District Councils, Parish Councils, etc.—with a leaning perhaps towards the more *local* authorities, because the needs of particular lands and the folk occupying them are likely on the whole to be better understood and allowed for in the locality than from a distance.

Let us suppose, in the parish which I have taken for my text, that by some kind of political miracle, all the lands on which rents are now being paid to absent landlords were transferred to the ownership of the Parish Council. Then at once the latter body would come into an income of £2,500 a year. At one blow the whole burden of the rates would fall off, and still a large balance be left for public works and improvements of all kinds. There is no danger of course of so delirious an embarrassment actually occurring! for any scheme of nationalisation would take a long time, and would only gradually culminate; and no scheme would place the whole lands at the disposal of a single body like the Parish Council. But the example helps us to realise the situation. Every farmer and cottager whose holding was under the Parish Council would know and feel that whatever rent he might have to pay, it would come back to him in public advantages, in the ordaining of which he would have a voice; he would know that he would be in no danger of disturbance as long as he paid his rent; and in the matter of capital improvements in land or building he might either make them himself (with the Council's consent), in which case if he should decide later on to quit the holding, the Council would compensate him, knowing that the rental paid by the new tenant would be correspondingly increased; or he could get the Council (if willing) to make the improvement, and himself pay a correspondingly increased rent to the Council for it. In either case he would have as good a bargain, and almost as free a hand, as if he were on his own freehold.

Security of tenure, largely through public ownership, must be one of the first items of a Land-reform programme. Another item, the importance of which is now being widely felt, is the making of some provision for the effective supply of Small Holdings. By small holdings I do not mean small *freeholds*, but I mean *any* holdings, freehold or leasehold, from 25 acres down to one or two acres in extent, each with cottage and buildings attached. Of this class of holding (largely owing to the "rolling up" policy of last century) there is an absolute famine in the land. The demand, the outcry, for them is great, but the supply is most scanty. Yet this class covers some of the most important work of modern agriculture, and a great variety of such work. It includes in its smaller sizes, market gardens, with intensive culture of all kinds, and glass, besides the kind of holding occupied by the professional man or other worker who supplements his income by some small cultivation; and in its larger sizes it includes nurseries, as well as small arable and pasture farms. The starvation that exists to-day in Britain of all these classes of industry is a serious matter.[1]

In the parish with which we are dealing, owing partly to its distance from a market, the demand for such holdings takes chiefly the form of a demand for small arable and pasture farms. But the need of these is great, as indeed it is nearly all over the country. A holding of this kind, of any size from five to twenty acres, forms an excellent stepping-stone for a farm labourer or farmer's son towards a position of independence. A second or third son of a farmer, not likely to follow his father in the occupation of the farm, has to-day only a poor prospect. Unable to command enough capital to stock a large farm himself, and unable to find a small one, he has but two alternatives—to drift down into the fruitless life of the farm labourer, or else to go off and try his luck in town. If, as is most often the case, he is twenty-five or so before the need of making a decision comes upon him, his chances of learning a town-trade are closed, and the first alternative is all that is left. Yet the small holder of this kind is often one of the most effective and useful types of agricultural worker. On a holding, say of fifteen acres, while he cannot get an adequate living for himself and family by ordinary farm

---

[1] It will be said that if there is such a demand for small holdings, the supply will soon by natural laws be forthcoming. But as a matter of fact under our present system this is not so—and for three reasons: (1) The slowness of the landed classes to perceive the needs of the day—even though to their own interest; (2) The want of capital among a great number of them, which makes them unwilling to face the breaking up of large farms and the building of extra cottages; (3) The fact that those who have money are careless about public needs, and do not *want* to see a sturdy population of small holders about their doors.

methods, yet he can gain a considerable amount, which he supplements by working as a useful hand for neighbours at harvest and other times. Being thrown on his resources, and not having *too* much land, he gains more than the average out of it, and his own ingenuities and capacities are developed ; so that, as a rule, he is the most resourceful and capable type of man in the district. It is of the most vital importance to the country that this type of man, and his class of holding, should be encouraged.

There is one method which I have so far neglected to mention by which both security of tenure and small holdings can be obtained—I mean co-operation. The formation of co-operative societies for the purchase of large farms, for the division of them, the building of cottages, and the leasing of the small holdings so obtained, is one of the most hopeful directions for the future. It ought to be easy for the public authorities to lend money on perfectly safe terms for this purpose. What co-operation has done and is doing for agriculture in other countries—in the way of establishing banks, land-holding societies, societies for butter-making, egg-collecting, buying of feeding stuffs and manures, sale of produce, etc., is now perfectly well known. Ireland even has left England behind in this matter ; but England and Scotland will have to level up. Any Government that will rise to a sincere and effective tackling of this land question, including the acquirement of lands by public bodies, their division into small holdings, the provision of cottages, security of tenure, encouragement and assistance of co-operative societies, and a thorough system of agricultural education throughout the country, will have a great and noble programme before it.

One of the very first things, I think, which ought to be taken up is this question of the commons. If ten million acres between 1760 and 1880 passed so easily from the public use into the exclusive hands of the land-owners, surely there ought not to be much difficulty in passing them back again. As I have said, they were appropriated mainly on the plea that being commons they were inadequately cultivated. The main cultivation they have received from the landlords has been of rabbits, grouse and other game! The public has been simply played with in the matter; and agricultural interests, instead of being extended and improved, have been severely damaged. When we realise, in addition to this, that owing to the increase of the general population and its needs, these tracts which passed into private hands with such slender compensation to the public, are now held up at ruinous prices, we realise that it is high time that the game should cease, and that the lands which Parliament voted away from the public in those days should now be voted back again—and with "compensation" on a similar scale. These lands are still *mostly* in the hands of the families to whom they were awarded; and the transfer could perhaps be most fairly and reasonably effected by their simple reversion to the public on the expiration of existing life-interests in them. But of course there would have to be Land-Courts to deal with and compensate special cases, as where the land had changed hands, and so forth.

The value of such ancient common lands to the public would now be very great. Large portions of them would be suitable for cultivation and for allocation in small holdings; the villages would again have a chance of public playgrounds and cricket grounds; the Parish Councils would have lands (so much needed and so difficult to obtain) for allotment gardens; the District Councils might turn many an old woodland into a public park; while the wilder moors and mountains could be held under County Councils or the State, either for afforestation, or as reserves for the enjoyment of the public, and the preservation of certain classes of wild animals and birds, now in danger of extinction.

Let a large measure of this kind be passed re-transferring the main portion of the common lands into public hands; and at the same time a measure compelling owners in the future to declare their land-values, and giving power to the public bodies to purchase on the basis of the values so declared; and already we should have made two important steps towards bringing the land of the nation into the possession of its rightful owners.

EDWARD CARPENTER

33

WAGTAIL AND BABY :

AN INCIDENT OF CIVILIZATION

A BABY watched a ford, whereto
 A wagtail came for drinking ;
A blaring bull went wading through :
 The wagtail showed no shrinking.

A stallion splashed his way across,
 The birdie nearly sinking :
He gave his plumes a twitch and toss,
 And held his own, unblinking.

Next saw the baby round the spot
 A mongrel slowly slinking ;
The wagtail gazed, but faltered not
 In dip and sip and prinking.

A perfect gentleman then neared :
 The wagtail, in a winking,
Rose terrified, and disappeared . . .
 The baby fell a-thinking.

THOMAS HARDY

MARK TWAIN

THE critic's sympathies with the subject of criticism should not be "imperfect," like Charles Lamb's sympathy with the Scottish people. With Mark Twain I am happy to possess many perfect sympathies : on some points I am less fortunate. My first acquaintance with him was memorable, because it illustrated varieties in the sense of humour. I was then an undergraduate, returning from Scotland to Oxford in the same railway carriage with my friend and tutor, Mr. Jowett ; later the renowned Master of Balliol. I bought at a bookstall a cheap little paper-covered book (not impossibly pirated), *The Celebrated Jumping Frog*, by Mark Twain. I opened it, and my conduct for half-an-hour was highly unbecoming a person *in statu pupillari*, who, accompanied by a leader in philosophy and theology, was returning to studious cloisters. I shrieked and exploded with laughter ; my eyes were filled with idle tears of pure mirth ; my gestures were convulsive, and, when I had reached *Finis*, I handed the volume to Mr. Jowett. He read through it with perfect solemnity combined with disapproval, and restored it to me without a word. The Master had humour enough for a whole University, yet he did not see the fun of *The Celebrated Jumping Frog*. He missed the joke which reached me without the aid of a surgical operation. Possibly he was painfully affected by the operation performed on the Frog. *The Celebrated Mexican Plug* affected me, in a room in an austere club, precisely in the same way as the Frog did. Members, disturbed over their studies by my explosions, glowered at

[1] Chapters from my Autobiography, by Mark Twain (North American Review, Sept. 15th, 1906, etc).

me with horny eyes of disapproval. I laugh as I write when I think of that Mexican Plug.

In a graver way my entire sympathies are engaged for

> " All Tom Sawyer did and planned,
> With him of the Ensanguined Hand,
> With Huckleberry Finn."

Tom Sawyer is the Iliad, *Huckleberry Finn* is the Odyssey, of life, not of boy's life only, in the rural Southern States ; with the Mississippi for the Mediterranean. Here we become conversant with great adventures, and yet greater aspirations : here is humour unstinted, and melancholy, and keen observation. Here nothing is stereotyped ; nothing is of convention ; the fun is not forced. At one point I must admit that my sympathies are not perfect—where Mark himself is out of sympathy with his environment. I never read, and never will read *A Yankee at King Arthur's Court.* What has such a one to make with Lancelot and Guinevere, with Galahad and Elaine, and all that gallant fated company of knights and ladies ? Let the Yankee chuckle with Dagonet at the battery : he has no place in the Quest of the Grail. Moreover I prefer Mark on the Mississippi, where he is at home and is perfect, to Mark on the Arno (he complains that there are too many bridges, and does not see that the Florentines are too good to wade). Mark on the Jordan is out of place : there is nothing funny to be made of the siege of Samaria, and the disappointment of " many a shoddy speculator in doves' dung." This kind of joke does not bear sea transport : it loses its qualities like Chianti, if indeed Chianti has any qualities. It looks like the stuff that gave colour to Rosamond's purple jar, which, I think, had the same taste as Chianti. On the other hand, Mark as a philologist, in his Excursus concerning the German language, is supreme, is ineffably excellent. Probably he has mastered German. By me, much as I have been obliged to read the works of German mythologists and Homeric critics, the language remains unmastered ; I find my way about in it doubtfully, like a man in a fog. It is almost, if not quite, as difficult as the Armenian alphabet. Byron tells us that twenty gallant young Frenchmen entered themselves as students in the Armenian convent at Venice. On the tenth day fifteen of the twenty fled ; it was a *débandade*. They had conquered and held the outworks as far as the twenty-sixth letter of the alphabet, and then the word went round *sauve qui peut !* " It is," says Byron, " a Waterloo of an alphabet." The German language is an Armageddon unto many : and they, poor defeated witlings, console themselves by reading Mark's masterly philological thesis.

It was not without trepidation that I opened Mark's romance on Jeanne d'Arc, which happened to appear at the. same time as a kind of novel of my own, concerned with the same heroine. Would he be able to keep his less sympathetic humours out of the tragic narrative ? His sympathy with Jeanne was perfect and entire ; and he, who does not usually plume himself on his erudition, had mastered Quicherat. He did, to be sure, introduce a tumble bug. I am no entomologist, but I doubt if fair France is the habitat of the tumble bug, and wonder what is the French name of that mysterious insect.

On another occasion Mark proved unexpectedly sympathetic. It was in the days of what Mr. Freeman called " chatter about Harriet." The " literary world " was rent by the problem of Shelley's treatment of his first wife ; Professor Dowden's biography of the poet had just appeared ; a valuable work, though the author, in doing his best for Shelley, had aroused Mr. Matthew Arnold to say his word for Mrs. Shelley. Not only Matthew, but Mark took up the bucklers for Harriet, and it is not easy to say which critic was the more acute, and (to friends of Harriet) the more amusing and acceptable. The biographer gave six grounds of offence in poor Harriet, trivialities such as her love of a bonnet, and her waning interest in culture. Mark tabulated the six grounds of offence, and opposite them wrote Harriet's six grievances, the six times repeated name of CORNELIA TURNER. He was perfectly right, the pretty young married woman who read Petrarch with Shelley, and sat up with him deep into the night—because he saw visions when alone !—was a grievance six times greater than all the six sins of Harriet. When it is added that Mark invented telepathy quite independently, and without assistance from Mr. F. W. H. Myers (Mark used the phrase " mental telegraphy "), it is plain that he is indeed sympathetic to this reader of *Chapters From My Autobiography*.

A critic less harmoniously disposed than myself might hint that this Autobiography is neither concise nor systematic ; that recent occurrences appear in the earliest numbers, while remote events are chronicled in the latest chapters that have appeared. This austere critic is met by the author's statement that he has "a deliberate system," "a complete and purposed jumble." When once that is understood, it becomes plain that the autobiographer is a coherent and consistent artist, and that his book, if "a mighty maze," like the universe in the opinion of the poet, is also "not without a plan," "sun-clear to him," like the dodges of Mr. Carlyle's most ruffianly heroes. An American, like a Scot, is full of genealogy, and, like a Scot, Mark opens with "an ell of pedigree." He does not, however, cite the evidence of the charters in his muniment room, but relies on tradition. His ancestors were pirates and slavers, like Drake, Hawkins, and many other gentlemen of England, in Queen Elizabeth's time. One of them was ambassador, the British Ambassador to the Escurial, under James VI. and I., or Charles I. Another, Geoffrey Clements, was a Regicide, "helped to sentence Charles to death," with Mark's filial approval. *Moi aussi*, I have a dim and disliked connection (not by descent, but by affinity), with two Regicides, Harrison and Mayne—my malison go with them ! There are "Clemenses who say they have examined the records," and Mark regards his regicidal kinsman "with pride." There is no accounting for tastes. The pedigree then skips all the generations till it comes to that of the American Civil War. An aristocratic kinsman then bade Mark remember that he was a Lambton (of the Durham family, by maternal descent). He has never forgotten it, but his branch of the Lambtons spell the name "Lampton."

Mark's parents married in 1823, and dwelt first in Tennessee, later in Missouri, where Mark was born in 1835. His father owned an estate of over 100,000 acres. It contained coal, copper, timber, iron, and oil, but, somehow, the entail has been broken, and Mark is a disinherited knight, *El Desdichado*. The value of the principality seems to have been overlooked by the family, except by Mr. James Lampton, Mark's uncle, the original of the honest, kindly and imaginative Colonel Sellers, in *The Golden Age*. Mark named the hero of the novel Eschol Sellers, thinking that no man's feelings could be hurt, but a Mr. Eschol Sellers in the flesh turned up and protested. There was nearly as much trouble with him, as a Captain M'Turk gave Scott on account of the Captain M'Turk in *St. Ronan's Well*.

The author of this autobiographical epic has already wandered from *Les Enfances Marc*, and we next find him dealing with his literary adventures in 1867. Thence he arrives by a retrograde movement, at his boyhood in 1849, when he dwelt in Hannibal, a city of the Missourians. His adventure with two young ladies who were unconsciously dressing in a room where he, unbeknown, was attired as a brown bear, a character in a domestic pantomime, is a good story, but rather long. Mark, like his brother Orion, had all Tom Sawyer's love of public notice. Failing to acquire histrionic renown as a brown bear, he ascended the platform of a lecturer in Hypnotism, and was a prize sample of supernormal obedience to unuttered commands. There was no hypnotism and no telepathy in the matter. Mark did any wild thing that came into his head, and then the lecturer explained that the feats were what he had silently " willed " him to do. The trick was never discovered, and when, long afterwards, Mark made a clean breast of it to his mother, she utterly refused to believe him. Nay, more, by brilliant dialectic she proved that the feats had been " honest Injun " ; the disclaimer came from the forked tongue of the Pale-face.

Mrs. Clemens' argument was based on a fact well known to psychical researchers. Some persons, if they see a spook, or dream a dream that is fulfilled, greatly exaggerate the facts, and richly embroider them, as time goes on. Their memories unconsciously magnify the adventure. Another class of minds as regularly minimise the adventure, and end by disbelieving in it. Lord Chesterfield said that if a man in

London rose from the dead, the Archbishop of Canterbury would disbelieve the fact before the end of the week. Mark's mother argued that he was like the Archbishop of Canterbury, or worse. In the course of thirty years he had come to disbelieve in his own miracles. The best had been a vision which he announced at the moment when a Dr. Peake entered the lecture hall. He "saw," and described in detail, a terrible fire which had deeply impressed Dr. Peake thirty-six years before Mark was born. Dr. Peake leaped up, " No collusion," he cried, " could produce that miracle." Now Mark had heard, unobserved, Dr. Peake describe the whole scene, two years before the night of the meeting at the lecture on Hypnotism. So much for public hypnotic marvels ! But Mark's performances are still matters of faith in Hannibal. " Carlyle said 'a lie cannot live.' It shows that he did not know how to tell them."

As far as the published Autobiography has gone, Mark tells us nothing about his education. The flight of the Autobiography, however, is as the flight of the boomerang, a thing of loops, and recurrent curves ; it may touch on the author's education later. But perhaps to give detail is superfluous : Mark was the original from whom he drew Tom Sawyer, and about Tom Sawyer's school-days we have abundant information. That he learned much Latin is improbable, and there are traces in the Marcian writings of but little knowledge of Greek. Mark was Tom Sawyer : he confesses to it, and what Tom learned, Mark learned. He nowhere gives us an account, to my knowledge, of his later literary studies. Who are his favourite poets ? What are " the books that have helped him " ? He has an enthusiasm for Shelley, so he must have read Shelley ; he has an enthusiasm for Jeanne d'Arc, and he has read Quicherat, in whose five stout volumes there is a great deal of Latin and of French. Beyond these facts, Mark's historical and literary studies remain to be revealed. Certain it is that in the course of his varied career he must have perused enormous quantities of journalism. His brother, Orion, by ten years his senior, was a printer. " Out of his wage he supported my mother and my brother Henry, who was two years younger than I," and who was the Sid of *Tom Sawyer*; the good boy who gets into trouble with Tom, not with his aunt. Mark, on his father's death, left school, and went as an apprentice into the office of *The Hannibal Courier*. The life was of a Spartan severity. In 1853, Mark, aged seventeen, fled to St. Louis, worked as a compositor in a newspaper office, and then came his *Wander-jahre*, still as a printer, to New York and Philadelphia. He then joined Orion, and worked in his little job office, a printer's office, in a city named Keokuk. He next tried Cincinnati, and was on his way to make a fortune in the cocoa trade—on the Upper Amazon—when he fell in love with the art and science of piloting a Mississippi steamer. Who that has read this account of his career does not envy him?

Meanwhile Orion had deserted printing for the Bar, where he was among the briefless. In 1861 a friend procured for him the post of secretary of the Nevada Territory, whither Mark accompanied him with all his capital in silver dollars. After prospecting for more silver, in its native rock (if silver grows in rocks: I am no geologist), Mark tried that refuge of the versatile, journalism, in Carson City (1863).

Here, thanks to the original method of the Autobiography, I lose the author for a while, but entertain the opinion that he contributed to the press in San Francisco and elsewhere. Anxiety for the freedom of the press, doubtless, caused him to write articles in which Liberty expatiated, and Truth, with her eye on political opponents and professional rivals, walked abroad undraped. The result was a challenge, but neither of the principals was anxious to shed blood, and a trivial incident served to stop a hostile encounter. The story has been told before. It involves the shooting, by Mark's second, of a small bird, at thirty paces, with a revolver. Artemus Ward was the pilot of Mark into the open waters of literature. Mark had told him (1865 ?) the story of *The Celebrated Jumping Frog*, and Artemus asked him to write it, and give or lend him it to pad out some book of his own. The publisher of Artemus, a Mr. Carleton, took Mr. Jowett's view of the Frog, and gave that immortal creature to the editor of a dying newspaper. The piece was quoted in the press of the English-speaking world, and Mark offered a collection of short tales to the unsympathetic Carleton. He declined the offer, and a Mr. Webb published the collection, " on a ten per cent. royalty." The results may have made up for the loss of the oil and minerals on the paternal estate. Yet it was with great difficulty that publishers were induced to launch *The Innocents Abroad*.

We have followed our author as closely as his system of writing autobiography permits. Several of his chapters contain matter of a nature too intimate, and too touching for comment ; or, at least, for comment by one who has had, even in a slight degree, the privilege of being acquainted with the lost kinsfolk who are commemorated.

"Mark's Autobiography," he says, " can never reach an end while I am alive, for the reason that, if I should talk two hours a day to the stenographer for a hundred years, I should still never be able to set down a tenth part of the things which have interested me in my lifetime." Arithmetical computations equally prolonged could not ascertain the number of people whom he has interested, amused, and delighted. Mark has usually a kind word for most conditions of men, but has the rare peculiarity of not liking reviewers. He expresses himself thus: "A generation ago, I found out that the latest review of a book was pretty sure to be just a reflection of the *earliest* review of it; that whatever the first reviewer found to praise or censure in the book would be repeated in the latest reviewer's report, with nothing fresh added. Therefore more than once I took the precaution of sending my book, in manuscript, to Mr. Howells, when he was editor of the *Atlantic Monthly*, so that he could prepare a review of it at leisure. I knew he would say the truth about the book—I also knew that he would find more merit than demerit in it, because I already knew that that was the condition of the book. I allowed no copy of it to go out to the press until after Mr. Howell's notice of it had appeared.

" I believe that the trade of critic, in literature, music, and the drama, is the most degraded of all trades, and that it has no real value—certainly no large value. When Charles Dudley Warner and I were about to bring out *The*

Gilded Age, the editor of the *Daily Graphic* persuaded me to let him have an advance copy, he giving me his word of honour that no notice of it would appear in his paper until after the *Atlantic Monthly* notice should have appeared. This reptile published a review of the book within three days afterward. I could not really complain, because he had only given me his word of honour as security ; I ought to have required of him something substantial. I believe his notice did not deal mainly with the merit of the book, or the lack of it, but with my moral attitude toward the public. It was charged that I had used my reputation to play a swindle upon the public ; that Mr. Warner had written as much as half of the book, and that I had used my name to float it and give it currency ; a currency—so the critic averred—which it could not have acquired without my name, and that this conduct of mine was a grave fraud upon the people. The *Graphic* was not an authority upon any subject whatever. It had a sort of distinction, in that it was the first and only illustrated daily newspaper that the world had seen ; but it was without character ; it was poorly and cheaply edited ; its opinion of a book or of any other work of art was of no consequence. Everybody knew this, yet all the critics in America, one after the other, copied the *Graphic's* criticism, merely changing the phraseology, and left me under that charge of dishonest conduct. Even the great Chicago *Tribune*, the most important journal in the Middle West, was not able to invent anything fresh, but adopted the view of the humble *Daily Graphic*, dishonesty-charge and all."

In this country (though even here unkind things are said about reviewers) nobody can accuse them of being unanimous in their verdicts.

ANDREW LANG

THE LORDS AND THE REFERENDUM

MR. J. A. HOBSON'S recent advocacy of the Referendum or popular vote as a solution of the House of Lords problem was so able and persuasive that one hesitates to oppose so specious a presentment of the case for direct democracy. But it is impossible to remain silent on a proposal which, beneath so fair an exterior, contains so many hidden dangers to the good government of this country.

Even Mr. Hobson gradually ceased in the course of his article to maintain as his chief argument for the Referendum that it will solve the question of the House of Lords. He perceives, of course, that to place in the hands of the House of Lords as at present constituted the power of compelling a Liberal Government to take a popular vote on every Bill with a disputed mandate would be to multiply the power of that House indefinitely. If the mandate of last year's Education Bill could be disputed, then no Bill is safe ; and we can take for granted that the number of popular votes under a Liberal Government would precisely equal the number of Liberal measures sent up to the Lords. In other words, Liberal government would be impossible : for no modern country could endure the expense and unrest of what would practically amount to an incessant general election.

To meet this difficulty Mr. Hobson holds out to us the prospect that probably the first measure under the Referendum would be a reform of the House of Lords. "One of the first and most important uses which a Liberal Government could make of the Referendum Act would be to reform the constitution of the Upper House, by forcing through a Reform Bill which the Lords would now be impotent to stay." There are those among us who see nothing in the present House of Lords on which you can build a reform—who believe that if you want a new Second Chamber you will have to start completely afresh, lock, stock, and barrel. But, putting that aside, does not the procedure become rather cumbrous ? First there is to be a Referendum Bill charged with a clearly-designed doom, which the Lords, being human, will resist to the uttermost. It is the wooden horse of Troy with a label affixed— "There are soldiers within." The Lords will reject the Bill, and you will have next to dissolve on the Referendum issue. Assume that you are again returned to power. Then, having carried your Referendum Act—perhaps by a creation of Peers—you will have to begin afresh with a new Referendum on the constitution of the House of Lords. If you are beaten, the House of Lords will emerge stronger than ever, with the added power of forcing you to endless Referenda if you should ever revive from your present defeat. If you win, you have to shoulder the task of re-constituting an assembly that will always be able to fire at you the new weapon with which you have armed them. The prospect is appalling. It would require a Tithonus to face it. And at the end of it where would be the British House of Commons ?

If you want a reply to this question you have only to look to Switzerland, the paradise of the Referendum. It is possible to share Mr. Hobson's admiration for that splendid little democracy, the one thing in the modern world which constantly reminds one of the best kind of Greek state, without in the least degree blinding oneself to its one clear and undeniable feature. The Referendum has entirely destroyed the prestige and power of what corresponds in Switzerland to our House of Commons—the Nationalrath, or National Council. A council that legislates under a storm of popular buffets—that undertakes every measure under a depressing sense of possible popular censure—cannot maintain the prestige of a great assembly. The logical course would be to abolish the Swiss National Council altogether, and have an ecclesia, or assembly of all enfranchised citizens. That is forbidden by the dividing mountains. So there has to be the farce of sending to Berne from the cantons every three years 167 representatives of the Swiss people. But under the amended Constitution of 1874 any 30,000 citizens may demand a Referendum by signed petition on any Bill of the Federal Assembly, while under the original Constitution of 1830 any amendment of the Constitution must compulsorily be submitted to Referendum, whether demanded or not. Since 1874 there has been under these two heads an average of nearly two Referenda a year. The rejections of Bills have been nearly twice as numerous as the acceptances. More than once a year, then, the Federal Swiss Government has been censured by the popular vote. According to our theory, no Government so censured could survive. But it has been plainly impossible that the Swiss Government should resign once or even twice a year. So the Swiss Governments have remained on and humbly readjusted their Bills, while the Federal Assembly has inevitably fallen more and more into the position of a body of most obedient servants to the Swiss people.

That result does not so much matter in Switzerland, where the only real political entity is the little democracy of three million self-reliant, self-contained, highly-educated. mountaineers. Switzerland, fortunately or unfortunately for herself, has no empire. Being neutralised by the consent of the chief Powers of Europe, she has no foreign policy. Her sole task is to govern herself. Not so very simple a task in a country of twenty-two sovereign cantons, sundered by snow and ice, speaking three languages, and professing two religions. It is a people in which the passion of self-government is as deeply rooted as the power of self-control.

The custom of government by assembly is there fixed in the customs of the past. It has been handed down, probably, from early Teuton ancestry. In some cantons it survives to-day in the form of the interesting Landsgemeinde, open-air assemblies of all the citizens which positively transact all the business of the communes, whose manhood they actually are. The great administrative problem of Federal government in Switzerland is to obtain the working consent and agreement of these scattered communities throughout the various valleys that make up Switzerland. That has been achieved by the Referendum.

The Swiss have probably been quite right in their choice. But, once more, it is necessary to bear in mind quite clearly the price they have paid. They have sacrificed the possibility of developing a ruling class. A Federal Assembly that has to prepare its measures under the shadow of a popular guillotine of that kind cannot enjoy the freedom of action or sense of responsibility that moulds and shapes the characters of public men. On the contrary, they will probably develope a habit of submissiveness verging on subserviency. They will, above all, stick to their places. The few independent men will rebel against such a system as intolerable, just as the Radicals in the Swiss Council rebel against the Swiss Referendum.

It is, perhaps, useless to add that the party system under the Referendum becomes impossible, for Mr. Hobson might possibly put that forward as its chief merit. But it is at any rate interesting to observe that in Switzerland the development of the party system has been entirely checked. Cabinets are formed out of both parties together. Public men, we are told, are chosen largely for their private characters. It is needless to turn out a party on the ground of political disapproval, when you can easily express that at a subsequent Referendum. The real politics of Switzerland centre round these popular votings on specific measures, and the proceedings of the Council are languidly watched and badly reported.

Transfer the same situation to this country, and see how it would work out. We have a great empire to be governed; and it is at present governed largely through and by responsible public men in the House of Commons. Weaken that authority, and the government of the empire must fall into the hands of a bureaucracy. Faced with the accomplished fact of a hostile popular vote, a Government would have to choose between two alternatives. It must either go on or resign. If it always resigned, stable government would be impossible. If it went on, then its prestige would be weakened, and would become weaker with each repetition of the process. The Referendum in Switzerland has nothing to do with any differences between its two Houses, which are adjusted with the characteristic phlegm and patience of the Swiss nation. It is the recognition of the right of direct government, existing already in all the principal cantons, and extended to the Federal Assembly as the result of cantonal suspicion. It is the popular veto on a selected governing class—the refusal to delegate its own government on the part of a people with an intense interest in its affairs and a very high political intelligence. It is directed not against the Upper House, but the Lower. It is a protest against the rule of Parliament. The Referendum would have the same effect in England. It would not weaken the House of Lords; it would simply destroy the House of Commons. And by that destruction it would scatter both parties to the winds, and vitally change, if not entirely undermine, the government of the empire.

But Mr. Hobson faces those possibilities with a cheerful gaiety. He does not profess to love or trust the British House of Commons. He has a rooted suspicion of the British Cabinet, though that is practically a creation of Parliamentary opinion. He has his eye on the inner Cabinet, a creation of the Cecil family which has virtually ceased to exist under the present Administration. Above all, he does not believe in the British Empire. His ambition for England is very much that it should become another Switzerland, self-contained and happy within its silver seas, and developing its political intelligence throughout the land by constant discussions and decisions on high political affairs.

The ideal is not without its attractiveness. It has its origin in the teaching of Jean Jacques Rousseau, himself a Swiss. It fascinated some of the best minds during the French Revolution. The still-born French Constitution of 1793 contained one of the best thought-out schemes for government by Referendum that has ever been placed before the world. France has suffered so much since that date from plébiscites of one kind and another that French public men have now gone to the other extreme. The Referendum has now few followers in France. But to us in England it has all the fascination of the untried and the unknown. It attracts Conservatives because, as Mr. Hobson points out, the results in Switzerland have been uniformly on the side of conservation. It attracts democrats because it seems the logical result of their ideal. But there is a logic of practice as well as a logic of words ; and the one often defeats the other. History and experience alike teach us that by laying too great a strain on the faculties of a democracy you may round the circle and complete your journey in full and complete autocracy.

It is only too probable that we should have some such result in England. Already the burden of elections lies heavy on the land, and it becomes increasingly difficult to get people to vote. We feel fortunate if, even in so sensational an election as that which has recently taken place in London, we can persuade half the electorate to come to the polls. What would happen if we had two national popular votes—call them Referenda or Dissolutions, it matters little —every year ? They might have some educational value, though quite as much would be lost by the consequent decline of debating power in the House of Commons and the loss of interest in big popular speeches. But the difficulty of explaining all the complex questions that arise in so great an empire—the immense and constant strain placed upon the mind and attention of a busy democracy—would inevitably lead to failure and disillusionment. The means would defeat the end. Even in Switzerland, with her smaller range of questions, close observers tell us that the system lays too great a strain on the people. They cannot grasp the issues, and consequently tend to follow the practice of giving the benefit of the doubt to the existing order. There is no adequate discussion ; no reason has to be given for the vote ; laws cannot be amended by the Referendum, but must be accepted or rejected *en bloc*. So there is a frequent failure of judgement.[1] But if that is so in Switzerland, how would it be in Great Britain with all the vast problems that arise from the government of an empire of 450,000,000 souls ! The strain would be intolerable. A

[1] See M. Signorel's *Étude de Législation, Comparée sur le Referendum Législatif* (Arthur Rousseau. Paris, 1896).

people so harassed would gladly hand itself over, as France handed itself over in 1851, to the first specious and plausible despot that came along.

The problem of government in this country is totally different from the problem in Switzerland, and therefore the lines of evolution have been in entirely opposite directions. The problem in Switzerland has been one of simple communal self-government—a community of little scattered hamlets sheltered from the outer world by a special international provision, and anxious that the national tie should be as weak as possible. The result is that the canton has been given the smallest possible power over the commune and the Federal Government as little as possible over the canton. But in this comparatively great country of ours, with its population of 40,000,000, and its great destiny of world-rule, the whole effort has been to evolve a strong central government. The problem has been to make that consistent with liberty, so often threatened in the process. The solution has been found in the representative system, which has given us the House of Commons. It would be impossible to hope that that body should always exactly represent the will of the nation throughout every septennial period. If there is a case for reducing that period, let it be reduced. But do not let us in our perplexity about the House of Lords adopt a method which will surely undermine the whole foundation on which the House of Commons rests. Let the Referendum be adopted freely in local affairs ; extend, as the Americans are extending, the principle already recognised in our Libraries Act to many other forms of local government, especially to licensing control. There the process has a real educational value. But for Imperial rule we must have an Imperial Parliament, and a trained set of rulers willing to accept responsibility for their actions. Our empire exists, and we cannot get rid of it. The problem of the moment is not to increase the burden of an already over-burdened democracy, but to simplify and quicken procedure, even if the only weapon at our hand is government by a single Chamber.

HAROLD SPENDER

RITUALISM AND DISESTABLISHMENT

THE title of an article should be short, and in the words at the head of this paper I have endeavoured to condense the task which the Editor set me. That task was to examine the *Report of the Royal Commission on Ecclesiastical Discipline* (1906) and then to estimate its bearing on the question of disestablishing the English Church. This, briefly stated, amounts to what I have called "Ritualism and Disestablishment."

Whatever else may be said or thought about the Commission on Ecclesiastical Discipline, this at any rate is certain—that its authors and promoters did not intend it to help the cause of Disestablishment. It was devised in the first instance to deliver a Gallio-like Minister from a parliamentary embarrassment, and it was enthusiastically adopted by the persecuting party in the Church, in the hope that it might enable them to destroy the outward and visible manifestations of a faith which they detest. When, in 1874, Archbishop Tait introduced his Public Worship Regulation Bill, with infinite palaver about paternal authority and proved abuses and peaceful reforms, Disraeli brushed aside all the flummery and exposed the naked truth —"This is a Bill to put down Ritualism." For "Bill" read " Commission," and you have the exact account of the Royal Commission on Ecclesiastical Discipline. It should be observed that no attempt was made to preserve even a semblance of impartiality in the selection of the Commissioners. The wretched Ritualists, whose alleged misdeeds were to be examined, and, if possible, punished, had not a single friend among the inquisitors appointed to harry them. The Commission was packed with Low Churchmen and Broad Churchmen (to use the traditional nicknames), and among these were included, in a minority so small that it could do no harm, three moderately High Churchmen. Ritualist, or friend of Ritualism, there was none. This studied and scandalous onesidedness, contrasting forcibly with the principle on which all similar Commissions in the past had been formed, has elicited an important protest from one of the judges of the High Court. Addressing a meeting of the English Church Union on the 23rd of January last, Mr. Justice Phillimore said: " The constitution of this last Commission was much less favourable to us than that of the Ritual Commission (1867), or, indeed, of the Ecclesiastical Courts Commission (1881). On the Ritual Commission the English Church Union had a member, Canon Perry ; in the late Commission, none. . . . Mr. Talbot, in the late Commission, may well represent Mr. Hubbard, or perhaps Mr. Beresford Hope in the Ritual Commission. Other sympathisers we had none." Even so, I think, Mr. Justice Phillimore concedes too much. Mr. Talbot, whose judicious moderation we all respect, seems scarcely to represent the founders of St. Alban's, Holborn, and All Saints, Margaret Street. If I were a Ritualist, I should omit the " other," and say " sympathiser we had none." This being the case, it is all the more remarkable that this Commission, appointed in the hope of alarming the nation about the virulence of Ritualism, and so packed and engineered, as, if possible, to justify persecution, was driven to record its conviction " that the evidence gives no justification for any doubt that in the large majority of parishes the work of the Church is being quietly and diligently performed by clergy who are entirely loyal to the principles of the English Reformation as expressed in the Book of Common Prayer." This being so, it might be reasonably asked, " What bearing has this report on Disestablishment ? " The Commissioners admit that the complaints laid before them relate only to a " small proportion of the 12,242 churches in England and Wales." If, in all the rest, " the work of the Church is being quietly and diligently performed by clergy who are entirely loyal to the principles of the English Reformation," what reason can there be for disestablishing such an orderly, diligent, and Reformation-loving Church ?

Perhaps some answer to this question may be found in the Minutes of Evidence laid before the Commission. It is difficult to grasp the effect which that evidence may produce on the mind of the Man in the Street. George Eliot observed, with cruel truth, that " the depths of middle-aged gentlemen's ignorance will never be known, for want of public examinations in this branch." A public examination in which the subject-matter should be the Church, its nature, its work, and its ways, would disclose some serious gaps in the knowledge of even educated men. Mr. John Morley, unexpectedly taking a hand at " No Popery," justified his plea for the Education Bill by dark allusions to mysteries of evil which the Report of the Commission would disclose ; and, when so experienced a publicist is scared, one can picture the perturbation of the Man in the Street, whose ignorance of the Church and the Prayer-book is only equalled by his ignorance of the Bible. If Mr. Bottles, for so Matthew Arnold named him, reads the evidence given before the Commission, he will discover, to his infinite astonishment, that the English Church enjoins a great quantity of ceremonial, permits more, and by implication suggests more still. He will further learn that no single clergyman obeys, or can obey, every rubric with literal exactness, and that High, Low, and Broad Churchmen alike are forced to offend against strict legality. Furthermore, he will learn that a few clergymen think fit to practise ceremonies which the Prayer-book does not sanction, but which they have seen, and thought edifying, in foreign churches. He will learn also—and this will astonish him more than anything else—that Ritualistic clergymen are enthusiastically and doggedly supported by their congregations, and that the laity are the people who demand increased ceremonial. Finally, he will notice—and, if he be a persecutor, he will admire—the fact that the Commission lavish their ponderous rebukes on breaches of the rubric which they hold to symbolise Roman doctrines, but deal very gently with those which tend in a Zwinglian, or Calvinistic, or Unitarian direction. "The balance of the report," says Mr. Justice Phillimore, " is wrong. The more dangerous breaches of order are in the other direction, yet not a word has been said suggesting vigorous enforcement of discipline in that direction."

These things and others like them Mr. Bottles will find in the evidence ; and, having found them, he will strut, and fret, and talk at large about purging the Church of traitors. But I doubt if, even under this pressure, he will begin to demand Disestablishment. If I know him, he will be for some short and easy method of abolishing Ritualism, but the very last reform which he will desire is the liberation of the Church from the State. "As long as the Church is Established, we can kick the parsons ; but once disestablish it, and begad ! they'll kick us." This is the doctrine of the Man in the Street, and no one can deny that it has a basis of truth. What then is the true bearing of the Report on Disestablishment ? The terms of the Report itself certainly do not favour any severance of the bond which binds the Church to the State. The evidence, as I have just said, may astonish the Man in the Street, but will not convert him to Liberationism. It only remains to consider the " Recommendations " with which the Report concludes, and these must be read in connexion with the "two main conclusions" at which the Commissioners arrive. The first of these is stated as follows :

"The law of public worship in the Church of England is too narrow for the religious life of the present generation. It needlessly condemns much which a great section of Church people, including many of her most devoted members, value ; and modern thought and feeling are characterised by a care for ceremonial, a sense of dignity in worship, and an appreciation of the continuity of the Church, which were not similarly felt at the time when the law took its present shape. In an age which has witnessed an extraordinary revival of spiritual life and activity, the Church has had to work under regulations fitted for a different condition of things, without that power of self-adjustment which is inherent in the conception of a living Church."

The second "conclusion" of the Commissioners is stated as follows :

> "The machinery for discipline is broken down. The means of enforcing the law in the Ecclesiastical Courts, even in matters which touch the Church's faith and teaching, are defective and in some respects unsuitable. . . . It is important that the law should be reformed, that it should admit of reasonable elasticity, and that the means of enforcing it should be improved ; but, above all, it is necessary that it should be obeyed. . . . If it should be thought well to adopt the recommendations we make in this Report, one essential condition of their successful operation will be, that obedience to the law so altered shall be required, and, if necessary, enforced, by those who bear rule in the Church of England."

In order to remedy the evils set forth in these two " conclusions," the Commissioners make ten " Recommendations." Most of them suggest sweeping changes in the laws which affect ecclesiastical jurisdiction ; and, seeing that the Tories on the Commission were twelve to two Liberals, it is not surprising that all these changes should be in restraint of freedom. They are aimed, in the first instance, against the freedom of the parochial clergy ; but, in so far as the clergy are acting in harmony with their congregations, they also threaten the freedom of the lay-people and their right to enjoy the type of worship which they find most helpful. The Commissioners recommend all sorts of coercive legislation—the abolition of the episcopal veto on ritual prosecutions, the " deprivation " of contumacious incumbents, the permanent exclusion from ministerial work of men who will not surrender their conscience at the bidding of a bishop ; but by far the most important of the " Recommendations," if only because it is the one which can be most readily carried into effect, is No. 2, which runs as follows :

> "Letters of Business should be issued to the Convocations with instructions : (a) to consider the

preparation of a new rubric regulating the ornaments (that is to say, the vesture) of the ministers of the Church, at the times of their ministrations, with a view to its enactment by Parliament; and (*b*) to frame, with a view to their enactment by Parliament, such modifications in the existing law relating to the conduct of Divine Service and to the ornaments and fittings of churches as may tend to secure the greater elasticity which a reasonable recognition of the comprehensiveness of the Church of England and its present needs seem to demand."

Now surely, as Master Shallow says, good phrases are, and ever were, very commendable. Divested of verbiage, Recommendation No. 2 comes to this—The Convocations, which, as every one knows, do not represent even the clergy, are to overhaul everything connected with public worship; the terms of the creeds, the language of the prayers, the dress of the ministers, nay, even the fittings and trappings of the churches; and then, when these clerical caucuses have done their worst, their handiwork is to be submitted, for correction or confirmation, to the judgement of the House of Commons.

The Government, whether frightened or cajoled by the Episcopate it is hard to guess, have weakly granted the " Letters of Business "; and the Convocations, duly manipulated by apostolic wire-pullers, will soon begin to tear the Prayer-book to pieces. It is easy to forecast the changes which will be proposed; and it is possible that, in a picked and packed assemblage, the Episcopal innovators may secure a majority for their proposals. If that were all, nothing could signify less; for the decrees of Convocation have no more force than the resolutions of the Oxford Union. It is at the next stage that the bearing of these things on Disestablishment will be seen. If the recommendations of the Commissioners are carried out, the House of Commons, rightly comprising Jews, infidels and heretics, schismatics of every shape and shade, and a great mass of men simply irreligious, will be invited to undertake the work of liturgical revision. The prospect is indeed amazing. Mr.

Healy will balance the respective merits of the Roman cotta and the English surplice. Mr. Rothschild will discuss the legality of the Crucifix. Mr. Lloyd-George will uphold the cope as the right garment for the Communion Service, while Mr. Masterman pleads, with tears in his voice, for the chasuble, amice, maniple, and stole. Sir Henry Fowler, with that lucidity which is his special gift, will prove that " before the table " means behind it ; and Mr. Morley, arguing for the disuse of the *Quicunque vult*, will cross swords with Mr. Haldane, who esteems it the most philosophical attempt to express the inexpressible. The language of prayer will be revised by men who believe that they die like dogs. The Creeds will be overhauled by men who acknowledge neither God nor devil. The words and the acts with which the Lord's Supper is observed will be discussed by men who regard all sacramental usages as pestilent superstitions ; and the Cross may be dethroned at the bidding of those who revile the Crucified.

This is the prospect which, if the Commissioners get their way, awaits English Churchmen ; and I ask, in all seriousness, if there is any sect in Christendom, the tiniest and the weakest—the Muggletonians, the Sandemanians, or the Seventh Day Baptists—which would submit to such unholy degradation ?

Just lately, some itinerant politicians, new to parliamentary life, have been stumping the country in the interests of religious persecution ; and the boisterous language of 1898 and 1899 has been heard again. We are once more told that " the Mass " and " the Confessional " are to be put down by law, and that in ten years England is to be free from the last trace of the accursed thing. But this millenium can only be secured by Act of Parliament. " Foul fall the day," wrote Mr. Gladstone in 1894, " when the persons of this world shall, on whatever pretext, take into their uncommissioned hands the manipulation of the religion of our Lord and Saviour." And, if Parliament lays its hands on the Eucharistic worship of the Church, or on the Ministry of Reconciliation, the demand for Disestablishment will be heard in quarters were it is least expected, and will shake some comfortable institutions, such as the Episcopal Bench, with unwonted tremors. If there be any Successors of the Apostles whose first care is for palaces and patronage, seats in the House of Lords, and the chief rooms at feasts, they had better take heed in time, for assuredly those cherished possessions will not long survive a second Public Worship Regulation Act.

But for the Church herself, and for those who believe in her spiritual character and claims, Disestablishment has no terrors ; while some of us have always longed for it as for a coming deliverance. We learned from a great ecclesiastic, John Wesley, that " the Establishment by Constantine was a gigantic evil," and we say with a great layman, William Gladstone—" Choose between the mess of pottage, and the birthright of the Bride of Christ."

The doctrine that the Church and the State are separate entities, bound together by a mutual alliance, but each possessing functions and prerogatives of its own, is not an invention of to-day. The spiritual independence of the Church in its own sphere was maintained by High Churchmen of the old school, such as Bishop Horsley, Archdeacon Daubeny, Oxlee, Wrangham, and Sikes of Guilsborough. " The Constitution of the Church and State, according to the idea of each," was expounded by Coleridge, with his customary wealth of philosophic amplification. The Oxford Movement of 1833 was, above all else, an attempt to recall men's minds to the conception of the English Church as a spiritual society, holding its essential constitution direct from Christ, and only accidentally allied with the secular State. This view of the Church appealed to spiritually-minded Churchmen quite outside the Oxford Movement. Whately had taught it in his *Letters of an Episcopalian*, some years before the Movement began. Dr. Hook, when Vicar of Coventry, maintained it, with characteristic force, against the Erastianism of Bishop Samuel Butler. Some of the more ardent spirits of the Oxford Movement—such as Hurrell Froude—felt the galling fetters of Establishment with special keenness ; thirty years later, Dr. Pusey declared that the time had come when the Church must demand her freedom from the State. In 1877 Mr. Mackonochie, the devoted protagonist of Ritualism, drafted a Bill for Disestablishment, and that staunchest of Tories, Archdeacon Denison, joined in the demand for Liberation. In 1881, Dr. Liddon gave it as his opinion, that few, if any, Churchmen desire to see the Church disestablished or disendowed; but, having regard to the actual state of things, and the tyranny exercised by State-made courts over human consciences, he added:

> "If it be a question whether it is better to be turned out of house and home, without any clothes, and even on a winter's night, or be strangled by a silken cord in a well-furnished drawing-room, what man, or Church, will have any difficulty in arriving at a decision?"

It is true indeed that there are certain dignitaries, and adherents of dignitaries, whose first article of faith is, *I believe in an Established Church,* and who would cheerfully sacrifice the faith for the endowment—the altar for the gold.

But there is an increasing number of faithful Churchmen who have learnt by the experience of recent years and by a widening acquaintance with non-established churches, the beauty of Cavour's ideal—a free church in a free state.

The Episcopal Church of the United States is one of the most vigorous, most orthodox, and best organized parts of Christendom ; and, like Bishop Hamilton forty years ago, we have found that we " had much to learn from closer contact with the faith and vigour of the American Episcopate."

As regards the Church of Australia, let us take the testimony of Dr. Thornton, Bishop of Ballarat, delivered at Dublin in 1896:

> "I am here to-day, after living for twenty years within, and helping in the administration of, an unendowed and unestablished Church, and I will say that, however great the disadvantages of such a condition of affairs are to the State, I am not prepared to say that they are a disadvantage to the spiritual well-being and

prosperity of the Church herself. I for one should be very sorry to take any price I can think of for the freedom of administration and government which we enjoy, the power to promote reforms, and the power of adaptation, more difficult to secure where there is a State connexion."

In 1899 the Bishop of Melbourne said :

"Let us suppose that the wealth of the Church was to be taken away, and that the Archbishops and Bishops were to lose their seats in the House of Lords, the Church of England would still go on. The Church was a great spiritual corporation, governed by bishops, priests, and deacons, and it might be that, if the Church was disestablished, she might become more powerful and energetic in saving souls for Christ."

As regards the Church of Ireland, in spite of all the difficulties and dangers through which it has had to pass, chief rulers give like testimony. In October 1882, Lord Plunket, then Bishop of Meath, and afterwards Archbishop of Dublin, addressing the clergy of his diocese at his annual Visitation, used these remarkable words in reference to the ordeal through which Ireland had passed during the previous three years :

"Before we give.way to querulous murmurings, let us remember that this dark cloud has not been allowed to burst over our country until, in the providence of God, and by ways that we should never have selected for ourselves, our Church has been prepared to abide the fury of the storm. Had we been called upon to face a Land League agitation at the time when our clergy, as ministers of a State-protected Church, received their tithes from the poor, or even when they drew their tithe rent-charge from landlords, some of them in very needy circumstances, how intolerable would have been our position both as regards the obloquy and out-rage we should have had to endure, and the cruel straits to which we should have been inevitably reduced !

Now, however, the very disaster which seemed to threaten our downfall has been overruled for our good.".

After ten years' experience and reflection, Lord Plunket said in 1892 :

" When I count up the advantages which have followed Disestablishment ; when I think of the strength and vitality which our Church has derived from the admission of the laity to an active and responsible participation in her counsels, in the disposition of her patronage, and in the financial departments of her work ; when I observe the spirit of unity and mutual respect which has been engendered by the ordeal of our common adversity, and the increased loyalty and love which are being daily shown to their mother Church by those who have had to make some sacrifice on her behalf ; when I remember, too, the freedom from agrarian complications which our disconnexion from all questions of tithe and rent-charge has brought about, and the more favourable attitude as regards our influence upon the surrounding population which we occupy, because of our severance from any State connexion, when I remember all this counterpoise of advantage which we enjoy in our new and independent position, and when I try to hold the balance evenly and weigh the losses and the gains on the whole, I say boldly and without reserve that, in my opinion at least, the gain outweighs the loss."

In 1899 Dr. Alexander, Primate of All Ireland, spoke as follows at Templepatrick :

" I must say, in striking the balance between loss and gain there is something to be said on both sides. There are, at all events, three or four circumstances of gain. Well, in the first place, an occasion like this reminds me that opportunities are much more frequent and more considerable for the interchange of ideas in our Churches between the bishops, clergy and laity, and our friends, also, of other denominations and schools of thought than there were in old times. I do not think there are many of our people, and I am sure not many of our friendly Presbyterian neighbours, who any longer look upon a bishop, or even that dreadful being, an archbishop, as a spiritual enemy. They know very well he has got no unusual wealth and no unusual privileges, and so they look upon him with patience and toleration at least. . . . Besides bringing together all the constituent parts of the Church I think there is another good brought about by Disestablishment. The life of ideas makes the great part of the life of a Church, and the only way in which it can be discovered whether the ideas are really vital, whether they have real life in them or not, is to show how they work, and whether they can last when clothed in totally different surroundings and investiture of circumstances ; and so is it with many of their Church's ideas. They all feel that they have an old Church, and they feel that that Church is able to act upon new lines.

"The third thing about Disestablishment to which I would like to refer is, that our present position gives our people scope for liberality, and I must say, after making all allowances, the liberality of Irish Churchmen has, on the whole, been very conspicuous. It is a very simple fact, about which there is no manner of doubt, that five millions of money have been raised in our parishes since the time of the Disestablishment in 1869, and when you take into account the building of churches, the five millions become six millions. That, I think, speaks well for liberality. And yet another privilege which the Disestablished Church enjoys, is that it is free to legislate."

These last words touch the heart of the present controversy. A disestablished Church can exercise the elementary rights of spiritual self-government, can formulate its own faith, and shape its own worship. It is free from Acts of Uniformity and Royal Commissions and State-made bishops and Parliamentary wire-pullers. It can discharge its Divine commission to the souls of men without let or hindrance from the powers which rule an unconverted world. So, if the issue of the present controversy is the Disestablishment of the English Church, what was intended to be a fresh yoke of bondage will prove to have been an instrument of emancipation. At length we shall be free from the interference of outsiders, and the worship of the Jumping Cat, and the appeal to the Man in the Street, and all the degrading incidents in which Establishment has involved us.

All but sixty years ago an English clergyman of high standing, and wide influence, renounced, as was said, " the Church which was his living and the pulpit which was his throne," because he saw that the Church's alliance with the State involved urgent and manifold danger to spiritual religion. Surveying the prospects of the contest which he believed to be impending, he wrote some memorable and exhilarating words:

> " Should we in this cause meet with some rude assaults, the cause is worth the conflict. The humble tomb at Thermopylæ speaks more to the generous traveller than the sky-pointing Pyramids. For, when the three hundred Spartans stood on the narrow causeway between Mount Œta and the sea, to guard the liberties of their country against an innumerable host of invaders, they did that which will live in the hearts of brave men while the world lasts. And the liberties of Christ's Churches are more precious than the civil liberties of Greece. Let each minister, and each Christian, who knows that the principles of the union [between Church and State] are corrupt and dishonourable to Christ, resolve that they will terminate the bondage of the Anglican Churches by destroying it ; and, with the aid of God, they will at last succeed."[1]

GEORGE W. E. RUSSELL

[1] Essay on the *Union of Church and State.* By Baptist Wriothesley Noel, M.A. 1848.

THE WORK OF THE HEALTH VISITOR

THE opening years of the present century have witnessed an important development in our methods of public hygiene—in the measures consciously adopted by our Sanitary Authorities for the prevention of disease and premature death. The nature and significance of these measures may best be apprehended by contrasting them with the great sanitary reforms of the reign of Queen Victoria. The latter consisted for the most part in the removal of unwholesome conditions of environment. The prompt removal of waste matter from the vicinity of human habitations, which is the beginning of sanitary wisdom, was accomplished by the provision of elaborate and costly systems of drainage and sewerage, and of refuse removal and destruction. The vast cess-pool, which in the early years of the nineteenth century formed an important feature of the basement of a London dwelling-house was ruthlessly abolished—although even now this survival of a pre-sanitary era is occasionally brought to light by systematic sanitary inspection. Plentiful supplies of pure water from carefully supervised sources took the place of the sewage-polluted wells and streams which supplied our great-grandfathers with such water as they found necessary for drinking purposes. Improved methods of street-paving and street-cleansing were introduced; open spaces were provided; the sanitary standard of building construction was raised; offensive trades were regulated, and the smoke nuisance was brought under some measure of public control. So far as these Victorian sanitary reforms can be described by any one phrase, it may be said that they were measures of *communal cleanliness*. The aggregation of increasing masses of the population into large towns brought with it increased susceptibility to disease, and in self-preservation the new city community evolved an elaborate organisation for the protection of the public health, the first aim of which was to secure communal cleanliness. The municipality itself assumed responsibility for the provision of sewers and sewage disposal, of dust-carts and dust-destructors, of street pavement and street scavengers; and in the pursuit of cleanliness it did not hesitate to send its sanitary officers to investigate and remove the insanitary conditions lying behind the sacred threshold of the Englishman's house. It is true that we are still far from having reached finality in the way of communal cleanliness: much yet remains to be done. But further progress in this direction must take place on lines already laid down by the Victorian sanitary reformers. The methods of environmental hygiene developed by Edwin Chadwick and John Simon were conceived on right lines and have been fruitful in results. The army of sanitary officials whose existence was pathetically deplored in one of Herbert Spencer's later books can at all events point to something real and definite as a result of their labours. Some diseases have been swept out of the country, others have been brought under control and are rapidly diminishing, the death-rate has undergone a great and progressive reduction, and the expectation of life has increased. In view of the immense alleviation of human suffering which these things imply, it is not difficult to share Lecky's belief that " with all deductions, the triumphs of sanitary reform as well as of medical science are perhaps the brightest page in the history of our century."

But great as have been the triumphs of environmental hygiene, it is far from covering the whole field of hygienic reform : it is now realised that there is an enormous wastage from disease and death which is comparatively untouched by the sanitation of surroundings. In spite of the elaborate and expensive reforms of the nineteenth century, to which we must unquestionably attribute the greater part of the reduction in the general death-rate, the last ten years of the century were years of exceptionally high infantile mortality. It is a striking fact that the highest infantile rate ever recorded in this country was reached as recently as 1899, when the number of deaths under one year per 1000 births registered was no less than 163. Measles and whooping cough are as destructive as ever, and although there has been a great reduction in the mortality from tuberculosis, it is now realised that this disease will not be controlled unless we can influence the personal habits of the patient. It is evident that the field of preventive endeavour must be extended so as to include not only the hygiene of the environment, but also the hygiene of the person. It is not enough to remove the insanitary surroundings of the people if the people themselves remain ignorant of the essentials of clean and healthy living. This is now fully realised, and for some years past sanitary authorities have employed various agencies for the popularisation of some of the more important aspects of personal hygiene. There has been a copious distribution of advisory leaflets on infant feeding and other health subjects, and in many districts a municipal warning against the injurious effects of alcohol on physical efficiency has been extensively placarded. But the mere distribution of printed matter, though it has its uses, leaves much to be desired. It lacks the one thing needful—the element of personal service, the personal relation between the teacher and the taught. A far more effective method of bringing the necessary hygienic knowledge to the homes of the less favoured members of the community is the employment of women health visitors to visit those homes, and in a kindly and sympathetic spirit to inculcate the advantages of clean and wholesome ways of life. Accordingly, many sanitary authorities have of late years supplemented the labours of the sanitary inspector by those of the sanitary missionary—the health visitor.

The first health visitors began their work in 1862 in Manchester, under the auspices of the Ladies' Health Society of Manchester and Salford, which, under the title of the Ladies' Sanitary Reform Association, was founded in that year at the suggestion of the late Mr. Thomas Turner, then one of the leading surgeons in Manchester. This Society has been the pioneer of many similar associations of voluntary health workers that have since been established in other towns, and its early history, which has been admirably told by Mrs. Hardie, a former president, affords a good example of the growth of that co-operation between the official sanitary authorities and voluntary health associations, which promises to become an important feature of modern public health work. The aim of the Society, Mrs. Hardie tells us, " was to popularise sanitary knowledge, and to elevate the people physically, socially, morally, and religiously. This it essayed to do by the united efforts of ladies of position and working women belonging to the class of those it endeavoured to influence." " Its beginning was most modest, and consisted in the distribution of tracts and leaflets on health topics by three or four ladies. In the course of time they found that this by itself made little impression, and a respectable working woman was, there-fore, engaged to go from door to door, among the poorer classes of the population, to teach and help them as opportunity offered." This " respectable working woman " was our first health visitor.

As the work of the Society gradually extended and developed, the number of health visitors increased. Man-chester and Salford were mapped out into districts, each district having its own lady superintendent and its health visitor, the latter being a working woman who was paid a small salary for her services. The bulk of the systematic visiting was done by the paid visitors, but the lady superin-tendents and other ladies attached to the various districts also took part in this branch of the Society's work. Some idea of the daily work of the health visitors in the early years of the Society's existence may be gathered from the following extract from the rules supplied to each visitor. " They must visit from house to house, irrespective of creed or circumstance, in such localities as their superintendents direct. They must carry with them the carbolic powder, explain its use, and leave it where it is accepted ; direct the attention of those they visit to the evils of bad smells, want of fresh air, impurities of all kinds ; give hints to mothers on feeding and clothing their children ; where they find sickness, assist in promoting the comfort of the invalid by personal help, and report such cases to their superintendent.

They must urge the importance of cleanliness, thrift and temperance on all possible occasions. They are desired to get as many as possible to join the mothers' meetings of their districts ; to use all their influence to induce those they visit to attend regularly at their respective places of worship, and to send their children to school."

But the work of the Society is not limited to domiciliary visitation—once a week in each district a mothers' meeting is held, at which simple health addresses, followed by con-versation, are given. The subjects discussed at these meet-ings are " such as personal and household cleanliness, thrift, ventilation, the prevention of infection, care of children, the feeding, washing and dressing of babies, cutting out, clothing, patching, etc., varied by demonstrations of sick nursing and cooking." Musical afternoons for the mothers form another feature of the Society's work, and every year there is a tea-party and entertainment, and, in the summer, a trip to the country. Anything in the nature of " pauper-isation " is studiously avoided. Independence and self-reliance are encouraged, and efforts are made to foster a spirit of civic patriotism. It will be seen that this health society interprets the word " health " in a broad sense, and that its work includes much that would not usually be called " sanitation."

In its early years the Society worked in complete inde-pendence of the official sanitary authority—the municipality —except that it had always been the practice to report cases of overcrowding, dilapidations, and nuisances generally to the municipal sanitary department. In 1890, however, the Society came to an arrangement with the Manchester Corporation which resulted in an important development of its work. Under this arrangement the salaries of some (now half) of the visitors were paid by the Corporation, while the supervision and direction of the work of the visitors generally was placed in the hands of the medical officer of health. The advantages of this arrangement were twofold : to the Society it gave a skilled supervision, and a substantial addition to its funds which enabled it to extend its work, while the Corporation secured a large increase in the number of its health workers at a small cost to the ratepayers. A few years later a similar arrangement was entered into with the Salford Corporation in respect of the visitors working in that Borough. The work of the Society has continued to extend, and it has now twenty-three districts in Manchester and Salford, each with it own health visitor.

Some idea of the nature and extent of the work carried out by the visitors may be gathered from the following particulars which have been extracted from the last Annual Report of Dr. Niven, the Medical Officer of Health of Manchester. The particulars relate only to the visitors, sixteen in number, working in Manchester, and do not include the work of the Salford visitors. It appears that during the year 1905 no less than 14,424 houses were visited in systematic house-to-house visitation, while 1746 special inquiries were made in cases of death, and 777 complaints of insanitary conditions were made to the sanitary authority. 14,554 leaflets on infant feeding, the prevention of consumption and other health subjects were distributed, and disinfecting powder was left at 12,104 houses. Lime was supplied and lime-washing brushes lent to tenants willing to undertake cleansing and limewashing, and in this way the visitors were able to get 5836 rooms, yards, etc., thoroughly cleansed and limewashed. One hundred and nine cases of neglected children were discovered, and where necessary the cases were reported to the Society for the Prevention of Cruelty to Children. At the end of the year 513 cases of consumption were being kept under observation by the visitors. This is an important part of the work. The visitors report monthly to the medical officer of health as to whether the houses occupied by consumptives are kept free from dust and dirt, and every three months they see that the house is thoroughly cleansed so as to keep down infection. The method of cleansing adopted is as follows :—the walls are rubbed down with dough, the floors and furniture well washed, and the bedding and personal clothing of the patient washed in boiling water.

The work of the Manchester health visitors, especially in its relation to the prevention of infantile mortality, attracted the attention of local authorities in other parts of the country. The high infantile mortality of the last years of the nineteenth century brought the whole question of the wastage of infant life prominently to the notice of the authorities responsible for the protection of the public health, and the more the question was studied the more clearly did it appear that one of the chief causes of the high mortality was to be found in the fact that many mothers take upon themselves the supremely important duties and responsibilities of motherhood in complete ignorance of the things that are requisite and necessary for the successful rearing of babies. When this was realised it became evident that to dispel this ignorance, to popularise infant hygiene, to bring home to the mothers the essentials of infant feeding and infant management was as much the business of the sanitary authority as the supervision of drains and damp-proof courses. It was necessary that in matters of infant hygiene the sanitary authority should be the education authority also. Accordingly, an increasing number of towns, St. Helens, Sheffield, and Birmingham being among the first, began to employ health visitors to give simple practical instructions to mothers in the feeding and care of infants. This movement has greatly developed during the last five or six years, and there are now more than fifty districts in which, under the title of health visitor or lady sanitary inspector, women are employed by the municipality in this educational work. Some of the first of these municipal workers resembled the Manchester visitors in that they were drawn from much the same class as the mothers among whom their work lay, but it soon became apparent that the best results were obtained by women of superior education, and at the present time the municipal health visitors include several University graduates and five qualified medical women.

The work of the health visitor is chiefly directed to the prevention of infantile mortality. From the local registrars the Medical Officer of Health receives weekly lists of the homes where births have taken place, and these homes are systematically visited by the health visitor. She leaves at each home a card or leaflet containing simple practical directions on the feeding and general management of babies, and her work mainly consists in explaining and amplifying these instructions. It might be thought that visits of this kind would be resented, but experience shows that where the health visitor knows her business the visits, far from being resented, are welcomed and the visitor is encouraged to repeat her visit. The health visitor calls not as an inquisitorial official, but as a sympathetic friend, and when once the ice is broken—a process which in nearly every case is easily accomplished by a competent visitor— she finds the mother ready enough to enter into a long and detailed discussion on the ups and downs of babyhood.

But the work is not limited to the teaching of infant hygiene. The health visitor investigates notified cases of consumption, and explains the methods to be adopted to prevent the spread of infection by the patient ; she endeavours to inculcate a high standard of domestic cleanliness, to teach the value of fresh air, and of the open window ; in short she spreads abroad the gospel that disease is largely preventible, and that much of it may be prevented by the exercise of cleanliness and common-sense. The work obviously requires certain special qualifications; sympathy, tact, insight and patience are essential, and it is equally essential that the visitor should have adequate knowledge of the subjects she has to teach. The training of a hospital nurse is valuable preliminary work for a health visitor, and it is desirable that the official worker should hold a certificate as a sanitary inspector. It is most important that the work should be done under medical supervision, and in the case of the municipal visitors this is secured by making the visitors responsible to the Medical Officer of Health.

The work of the municipal health visitor has been supplemented in several towns by the formation of associations of voluntary health workers, somewhat on the lines of the Ladies' Health Society of Manchester. Some of the associations have organised bodies of voluntary health visitors who work on the methods already indicated. The local health association usually co-operates with the local sanitary authority, and its health visitors work under the supervision of the medical officer of health. One of the best examples of this co-operation between the municipality and its officers on the one hand, and the association of voluntary health workers on the other, is afforded by Huddersfield, where the Mayor, Mr. Broadbent, has built up one of the most complete and comprehensive organisations for the prevention of infantile mortality that can be found in any country.

The Huddersfield scheme came into operation in October 1905, when the Corporation appointed two qualified medical women as health visitors. These ladies visit the homes of the newly-born babies soon after birth, and present the mother with a card on infant management drawn up by the Medical Officer of Health, supplementing the printed directions by simple, practical oral instruction. Subsequent visits are paid by the voluntary helpers, members of the Huddersfield Public Health Union, of whom there are over eighty. Each of the nine wards composing the borough has been taken as a district, each district having its band of voluntary health visitors consisting of a lady superintendent, who arranges the work of the district, and a number of helpers. Every week each lady superintendent receives from the Medical Officer of Health a list of cases that have already been visited once by the Corporation lady doctors, and these she distributes amongst her helpers, who keep the babies under observation and if necessary invoke the aid of the Medical Officer of Health, under whose supervision the work is carried on. It should be said that the work is preventive, not curative : the visitors do not prescribe drugs, and if a baby is ill the mother is advised to consult her doctor. Dr. Moore, the Medical Officer of Health of Huddersfield, from whose Annual Report for 1905 the facts relating to that borough have mainly been extracted, is careful to point out that "great care is exercised to avoid touching upon the domain of the family doctor, and also to avoid any action which even might have the appearance of diminishing parental, and particularly maternal, responsibility."

The work of the Huddersfield visitors is facilitated and rendered specially effective by the provision the Corporation has made for the early notification of births to the Medical Officer of Health. From a public health point of view the system of birth registration in this country is defective, in that it permits a birth to be registered as late as six weeks after its occurrence. A large proportion of infant deaths occur within the first month of life, and many a child is already dead by the time the fact of its birth has been communicated by the parents to the registrar and by him to the sanitary authority. It is evident, therefore, that the full effect of the health visitors' ministrations can only be secured where special provision has been made for the early notification of births to the sanitary authority, so that the visits may be paid while there is still a chance of saving the child's life. In Huddersfield such provision is made by a local Act, passed in the last Session of Parliament, which provides that the birth of every child born in the borough shall be notified to the Medical Officer of Health within forty-eight hours of its occurrence, a fee of one shilling being payable to the person making the notification. Huddersfield is the only town possessing statutory powers to enforce the notification of births, but a system of voluntary notification has been adopted by several sanitary authorities, and it is probable that future acts will extend the compulsory powers obtained by Huddersfield to other districts, if not to the whole country.

The number of health visitors, official and voluntary, has much increased since the close of the last century, and there is little doubt that there will be a much greater increase in the near future. The value of the work has been amply proved, and in no branch of social service is there brighter promise of worthy results. The association of voluntary agencies with the local authorities in the movement for the prevention of disease is in itself a social development of much importance. It is necessary of course that the work should be done with organisation and method, and that certain precautions should be observed. There is some tendency for voluntary health visiting to be associated with alms-giving—a tendency which should be resolutely resisted. It is important, too, that all visitors should possess adequate knowledge of their work. The Hampstead Health Society have adopted the excellent rule that all their health visitors shall have attended a course of instruction in the feeding and care of babies before beginning their ministrations. For an official health visitor a hospital training is highly desirable. In this respect the Huddersfield Corporation has set an example by appointing as its health visitors two qualified medical women, and this example has been followed by Glasgow, Croydon and St. Helens. These appointments, which have all been made within the last twelve months, are indicative of the tendency of sanitary authorities to enlist the services of medical women in the administrative work of preventive medicine. In health-visiting, in the supervision of midwives, and in the important work of school hygiene, the "lady doctor" has given proof of special capacity, and the number employed in such duties is bound to increase. Medical women are not only exceptionally well equipped health visitors, but they have the further advantage of being well qualified to supervise the lay visitors. It is important that health-visiting should always be done under competent medical supervision, but the number of voluntary visitors is increasing so rapidly that there is some danger that proper supervision may not always be forthcoming. I have known of one or two instances where voluntary health visitors, working without medical supervision, have displayed more enthusiasm than knowledge, and have given advice which if followed would have been productive of more harm than good. In health-visiting, as in other philanthropic movements, enthusiasm must be tempered with knowledge, and both guided by method. Speaking generally, however, it can be said that the work of the health visitor fulfils these conditions. Its development is one of the most hopeful signs of our times, and it is already exercising a notable influence on the national well-being.

G. F. McCLEARY

(*Medical Officer of Health, Hampstead*).

A ROMANCE OF 1821

CONSCIOUS as we all are of our elders' short-comings, we are sometimes inclined not to credit our more remote ancestors with qualities that our elders did not possess. In our day we are all a little pleased with ourselves because we have broken down something of the barrier which was supposed to divide the sexes in what Mr. Wells has unkindly called an era of " sham delicacy, nasty sentiment, and giggles." Our young ladies read and attend the plays of Mr. Bernard Shaw and sundry other authors from whom they hope to derive a knowledge of the world. They share masculine recreations, and are able to discuss masculine topics. We may legitimately pride ourselves on this emancipation. Indeed it is only to be regretted in the interest of female hygiene that Mrs. Grundy should still frown upon pipes and cigars, even if she may occasionally connive at the insidious cigarette.

At the same time we are a little unfair to the ladies of the pre-Victorian age, and the conventions of 1840 to 1860 loom a little too conspicuously in our horizon. During that period political power and social influence came to a number of most estimable persons who did not exactly know what the proprieties demanded. The poor, who have no time for pretences and euphemisms, accept and discuss the obvious facts of life with a certain frank rationality. The properly civilised and educated person may have recourse to euphemisms, but endeavours to discard pretences. Our immediate ancestors rather fell between two stools, and their attitude was undoubtedly responsible for a certain amount of sentimental hypocrisy which frequently led to unhappy marriages.

75   G 2

But this was, after all, merely a passing phase in English life. Kate Nickleby is not the typical girl of English literature, and, as an antidote to her, we may do well to recall some of Shakespeare's most fascinating heroines, the memoirs of Lady Fanshawe, the letters of Dorothy Osborne, Fielding's adorable Sophia Western, and even Miss Jane Austen's young ladies.

These reflections are to some extent suggested by a very human document which I recently unearthed from a number of old manuscripts. It consists of a tiny little book bound in red leather, and written in a flowing Italian hand by a girl of twenty-one to a youth of twenty-two, to whom she was then engaged, and whom she married soon afterwards. It certainly shows a laudable ambition to settle all outstanding differences as much as possible before the irrevocable act of marriage, and it records the results of " five months' strict observation." The book begins as follows :

CHRISTMAS 1821

> " These desultory remarks on your character, my beloved ——, were suggested to me by your so repeatedly asking my opinion of the character given you by Miss F——. I know with your primitive notions of Love, you will think *my* affection for you ought to blind me to all your little failings, but if I am less lenient to them than Miss F——, remember it is because I am more anxious than she could possibly be that your merits may be seen in their proper light and not obscured by any failings."

The lady displays peculiar wisdom in warning her lover, who afterwards achieved some eminence, against the way in which young men sometimes resent the unreadiness of the world to take their good qualities for granted, though she might perhaps have added some reflections on the unreasoning acceptance of old age for its own sake which may also be observed :

> " She has justly ranked Pride as one of the leading features of your character. I admit that in some

instances it may operate beneficially on you and save you from follies . . . which a man of less pride would not hesitate to commit ; still, carried to the excess which I have sometimes seen in you, it becomes a vice, by generating hatred, revenge, and all their hideous feelings, and occasionally so fetters your excellent judgment as to induce you to regard the natural reserve which many people feel for the virtues or merits of a young man, when experience has not convinced them of their existence, as a Personal Insult."

The young gentleman appears to have professed a Byronic misogyny which was perhaps fashionable in the cultivated youth of the period, but was somewhat disconcerting to his future wife :

"However much you may smile at me and call me the champion of my sex, still I cannot help noticing to you the contempt which you so often express, and still oftener evince by your manners, for women. That my opinion of them may perhaps be more exalted than they actually deserve I do not dispute, but surely it is neither flattering nor pleasing to hear a young man who contemplates marriage strenuously endeavouring to depreciate that sex from whom he will derive most of the comforts of his future life. I know and acknowledge that you feel an individual respect for the virtues of a few of the sex with whom you happen to be intimate, but your judgment has been so allured by the fine poetry of Lord Byron, warped by prejudices contracted in early life in those climes where sexual slavery prevails and profligacy is tolerated and practised, from reading works which describe only the feelings and passions of those women whose laxity of principle reflects a partial disgrace on the whole sex, and lastly from living in a metropolis without the comforts of home and comparatively secluded from society where the mild radiance of female virtues shines the most conspicuous, and forced into that, which corrupts the heart and greatly influences the opinion. How different would be the sentiments of a man who had been fostered in the bosom of a domestic and united family, who could reflect with gratitude and love on the numberless little incidents which press on his memory, where an affectionate Mother has cheerfully sacrificed her personal feelings or deprived herself of some enjoyment for his sake, while the silent admiration painted on the cheek of a favourite sister, who probably shares the deprivation, reveals the unfeigned pleasure which she can derive from a Brother's gratification."

The writer goes on to vindicate the qualities of women in a clear-sighted way almost worthy of Jane Austen :

" To say that a Mother will lay down her life for a child gives but a faint idea of what she is capable. Although such a sacrifice may add splendour to a tale of heroism or romance, there is but one effort required, and pride lends its powerful aid in the accomplishment of that effort ; but to bear patiently and cheerfully a succession of petty inconveniences and wounded feelings, daily privations, loss of fortune . . . are evils which require more strength of mind to bear, inasmuch as the struggles are more frequent and derive no support from those powerful agents of the human mind, pride and ambition.

" That mind which has been accustomed to find these excellencies in part of the sex, will easily credit the whole of the better part for the possession of them, and will find that they exist in nearly all, and that they only await time and circumstances to bring them into action."

It is only to be added that the writer of these words proved herself more than worthy of them in later days.

The digression, however, does not lead her off the track, and she rapidly proceeds to a less academic subject of apprehension :

" You have a quickness and asperity of temper, my ——, which I sincerely wish did not exist. If your future companion were too amiable to notice, or too callous to be wounded by, its effects, it would not be worthy of remark, for it would never subject you to the imputation of ill-temper, but unfortunately I am neither the one nor the other, and when that ungraceful asperity is exercised to me I cannot help thinking it the germ of future uneasiness ; for in proportion to the happiness I feel in your unbounded kindness, so great is my wretchedness when that kindness is withheld, and that too by one on whom I have every claim which unlimited confidence and the sacrifice of friendship can exalt. I know your deep and almost romantic sense of honour, and to that I trust. Miss F—— says you have great command of yourself, and I shall willingly agree in her opinion when I see that self-command exercised in checking these virulent and sarcastic feelings."

Some further sentences follow on the dangers of Ambition and the possibilities of disappointment it brings, which are precociously wise, and to some extent, I fear, prophetic. She thus closes her discourse :

"You will see, my dear ——, that these remarks have been carelessly put together. I appeal, therefore, to you to pardon any inaccuracies which your better sense may discover. Every merit, or failing, I have noticed I firmly believe has its existence in your mind. Jealousy I have not noticed, because in a lover it may be tolerated, and I hope it will be discarded when you are united by a nearer tie. The latter are only venial errors which I am well convinced you can banish as soon as you please, and by so doing give me the highest satisfaction which the world can give by making that man pre-eminent for his virtues, loved by his friends, and respected by his enemies, whom I have pledged myself to love as my husband, and esteem as my friend.

" Should you be disposed to follow my example, I shall patiently listen to any follies which you may object to and will endeavour to eradicate them."

Here follows the date, " Monday, December 24th, 1821, and the name and address of the writer, and on the next page :

"Oblige me by preserving this little memorial, that when years have chilled the ardour of youth and an increased intercourse with the world has dissipated our more romantic feelings, we may ensure that half-hour's enjoyment which a retrospective view of our earlier years is sure to create, and thus give vitality to some latent spark of youthful fervour which even the icy breath of Time cannot extinguish."

Unhappily history does not relate if the young man was ever disposed to follow his future wife's example, or if on the other hand the little homily gave rise to any manifestation of the "quickness and asperity of temper" to which she refers. But as "extreme candour" was one of his characteristics, let us hope that he enjoyed the prospect of a candid wife. The pleasing fact remains that their marriage was singularly happy and affectionate. The style of the little book resembles, I have been told, that of the theme which the school girl of the period was taught to write, and, if this be the case, one may be old-fashioned enough to wish that school girls were still taught to write so precisely, even if the precision sounds quaint to modern ears.

I have had some qualms about unveiling the privacy of this old romance, but the ordinary objection to the publication of love letters does not apply to this case. As Mr. Chesterton has recently said, the affection of marriage is to some extent associated with a mutual fondness for amiable follies in each of the parties which neither interests the world at large nor exhibits the persons concerned quite as they would wish to be seen by their friends and acquaintances. "Dulce est desipere in loco" is an excellent motto for lovers, but they naturally prefer to be by themselves. My little book, however, is sternly practical, and I cannot help feeling that its engaging, if slightly didactic, author might have experienced some pleasure in the thought that an anonymous reproduction of her ingenuous exhortations should be given to the young men and maidens of another century.

E. S. P. HAYNES

FRAGMENT FROM A BALLAD EPIC OF "ALFRED"

THE Northmen came about our land,
    A Christless chivalry ;
    They knew not of the arch or pen,
    Great beautiful half-witted men
    From the sunrise and the sea.

Our sea was dark with dreadful ships
    Full of strange spoil and fire,
And hairy men, as strange as sin,
With hornèd heads, came wading in
    Through the long low sea-mire.

Their eyes were sadder than the sea,
    And they were speechless men ;
Their helms and arms were grey and green
    Like the sea slime on the fen.

Their souls were sadder than the sea,
    And all good towns and lands
They only saw with heavy eyes
    And broke with heavy hands.

Their gods were sadder than the sea,
    Gods of an empty will
That cried for blood like beasts at night
    Sadly, from hill to hill.

They seemed as trees that walked the earth,
   As witless and as tall,
But they took hold upon the heavens
   And no help came at all.

They bred like kine in English fields,
   They rooted like the rose,
When Alfred came to Athelney
   To hide him from their bows.

There was not English armour left,
   Nor any English thing,
When Alfred came to Athelney
   To be an English king.

His spear was broken in his hand,
   But his belt bore a sword ;
His heart was broken in his breast,
   But he cried unto Our Lord.

He cried to Our Lady and Our Lord
   Seven times in the sun,
And the boar and the black wolf answered him,
   And his tears began to run.

     *   *   *

Fearfully plain the flowers grew
   Like a child's book to read,
Or like a friend's face seen in a glass;
He turned, and there Our Lady was ;
She stood and stroked the tall live grass
   As a man strokes his steed.

Her face was like a spoken word
   When brave men speak and choose,
The very colours of her coat
   Were better than good news.

" Mother of snows and seas," he said,
   " I am but a common king ;
I do not ask what saints may ask,
   To see some hidden thing.

" The gates of heaven are fearful gates,
  Worse than the gates of hell ;
I would not break the portals barred,
Or seek to know the thing they guard
  Which is too good to tell.

" But for this earth most pitiful,
  This little land I know,
If that which is for ever is,
Or if our hearts shall break with bliss,
  Seeing the stranger go ?

" When our last bow is broken, Queen,
  And our last javelin cast,
Under some sad green evening sky,
Holding a ruined cross on high,
Under clean Christian grass to lie,
  Shall we come home at last ? "

" The gates of heaven are lightly locked,
  We do not guard our gain ;
The heaviest hind may easily
Come silently and suddenly
  Upon me in a lane.

" And any little maid that walks
  In good thoughts apart,
May break the guard of the Three Kings,
And see the dear and dreadful things
  I hide within my heart.

" The meanest man in grey fields gone
  Behind the set of sun
May hear fall out twixt star and star
Through the door of the darkness dropped ajar,
The council eldest of things that are,
  The talk of the Three in One.

" The gates of heaven are lightly locked,
    We do not guard our gold ;
A man may learn how worlds begin
Or learn the name of the nameless sin ;
But if he fail or if he win
    To no good man is told.

" The men of the East may spell the stars,
    And times and triumphs mark,
But the men marked with the cross of Christ
    Go gaily in the dark.

" The men of the East may search the scrolls
    For sure fates and fame,
But the men that drink the blood of God
    Go singing to their shame.

" The wise men know what wicked things
    Are written in the sky ;
They light sad lamps and touch sad rings,
And hear the heavy purple wings
Where the forgotten angel kings
    Still plot how God shall die.

" The wise men know all evil things
    Under the twisted trees,
Where the perverse in pleasure pine,
And men are weary of green wine
    And sick of crimson seas.

" But you, and all the kind of Christ
    Are ignorant and brave,
And you have wars you hardly win,
    And souls you hardly save.

" I tell you naught for your comfort,
    Yea, naught for your desire,
Save that the sky grows darker yet
    And the sea rises higher.

FRAGMENT FROM A BALLAD EPIC OF "ALFRED"

" Night shall be thrice night over you,
  And heaven an iron cope ;
Do you have joy without a cause,
  And faith without a hope."

She faded even as Alfred heard,
  And never a word said he,
Only he heard still as he stood,
Under the old night's starry hood
The sea-folk breaking down the wood
  Like a high tide from sea.

Only he heard the heathen men
  Whose eyes are blue and bleak,
Singing about some cruel thing
Done by a great and smiling king
  In daylight on a deck.

Only he heard the heathen men
  Whose eyes are blue and blind
Singing what shameful things are done
Between the sunlit sea and the sun
  When the land is left behind.

G. K. Chesterton

A RUSSIAN MOTHER: A PERSONAL NARRATIVE (1897–1905)[1]

I KNOW that these reminiscences will be a fresh source of suffering to me, forcing me to live through the past again. But these sufferings have not been mine only. . . . Not I alone have felt the iron hand of the government heavy upon me. There are other mothers as unhappy as I—thousands of others. And so, my true story may have a certain value.

The first blow fell upon our family in 1897. Until that year, we had lived as everybody lived in those days in the provinces: with no special cares, or public interests—in an easy-going way, as well-paid officials mostly do live.

My husband had a post in the Ministry of Justice in the Western Region. He was a man of intellectual tastes and liberal ideas, who refused to recognise any distinction between Jews, Russians, and Poles, between the rich and the poor. As a magistrate, he soon became popular among the downtrodden and intimidated peoples of that Region, and used to be called to his face and behind his back " zatsny sendzya," that is, the honest judge.

During his twenty years of service he decided every case according to the law, acting on his own convictions, without regard to the wishes of the higher authorities, so that he soon gained the reputation of being a man difficult to manage and a " Red."

As long as our children were at home, our life was free from all but the little everyday anxieties about the children's health and welfare. But at last our two elder boys had been sent off to St. Petersburg—one to the School of Mining Engineering, the other to the University—and at once there was a break in our life. Our peaceful existence was at an

[1] *The following narrative is a record of actual fact. The writer is still living.* TRANSLATOR'S NOTE.

end and a perfect tempest of new troubles and apprehensions burst upon us.

In St. Petersburg, the unsatisfactory conditions of higher education, the restrictions that thwarted the students in every effort for the public good, the stupid tyranny that fretted the nerves of the young—all this was beginning in those days to stir up the agitation that has ended in the revolution we are living through now.

An outburst of resentment was provoked by the monument in Vilna to Muravieff. The erection of a monument to Muravieff by the government might, in spite of its monstrous lack of tact, have possibly had no serious consequences, had it not been for the action of a few of the Warsaw professors who basely sought to ingratiate themselves with the government and to display their "patriotism" by sending a telegram of congratulation to the government on the occasion in the name of the University.

When one remembers how hateful the name of Muravieff was to every true Pole, since almost every family cherished the memory of some member who had died at the hands of the executioner, and how fresh these wounds were in the hearts of a people so sensitive, one realises the bitter insult that was given to the whole nation by this memorial to the "Hangman," as the Poles called him.

But the crushed people made no sign, and it was only among the students that there were outbreaks of discontent. These disturbances were followed by sympathetic agitation in the other universities. From the time of the Muravieff episode up to the present day, the students of Russia have never been at rest—though the causes of their unrest have been various.

This incident decided the fate of my children. Their first arrest and the police raid that accompanied it have left an impression on me that nothing can ever efface.

It was in 1897. The Christmas holidays had come and my husband and I were eagerly expecting our sons home. They were so young and had so lately left the home of their childhood. It was interesting for us to see what influence the busy life of St. Petersburg had had on them, what use they had made of their freedom. Three days before Christmas they arrived in the liveliest spirits. We should hardly have known them, they had so grown up and developed in this period of separation. They were intensely interested in public questions, and as we listened to their keen, spirited talk, my husband and I stole glances of pride at each other. We saw nothing to find fault with in them, and we felt how happy we were that our children were turning out fine, honest, vigorous men, useful citizens of their country. We had no suspicion of the bitter mistake we were making. Their country had need of ardent, honest, vigorous men, but the government did not need them. We were to realise this only too soon, but that evening we were happy. Alas ! how could we guess that it was to be the last happy, untroubled evening in our lives ?

After the liveliest conversation, about one o'clock we thought it time at last to go to our rooms. The lamps were put out ; I had begun to undress. All of a sudden the stillness of the house was broken by a violent ring at the bell. Thinking it must be ·a telegram, I hurried into the hall. The maid was already at the door, asking " Who is there ? " " The police ! " I heard shouted in a loud, peremptory voice. Our life had passed so peacefully and we had so little to do with that department, that I was simply surprised and felt no alarm. While the door was being opened, I rushed into my sons' room : they were hurriedly dressing, their father standing by them in perplexity. At that moment we heard the clink of spurs and the colonel of gendarmes marched into the room, accompanied by policemen, clerks and the dvornik. " Excuse me," he explained, with an elegant scrape, " by instructions of the head authorities, it is my duty to make a search."

My husband and I looked at each other in horror. In those days things were not as they are to-day, when police raids and arrests have become an everyday occurrence. At that time a raid on the house of an official was a rare event. How can I describe the feeling of humiliation and indignation aroused by this first outrage ? To see everything in your house pried into, nothing in it left sacred, every object fingered, the photographs of your dearest and

nearest turned over and flung about, your private correspondence read, your children pawed all over by the coarse
hands of strangers! I felt as though I had been stripped
naked and thrust into some public thoroughfare.

Even now at the thought of that police search, I cannot
shake off the agonising feeling of shame and insult! It was
conducted too in the presence of an extraordinary number
of persons. A dozen were tramping to and fro in our rooms,
another half-dozen were kept in the kitchen in reserve, at
every door there was a gendarme, and the house was surrounded by a cordon on every side. All this simply to
apprehend two defenceless boys. . . . When the colonel
rummaged in my sons' travelling basket, he found there
several copies of an appeal from the students to the Warsaw
professors on the subject of the telegram of congratulation.

At five o'clock in the morning, after the most scrupulous search, in the course of which my younger children,
aged six and seven, were lifted out of bed by the gendarmes
that their mattresses and pillows might be examined, the
colonel turned to our sons : "Take leave of your parents,"
he said, "you are to come along with me."

Sobbing, we embraced our boys. They were pale but
calm. The colonel saw them out before him, all the rabble
followed him out . . . and our boys were gone !

I wandered miserably about the rooms; everything was
out of place, the tablecloths had been flung off the tables,
the sofa cushions had been slit open ; everywhere there were
the marks of dirty boots . . . one could hardly believe this
was our snug little nest! I looked at my husband, and was
alarmed to see him pale and gasping. Getting him hastily
to bed, I sent for the doctor.

The night passed, my husband fell asleep, but I could
not rest. . . . Where were my boys? What was in store
for them ? But with my anxiety was mixed a feeling of
intense indignation. Even if our sons were guilty, we had
nothing to do with it. Why had they not searched them
in St. Petersburg, or even in the train on their journey?
Why let them come home in order to rouse up a whole
household in the middle of the night? If the protests
were to be looked upon as a crime, why were they not

taken from them sooner, before they had reached their
parents' home ?.

Choking with indignation, I went to my own room,
and writing a letter of complaint to the Governor, stamped
it and posted it myself.

At that time the Governor of the Western Region was
Prince Imeretinsky, one of the most humane governors of
that unhappy district—unhappy, because a whole series of
governors—foremost among them Gurko, and only second
to him, Tchertkoff—had carried out in it the idea of
" Russification."

The mere fact of being " Russian " brought with it a
mass of privileges, and put a person above the law. In the
twenty years of our life there, we had seen violence,
brutality, coarse abuse, blows, everything sanctioned, everything allowed to pass in a Russian. More than once my
husband has told me with indignation of the incredible
lawlessness of the police against which there was no redress.
Often he has witnessed incidents that made one ashamed of
being Russian. Under Prince Imeretinsky's rule, the Poles
for the first time obtained something like an indulgent
hearing. He received Poles graciously, was ready to discuss
things with them, and gradually introduced some alleviations
in the position. Thus, he gave permission for prayers to be
said in schools in the native tongue, and gave up punishing
the children for speaking Polish in their playtime.

Later on, in General Tchertkoff's time, it would never
have occurred to me to protest, as then such arbitrary
proceedings received support and commendation.

To the credit of Prince Imeretinsky I must add that he
did not leave my letter unanswered. He demanded an
explanation from the Procurator and from the General of the
Gendarmerie, and sent his own adjutant to express his regret
at what had occurred. Three days later our sons were
released from the citadel.

But the police search and arrest had left traces in their
hearts. They were continually talking of them, and their
eyes flashed with hatred of the capricious despotism which
sanctioned the erection of a monument to a man hated by
the whole population, and refused to allow any protest

against it. We could not condemn their indignation : the facts spoke for themselves, and there was no gainsaying them. With heavy hearts we saw them set off for St. Petersburg : we could see that they were not in the mood for passive acquiescence.

Less than two months later, in February 1898, we received from our younger boy the news that the elder had been arrested. I set off at once for St. Petersburg.

I was completely ignorant of the world in which I was destined from that day forth to move. Prison, bayonets, soldiers, gendarmes, had been abstractions for me, known only by name. And so on my arrival in St. Petersburg I wasted a lot of time at first from inexperience.

If I applied to the Office of Public Security, they referred me to the Gendarmerie Department, and from there I was sent back to the office I had just come from. Then I was advised to apply to the General of the Gendarmes. On applying there, I learned that he only saw applicants on certain days at certain fixed hours. In my distress all this was a real torture to me. Finally, being myself the wife of a magistrate, I resolved to try the Department of Justice and applied to the Procurator of the Palace.

The Procurator at last gave me permission to see my son. By that time I had been thoroughly alarmed by the air of mystery with which the gendarmes love to surround the simplest affair, and so it was with a sinking heart that I went to the House of Preliminary Detention. The feeling that this was a prison, and that my son was locked up in it, had an unnerving effect on me, and my complete ignorance of his offence made me dread the worst. Over a door in the quadrangle I saw the inscription, " Office," and going in I found the room crowded with people of all classes. There were richly-dressed ladies and very poor-looking old women, students and many girls, whose interesting faces made me guess them to be " kursistki." They seemed quite at home here, and evidently knew the rules of the place : they had nosegays of flowers and parcels for the prisoners. The novelty of my surroundings and the agony of apprehension I was in overcame me so much that I sank on to the nearest bench in tears. The young girls surrounded me at once with sympathetic inquiries. At that moment my number was shouted.

I followed the warder. There were about a dozen of us, persons of all sorts and conditions. A soldier walked behind us.

The warder showed the permit at the gates, and there was much grating of locks and bolts. I expected to see my son at once, but after passing through the gates we came to more bolts and bars, and the same process was gone through. At last we were led into the prison itself, and at that moment two gendarmes passed us with drawn swords, and walking between them a quite young, boyish little student, with the flush of childhood still on his cheeks.

" Aye, what a youngster ! " an old woman beside me murmured commiseratingly, crossing herself.

We all sighed: every one of us had a boy locked up here.

" And what do they shut boys like that up for ? " said a merchant wrathfully, but the gendarme looked round at him sternly and replied reprovingly, " Well, why do they resist the authorities ? "

At the end of a corridor an officer was sitting at a table with a group of soldiers by him. My muff and umbrella were taken from me. The officer looked me up and down suspiciously. Then I was taken into a dark, sunless room, six feet across. It was empty. I looked in surprise at the gendarme.

" Coming directly," he replied briefly.

The door opened, and I saw my son. With what anguish I embraced him !

One may get used to anything. Later on I grew more or less accustomed to prison. But this first interview with the boy who had been snatched from us made a lasting impression. . . . The prison had tight hold of him, and none could force open its walls for me.

Our time was short. Hurriedly I gave my son news of the outer world, but as soon as I spoke in French, I heard at once : " Speaking in foreign languages prohibited." We were of course not alone. . . . I had been warned in the office that I must ask no questions, must not speak of my son's case, must not mention proper names . . . and many, many more absurd " must nots ". . . .

Looking at my boy, I saw with distress that solitary confinement was already showing its effects on him. He was very pale, and his face looked swollen. He had not once been questioned, and I was the first living soul he had had to speak to since his arrest.

And the time seemed long from one interview to another. In those days it was better than later on. Parents coming from a distance were allowed interviews of twenty minutes twice a week, and they might bring books, cigarettes, and parcels for the prisoners. Letters might be written and received.

Every interview confirmed the miserable conviction that my son's health was breaking down. I called upon the Procurator and spoke of the disastrous effects of prison upon my son's health. He listened politely, but said that it was not in his power to release my son, that the preliminary investigation was only just beginning, and on my inquiring what my son was accused of, he shrugged his shoulders and replied that he was not at liberty to answer that question.

The time dragged on and still my son was not released : he had been two months in prison. Meanwhile I was needed at home : my younger children were taken ill, and my husband with his official duties had not time to look after them. I was forced to go, but I felt heart-broken at leaving my boy alone. In vain I addressed petitions to the Procurator, to the Gendarmerie Department, and to the Office of Public Security. Everywhere they tried to get rid of me by declaring they knew nothing about the case.

Only the General of the Gendarmerie inquired :

" And why do you want to know when the case will be tried ? "

I explained that I had to leave St. Petersburg and that I was in despair at leaving my son in prison. He gave a coarse laugh.

" Well, madam," said he, "if we were to consult the feelings of parents, our prisons would be empty."

Our relations with our acquaintances and with society

generally had undergone a marked change since our son's arrest. Being now for the first time in real trouble, we began instinctively to draw away from people holding the correct official views, and a small but very intimate circle of friends of our own way of thinking began to form around us. My husband and I, led by the events of our own lives, began to keep an anxious watch upon the policy of the administration, and from contented people, well satisfied with our own official prosperity, we gradually found ourselves maintaining a critical attitude to the wanton despotism of the government. It was the facts of life itself that drove us to this.

Meanwhile my letters to and from my son were little satisfaction to us. What could we say to each other with the thought that every word would pass first under the eyes of the gendarmes? His letters were sometimes blotted out in parts, and at the bottom was always the official stamp: "Permitted."

Four months went by. We heard that the police had made a descent upon my younger son's rooms, and though he was still at liberty, this piece of news did not add to our tranquillity. Our nerves were continually on the rack. As I lay in bed, I pictured to myself the prison, my son's cell, the tramp of the sentinels and the grating of locks. What was my poor boy doing? Was he asleep? Was he walking about his cell? Was he miserable? . . . And I turned from side to side and could not sleep. I was continually recalling my boy's wasted figure and worn face, and the longer his solitary confinement lasted, the more anxious I became about his health. And not without good reason.

At the end of the fifth month, I got a letter advising me to make an effort to get my son released if only on his parents' security, as his health was breaking down. I packed my things at once, and reaching St. Petersburg went straight to the Police Department, as it happened to be on Friday, the day for seeing applicants. One had to wait several hours to see the Chief of the Police ; the waiting-room was crowded with people of all sorts trying to obtain a personal interview with the Chief.

The Chief of the Police Department at that time,

Zvoliansky, rose on seeing a lady, set a comfortable chair for me, heard me with courteous attention, shook his head, threw up his hands, talked in a sympathetic tone of unhappy parents and erring children, promised that to-morrow, not a day later, my son should be examined, and if he were ill, should be at once released, and scraping and bowing in the most gallant manner, he conducted me to the door.

I went away in an ecstasy of joy. . . . I forgot my fatigue, my anxiety, my grief. . . . The thought that my boy might . . . perhaps even to-morrow . . . be released, made me delirious with joy! I went back to my hotel comforted. . . .

Alas! another Friday passed, and another and yet another, and one weary month and a second before I succeeded, after endless applications and petitions, in getting my son out of prison.

I soon obtained leave to see him, however. My God! how my heart ached when after four months' absence I saw him again. . . . I should hardly have recognised him in the street; thin, pale, bent, with a greenish pallor in his cheeks. . . .

" My darling! But what have you done that they should torture you like this ? " I cried.

" No allusion to the case permitted," I heard an indifferent voice repeat.

I spent weary weeks tramping about St. Petersburg from one department to another, and waiting hours at a stretch for a moment's interview with the authorities, before my son, his health completely shattered, was at last let out on bail.

There was intense dissatisfaction at this time among the students. The numerous arrests, the spies who were dogging suspected students at every step, the wretched University regulations, the deadly pedantry of the Minister of Education, the frequent cases of banishment and expulsion from the University, which was accompanied by loss of the right to enter any other educational institution, all this combined to arouse intense indignation. The reasons for discontent were too obvious and the stern measures taken to suppress it had exactly the opposite result. That year there was the mass meeting of students before the Kazan Sobor.

On the day of that meeting I was out walking when I saw an immense crowd in the Nevsky Prospect running in the direction of the Admiralty. I asked a policeman what was the matter.

" The students are rioting at the Kazan Sobor," he answered calmly.

I thought of my younger son, and calling a sledge, I hastened to the quarter where he lived with his wife and a tiny baby. We could not drive along the Nevsky, but the side streets were quiet, though down the turnings we could see crowds gathering in the main thoroughfare.

I found neither my son nor my daughter-in-law at home. Taking my little grandchild in my arms, I walked up and down, anxiously awaiting their return. Hours passed, my uneasiness grew ; several times I sent the nurse out into the street to find out what was going on, and every time she brought back more alarming news:

" The students have marched to Anitchkovo. They're beating them in an awful way ! Lots of them have been trampled under the horses ! They say they are carrying some away dead ! "

I was terribly alarmed.

At six o'clock my son and his wife at last came in. But what a state they were in ! My daughter-in-law had her arm bruised and swollen and her cloak torn. My son had received a blow on the head. They had both rushed to protect a girl-student, and so had come within reach of the Cossacks' nagaikas. They described with indignation the revolting treatment of the unarmed students by the police and the Cossacks.

My son's comrades came in one after another, all more or less injured. As I listened to their boiling indignation and fury against the government, I felt that no prophet was needed to see that that day's event was only the precursor of much more in the future.

At last my eldest son was released. I said good-bye to my younger boy with an anxious heart. He had been deeply stirred by recent events.

A RUSSIAN MOTHER

"There is trouble ahead," I thought, and I was not mistaken.

I had not been a week at home with my eldest boy, before I got a letter from my daughter-in-law to tell me that my younger son had been arrested, and sent to the fortress. The brave girl did her best to put the matter in the most reassuring light, but the fact that he was in the fortress spoke for itself. She urged me, however, not to come to St. Petersburg as I could be of no use ; for even she, his wife, was not allowed to see him. I need not say that the news of this fresh calamity almost drove me to despair ; but to spare my husband and my elder son, I concealed from them that the younger boy was in the fortress, and told them simply that he had been arrested.

Mournful days followed. My eldest son's ruined health, my husband's nervous condition, my younger son's imprisonment—all made our life a sorrowful one. Moreover, my heart yearned towards my second prisoner ; the fortress is a living tomb. My son used to tell me later on that after some months in the fortress, he had grown so used to the deathlike silence and stillness, that when he was removed to solitary confinement in the House of Preliminary Detention, where a few sounds such as footsteps, voices and sledge-bells reached him, these trifling noises at first seemed deafening.

Of the disastrous effects of solitary confinement, I had a living example always before my eyes in my elder son. From a vigorous young man, radiant with life and health, he had become a living shadow, starting at the slightest sound, unable to bear conversation, and shrinking from society. In the past he had been particularly energetic and efficient at his work. Now he could settle to nothing, and his temper was of the gloomiest. I understood the bitterness of his position. There was no getting any work in his own line in our town, and to return to the School of Mining Engineering was of course out of the question, since he was not allowed to be in St. Petersburg. Though time did much to restore his physical health, he still remained so depressed that it made my heart ache to see him. I consulted doctors. They advised change of climate and surroundings, and interesting work in the open air.

I suggested to my son that I should try to get permission for him to go, before his sentence, to the Ural mines, where he had more than once in previous summers worked as a mining engineer.

His case had been "by administrative order," and so there was no court to appeal to, and we could only await what the Public Security Office and the Gendarmerie might think fit to decide.

My son welcomed the suggestion eagerly and we sent in our petition. A long time passed before we received a reply.

Meanwhile my younger son, after five months in the fortress and four in the House of Preliminary Detention, was sent by administrative order to Vologda to await his sentence there, and obtained permission to come for three days to say good-bye to his parents. He too was terribly changed, thinner, paler, and much more nervous. But he was tougher than his brother, and he was buoyed up by the thought of having his wife and child with him in Vologda.

At last permission arrived for my eldest son to go to the Ural works before the final decision of his case. The thought of setting to work and being of some use again roused him from his apathy, and he began eagerly preparing for the journey; he bought books, got himself a violin and set off, happy and eager, promising to send us a telegram from Moscow. Sorry as we were to part with him, we could feel nothing but gladness at the improvement in his health and spirits. We waited patiently for news. Several days passed. Still no telegram, and no letter. According to our calculations, he ought long ago to have left Moscow.

Why did he make no sign? We waited on. Still the same sinister silence. Then we sent a telegram to friends in Moscow to ask whether he had been to see them, and what was wrong with him.

What was our consternation and despair when in reply we learned that our son was in Moscow, but immediately on his arrival had been arrested and was again in prison!

He had been for nine months with us, scarcely leaving the house, and seeing no one but our most intimate friends. There had been absolutely nothing suspicious in his actions, and we knew every detail of his life. . . . We thought of the faith, of the joy with which he had set off. . . . We were choking with indignation. . . . But it was no time for delay; one way or another, we must help him : in his nervous state, another spell of prison might be the destruction of him.

Setting my household affairs into some sort of order, and confiding my heartbroken husband to the care of our friends, I set off for Moscow.

I arrived in the evening. But I was in such despair that I could not wait till morning. The Procurator of the Palace of Justice was at that time Klugen, with whom I had had some slight acquaintance in the past . . . and so, though it was nine o'clock, I sent up my card to him. I was at once asked to walk up, and the Procurator came affably to meet me. He welcomed me as an old friend, and in spite of his wife's absence asked me to stay with them. The usual questions followed : " Had I come for long ? How was my husband ? What were the boys doing ? "

While he was putting me into a chair, I could not speak, tears choked me. He looked at me more closely and asked, " Why, what is the matter ? Mercy on us, what is wrong ? "

But when he heard that my son was a political prisoner, his face changed, his voice grew colder, and finally he passed into the regular official tone, and explained that he knew nothing whatever of my son's arrest, and could do nothing for me, as this was a case in the Gendarmerie Department. I could see that as the mother of a political prisoner I was in his eyes a person inconvenient to know. Those were the days of Plehve, and human feeling in an official was a crime ! More than once afterwards it was my lot to see a similar transformation among my kind acquaintances of the official world.

The Procurator, nevertheless, " did what he could " for me: he took out his visiting card and, scribbling a few words on it, advised me to take it to the Head of the Gendarmerie Department.

I was thankful to get as much as that. Seeing me out in a manner which was a strange contrast to the effusiveness with which he had greeted me at first, the Procurator informed me that should I ever wish to see him again, he saw applicants at the Palace of Justice on such a day: I understood: our personal acquaintance was at an end. . . . I did not sleep all night. . . .

At ten o'clock next morning I was on the steps of the Moscow Gendarmerie Department. I was familiar already with the manners and customs of the gendarmes; I had had to meet humiliations, brutal rebuffs, and callous indifference. But the methods of the Moscow gendarmerie, their heartlessness, their scoffing enjoyment of the sufferings of others, made me almost regret the St. Petersburg gendarmes, and think of them as comparatively humane.

I shudder when I recall all that I underwent in Moscow.

There was no room set apart for applicants. All who came were crowded in a small, half-dark entry together with the non-commissioned officers of the gendarmerie. There one had to spend hours at a stretch before the officer one wanted made his appearance. And during this long, weary waiting, one could hear the officer in the next room gossiping at his leisure about the entertainments of the previous evening. Sometimes he would stroll out with a cigarette between his teeth, and scanning the weary visitor with an insolent grin, would vanish into another room. If one slipped half a rouble into a gendarme's hand, and begged him to remind the officer one had been waiting over an hour, one heard the reply, intentionally shouted so as to be overheard, " Let her wait! " followed by approving guffaws.

Sometimes, after hours of exhausting suspense, I have seen the officer come out into the entry, put on his overcoat, and slam the door after him. Then a sergeant would come up and say, " The lieutenant has gone for to-day! Come again to-morrow."

And the next day I would have to wait again. There was no escaping the gendarmes. Money, books, and parcels could only be sent through them to the prisoners, permission for interviews could only be obtained through them. I had to face the gendarmes!

On my first visit I came upon a terrible scene. In the entry a middle-aged woman, very well dressed, was walking to and fro. I shall never forget the look of misery in her great eyes. She was not weeping; but as she paced up and down, her face grew whiter and whiter.

At last a captain came out, and, not looking at her, put a slip of paper into the sergeant's hand. " Tell So-and-so," he mentioned the surname alone without any prefix, " that the interview is refused! "

The unhappy lady stood still at once as though she had been shot.

" What? Refused again! " she cried. " Monsieur le Capitaine! In God's name! "

" Impossible! " answered the captain, smiling most malignantly.

" Then God's curse be upon you all! " shrieked the lady at the top of her voice. The faces of officers appeared at all the doors.

" God's curse be upon you all! " the poor woman screamed in a frenzy of grief. " Arrest me too; put me too in fetters, but don't part me from him! I must be with him! . . . Where have you hidden him? Let me go to him. . . . Oh, for a knife! "

She was beside herself, but in her screams there was something so heartrending, such a depth of woe, that the gendarmes did not arrest her, but merely muttered: " Semyonov! take her out! "

And Semyonov, who had seemed to me impenetrable to every human feeling, took her by the elbow, and said almost tenderly: " This way, please! Don't upset yourself so! What's the use? Why, they'll be arresting you next! "

S. A. SAVINKOV
(Translator, Mrs. Garnett)

(The remainder of the narrative will be found in our next number)

THE FIRST EARL DURHAM[1]

WHAT does the ordinary English citizen know about Lord Durham? He has seen his Lordship's head as the sign of a public house, or he has heard that we ought to have had a Lord Durham in South Africa to settle differences between the Briton and the Boer, or he may have heard that Canadian self-government was originated by Lord Durham. He will probably have a good opinion of him, but it will be founded on vague information, and it is not likely that he will place him in the first rank of statesmen. He may not judge him as harshly as he was judged by some of his contemporaries, but he will not rank him on a level with Lord Grey or Lord John Russell or even with Lord Melbourne. But what place does he deserve? On inquiry we find that he was a radical when radicals were scarce and unpopular, that he was associated as a responsible statesman with the philosophical radicals who numbered amongst them Grote, Roebuck and Mill, that he was the real author of the Reform Bill, that, at a time when Home Rule was unknown, he supported a national government for Ireland, that he was the first to discover that to grant responsible government to the Colonies was the only way to make them contented, to develope their resources and to render them loyal members of the British Empire.

If we wish to enlarge our knowledge of Lord Durham, what do we find? He is frequently mentioned in the lively pages of Mr. Creevy, where he enjoys the sobriquet of "King Jog." He knew him well and describes him

---

[1] *Life and Letters of the First Earl Durham*, 1792–1840. By Stuart J. Reid. (Longmans, Green & Co. 1906.)

in 1827 as full of good qualities and very remarkable, but subject to volcanic eruptions of temper. Finding no water where he expected some, he belaboured the bell in a manner which Creevy thought must inevitably bring the whole concern down, and then proceeded to strike his valet with a stick. Creevy has a scene with him at the dinner table, and thinks he must leave the house. Durham has a terrible quarrel with his father-in-law, Lord Grey, at a Cabinet dinner, in which he accuses Grey of being the cause of his son's death by obliging him to attend Cabinets. If, leaving this gossip, we turn to the sober pages of the *Dictionary of National Biography* we find the statement that "his undoubted abilities were rendered useless by his complete want of tact, while his unstable temper and overbearing manner made him a most undesirable colleague." Charles Grenville, in his memoirs, omits no occasion of disparaging him, and his censures have undoubtedly had a great effect upon the estimation in which he is generally held.

It is this judgement which Mr. Stuart Reid sets himself to remove, and he has undoubtedly done so with success. He has written an admirable biography, most valuable for the history of the time, and from it Lord Durham emerges, if not a statesman of the first rank, at least worthy to hold his own with others who have been placed before him. He was before his age. He held views which time has endorsed, but which were then too positive and too much advanced for those with whom he had to act. He showed a rare prescience in political affairs. If he erred in reluctance to accept a compromise, he at least saw the hollowness of many proposed accommodations, and clearly grasped the essential conditions on which democratic government must be based.

No period of English History is more dismal and in many ways more discreditable than that which followed the downfall of Napoleon, a catastrophe to which the English-government so largely contributed. In his maiden speech Lambton denounced the foreign policy of the Liverpool and Castlereagh administration and attacked the surrender of Norway to Bernadotte, the disastrous effects of which have reached a climax in our own day. In those times, " an awful period for those who had the misfortune to hold liberal opinions," he was in common with others "assailed with all the Billingsgate of the French Revolution," called "Jacobin leveller," atheist and regicide and shunned as unfit for the relations of social life. At this time, as Mr. Reid tells us, poverty was widespread, taxation was excessive, labour was cheap, work scarce and wages low. In some towns one out of every seven was a pauper and in some villages almost every one was bankrupt. It was in the darkest season of this humiliation, just after the passing of the Six Acts, that Lambton proposed in Parliament the repeal of the Septennial Act, the extension of the franchise to all copyholders and householders paying direct taxes, and the destruction of rotten boroughs.

The realisation of these proposals did not take place till Lord Grey assumed office in November 1830. He gave the preparation of the Reform Bill to Lord Durham in conjunction with Lord John Russell, assisted by Sir James Graham and Lord Duncannon. They formed the famous "Committee of Four" by whom the Bill was drafted, and they met in the library of Lord Durham's house in Cleveland Row. The result was naturally a compromise, but the Bill contained a provision for the ballot which was not finally carried till many years after. If Lord Durham had been a member of the House of Commons the Bill would have been introduced by him and not by Lord John Russell, and his name would have been more closely connected with it. The Bill received the royal assent on June 7, 1832, and effected a bloodless revolution. Durham always attributed the victory to the statesmanlike firmness of the Political Union of Birmingham.

Unfortunately the reformed Parliament which met in January 1833, and did such admirable work in the domain of liberal legislation, did nothing on a large scale to remedy the political grievances of Ireland, but adopted a policy of coercion. Durham was at this time so often in a minority that he received the name of the " Dissenting Minister," and in March resigned his place in the Cabinet. Out of office he continued to take the lead in reform, and in 1834 he supported the petition against religious tests presented by the University of Cambridge. Similarly at a great banquet held at Newcastle he declared that the Reform Bill was not an end but a means, and supported the shortening of Parliaments, the ballot and the reform of Church abuses.

The last and the best known action of Durham's life was his work as Governor-General of Canada. He was sent there to put a stop to a dangerous rebellion arising from the racial quarrels of French and English, as the Boer War arose from racial quarrels between the English and the Dutch. He acted with a wisdom, which has been ever since a landmark in politics, but which was unfortunately absent in the recent repetition of similar difficulties. The idea of the ministry was to give Durham a free hand. The existing constitution had been suspended and the new governor-general was to make new arrangements. Lord Melbourne and his colleagues were pledged to give him the firmest and the most unflinching support. He was accompanied by Charles Buller, one of the most brilliant of academical politicians, whose memory remains in Cambridge to our own day. On his arrival in Canada he found that his difficulties were increased by the sympathy of the Americans for the revolted Canadians, and that a war between Great Britain and the United States was not impossible. Durham dispelled this danger by declaring in the clearest manner his confidence in the friendly feelings of the United States towards England. Unfortunately his mission, begun with brilliant hopes, was wrecked on a comparatively small issue, the fate of the political prisoners, who ought to have been dealt with before his arrival. The leaders of the revolt were regarded by many as popular heroes, and might have been acquitted if tried in the ordinary course of law. Some had fled from justice, and were still engaged in rebellious acts, so that a general amnesty was impossible. Durham had to steer a middle course between universal pardon and a severity which would have made the prisoners political martyrs. He therefore issued a proclamation on June 28, 1838, the day of Queen Victoria's coronation, which forbade the return of Papineau, the leader, to Canada under the penalty of death and gave an amnesty to all the rest excepting eight who were exiled to Bermuda. Lord Durham's action was approved of both by British and French in Canada; it put a stop to all danger of war with the United States. But it was opposed in the English Parliament by Durham's personal enemies on the ground that in sending the prisoners to Bermuda he had exceeded his legal powers. Unfortunately the Ministry was too weak to support him, and the proclamation was disallowed. Lord Durham had no alternative but to resign, after he had held his office for only five months.

However, the influence of Lord Durham's principles was not at an end, but was destined to take a new and more vigorous departure. In January 1839 was laid before Parliament Lord Durham's famous report on the affairs of British North America, one of the few state papers which has become a political classic. It marked a turning point in the relations between England and the Colonies, and laid down the lines on which the government of our colonies should in future be based. It has become the text book of every advocate of Colonial freedom in all parts of the globe. It lays down the principles of Colonial self-government. Durham had found in Canada two races at war, differing in origin, in language, in religion, and education. He looked forward to an ultimate federation of all the Canadian provinces such as has been realised at a later time. But the proper season for this had not arrived. All that was possible was the union of Upper and Lower Canada, the creation of an executive council responsible to the new assembly, which he proposed to create, coupled with state-aided emigration, the abolition of the clergy reserves, and the establishment of an intercolonial railway. These measures he said would turn Canada from a barren and injurious sovereignty into one of the brightest ornaments of the young queen's crown.

There can be no doubt that this report was written mainly by Lord Durham himself, however much he may have been assisted by the brilliant intellect of Charles Buller. It was the culminating service which he rendered to his country and to the empire. It was also the last.

Five days after the Bill was passed which gave effect to Lord Durham's recommendations he died by a sudden illness. We cannot be too grateful to Mr. Reid for having given us the history of a man who, calumniated and misunderstood during his lifetime and neglected after his death, has an undoubted claim to stand in the first rank of the statesmen who changed the government of England from an outworn oligarchy to that of a contented and prosperous democracy.

Oscar Browning

THE OUTLOOK IN IRELAND [1]

FIFTEEN years ago, even ten years ago, Irish politics were a simple business; simple for the observer ; not of course simple for the statesmen who had either to do things or to prevent things being done. To-day Irish politics, without being a whit less difficult for the statesman, have become immensely complicated, and therefore very interesting for the observer. For instance, Lord Dunraven makes a profession of faith. " I am a landlord, a Protestant and a Unionist. I hold to my class, my creed and my political faith." Ten years ago such a confession would have sufficed. We should have placed the man who made it. We should have required no more words to tell us what he believed, what he felt, what he hoped. To such a man then " nationalist " and " blackguard " were interchangable terms. All nationalists were necessarily blackguards, and every kind of blackguardism known in Ireland drew its essential spirit from nationalism. In those days the Protestant, Unionist landlord believed whole-heartedly that the system under which Ireland is governed was perfect, and that nothing was wanting for the peace and prosperity of the country except the determined administration of law as

[1] *The Outlook in Ireland.* By the Earl of Dunraven, K.P. (John Murray. 1907.)

it stood. Ireland's troubles were to be attributed to the feebleness and vacillation of the men who administered, not to any flaw in the system of government itself. Ireland for the Unionist of those days was a bit of England, another Yorkshire, an Isle of Wight with a rather wider stretch of water between it and the mother island. What suited England must of necessity suit Ireland.

To-day things are quite different. Our Protestant, Unionist landlord has realised that he is an Irishman in a sense like that in which his great-grandfather understood the word in 1780; and, realising this, has come to see some very startling things. " With marvellous but mistaken pertinacity England has laboured to anglicise Ireland for some eight hundred years and has failed." The sentence reads like an extract from the propagandist speech of a Gaelic Leaguer. It is a quotation from the book of the Unionist landlord who speaks for the " Irish Reform Association." And the conviction that Ireland is in some sense a distinct nation is not peculiar to Lord Dunraven and his little band of associates. It has laid hold upon the minds of many Irish Unionists who still hesitate to throw in their lot with Lord Dunraven. Of course there is a remnant, a respectable and not uninfluential remnant of the old Unionist Party. An angry outcry was raised the other day against the declaration of the President of the Gaelic League that Ireland must be " de-anglicised." But the outcry didn't terrify anyone. The younger men of the class which ought by tradition to belong to the irreconcilable Unionist party are beginning to think, and whether they accept the devolution plan of dealing with the Irish question or not, are becoming convinced that there is a good deal of truth in the premises from which Lord Dunraven argues. It is no longer possible to feel sure that a Protestant Unionist landlord will be in full sympathy with Mr. Walter Long's administration; just as it is no longer safe to assume that every man who calls himself a nationalist is prepared to accept Mr. Redmond as his leader. Irish political opinion is in a confused state. Men are no longer ranged opposite each other in uniformed rows. The country is full of skirmishers whose inclination is for sniping shots into both the old camps ; who are very little amenable to strict party discipline. A considerable number of Irishmen are beginning to think for themselves in political matters, and such independence will surely in the end be an advantage, even though at present it finds expression in a good deal of disrespectful language about the old standards and watchwords.

But the power of the old watchwords is not wholly gone. A nationalist may be a great deal more interested in questions of social reform at home than in the tactics of the parliamentary party at Westminster, and yet find it convenient to give a formal adherence to the official creed. A Protestant landlord may make a lot of startling discoveries about the state of Ireland, and yet be most anxious to convince everybody that he is a sound Unionist. Lord Dunraven and the gentlemen of the Irish Reform Association want to be classed as Unionists, being thoroughly convinced that they are Unionists, and that their policy is the only sound policy for Unionists. One does not deny their honesty or refuse to accept their assurances. But it may very well be asked whether it is really possible for most men to remain Unionists once they have understood all that Lord Dunraven understands about Ireland. Take the matter of the taxation of Ireland. Lord Dunraven devotes a whole chapter of his book to Ireland's financial burdens. He argues that Ireland is overtaxed to the extent of more than four millions annually. He lays it down elsewhere that " It is not kindness we are pleading for ; we want justice." How is justice to be done in a case like this ? Lord Dunraven, clinging to his Unionism, thinks that the taxable capacity of Ireland " should be increased by a wise application of public money to the development of the country." In other words, " Help Ireland to grow rich and then the taxation will cease to be excessive." The idea is attractive and undoubtedly consistent with the Unionism of Mr. Balfour and Mr. Wyndham. But will any considerable body of Irishmen ever be got to accept it ? An Irish Unionist party which says boldly that Ireland is no more overtaxed than Essex is may find, and does find, adherents. An Irish Home Rule party which says that Ireland is overtaxed, and must therefore get clear of her fiscal union with

England, will certainly find adherents in Ireland. But how will the common man, once he has grasped the fact of the over-taxation, ever come to accept the doctrine of the Reform Association? He, poor fellow, has perhaps himself been living in too expensive a house. He hopes some day to be able to afford the rent of it; but meanwhile he understands the wisdom of moving into a cheaper one.

There is a note of pathos in this devolutionary Unionism. It is the political creed of honourable men still loyal to the traditions of their class, but cursed with a fatal clearness of vision. For no one sees more clearly than Lord Dunraven and his fellow-reformers that Ireland is sick. No one enumerates more convincingly the symptoms of her disease. "The broad fact is that the best in Ireland is flowing outward; the worst is drifting in increasing proportions to the lunatic asylums; and the balance remains in Ireland of necessity rather than of choice." "At present the whole educational system of Ireland is an anomalous botch." "Head for head the government of Ireland costs more than the government of any civilised community on the face of the whole earth." "While in Great Britain direct and indirect taxation are fairly evenly balanced, in Ireland the poverty of the country is so great that 72·2 per cent. of the amount which she pays into the Imperial exchequer is raised by taxes upon such commodities as are in daily use among the poorest people." The decay, the confusion, the ignorance, the government extravagance, the crushing weight of taxation, the whole list of ills against which Ireland has struggled, are plain to the gentlemen of the Reform Association. They have seen them and seen more. They have realised the underlying fact that "Ireland differentiates." They understand the spirit of nationality; "the natural pride in the mere fact that, in spite of every effort to deprive her of nationhood, Ireland remains Ireland to this day." It is very wonderful, considering the history of the last thirty years, that Protestant Unionist landlords have understood so much. It is more wonderful still that having seen what they do see they can remain where they are; can be content to advocate their Devolution as a remedy for the evils they deplore. It is quite incredible that their policy can ever attract the mass of the Irish people or even secure the allegiance of the majority of their own class. It is doctrinaire, in spite of its underlying sincerity of feeling ; it is of the library, not of the market-place ; a conception of the student, not of the man of affairs. The old Unionism was and is a practical policy. It appeals to the men who were driven against the wall by the pressure of lawlessness in the " bad times." The dualism, the restoration of Grattan's Parliament, which is the avowed aim of the Sinn Féin party, is intelligible and therefore attractive. Even the vaguely formulated aspiration after federation and the status of a self-governing colony which some of the Irish Parliamentary party have expressed, is good enough to work for and vote for. But Devolution, as the members of the Reform Association conceive it, Devolution as an end in itself, makes no appeal to Irishmen of any class, cannot be thought of as the final cure of Ireland's sickness.

JAMES O. HANNAY

THE AMERICAN SCENE [1]

"FROM the moment the principle of selection and expression, with a tourist, is not the delight of the eyes and the play of the fancy, it should be an energy, in every way much larger; there is no happy mean, in other words, I hold between the sense and the quest of the picture, and the surrender to it, and the sense and quest of the constitution, the inner springs of the subject—springs and connections social, economic, historic : "—so Mr. James wrote in the preface to that delightful record of the pleasures of perception, *A Little Tour in France*. On that journey he confined himself to the quest of the picture ; in *The American Scene*, he searches for the inner springs of his subject. His testimony is of extraordinary interest because it is the result of a direct personal vision. To describe these pages simply as personal " impressions " would not

---

[1] *The American Scene*. By Henry James. (Chapman and Hall. 12s. 6d.)

suggest the stability of judgement and consistency of view, which lies behind them; for impressions are at the mercy of moods, and moods are the playthings of chance; but the temperament of the artist, however complex it may be, is stable. We may marvel at the abandonment with which Mr. James yields himself to his sensibilities, confident that they will not betray him, and at the temerity with which he will follow an intuition beyond the point of possible verification; but these are precisely his characteristics as a novelist—to be besieged by swarming impressions, yet to remain fundamentally collected, to be so determined in following the most evanescent of clues to the very end.

It is this intellectual determination which saves him as an artist, while it loses him many a reader; for without it a man of such extraordinary receptivity would become either bewildered and incoherent amidst the press of hints, perceptions and criss-cross clues, which his imagination continually presents to him, or he would find at last only a meagre expression of himself, at the cost of deliberately strangling nine-tenths of his perceptions in their infancy. Thanks to his extraordinary mental tenacity Mr. James has not been driven to such Herodian methods. He has the power of clutching a perception, however swift its passage across the mind, and of holding on to it through all its Protean changes and twists till it yields up its meaning. These intellectual wrestlings are not to be followed by the reader without a painful effort of attention.

The book itself is a monument to the artist's confidence in the imaginative reason as a means of discovering the significance of things, a confidence which translated into words might run thus : " If I can but faithfully record what I have felt in my travels, I have no more need to verify my conclusions by referring to the works of economists, historians, and social philosophers, than I had need of their generalisations to help me see what I saw; if I can but keep the mirror of my imagination clear and flawless, the pictures reflected there will express the substance of those truths that anatomists of the body politic by their figures and theories strive to represent indirectly."

Mr. James has studied the life and manners of a whole

nation precisely in the way he would have studied the behaviour and surroundings of a family whose story he wished to write. He has made no use of figures as warrants, or of American literature as documents, no more than he would have required to examine the accounts and correspondence of a family in order to tell their story. He trusts his imagination to reveal the lurking significance of what he sees and to lead him farther and beyond.

This, then, is the supreme interest of the book, that it is an account of the manners (in the widest sense) of a huge complex society, written by one haunted by the obsessions of a story-teller, who trusts his art to represent not only individual lives, but to suggest the life of a community. In form it is the journal of a voyage of imaginative discovery, in which the reader shares the excitement and suspense " of the restless analyst " himself, his delays, his defeats, and the fruits of his triumphant penetration. In it we are invited not only to partake of the spoil, but to join in the chase; and those who read idly for the sake only of the conclusions will lose half their pleasure.

The central interest of *The American Scene* defined itself once and for all to the inveterate story-seeker on a drive, taken soon after arrival, through the immense rich suburb of New York.

" Here was the expensive as a power by itself, a power unguided, undirected, practically unapplied, really exerting itself in a void that could make it no response. . . . Nothing could be of a livelier interest —with the question of manners in view—than to note that the most as yet accomplished at such cost was the air of unmitigated publicity, publicity as a condition, as a doom from which there could be no appeal. . . . The highest luxury of all, the supremely expensive thing, is constituted privacy—and yet it was the supremely expensive thing that the good people had supposed themselves to be getting. . . . For what did it (the scene) offer but the sharp interest of the match, everywhere and everlastingly played, between the short-cut and the long road ?—an interest never so sharp as since the short-cut has been able to find itself so suddenly backed by money. Money in fact *is* the short-cut. . . . Yes ; it was all actually going to be a drama, and *that* drama . . . the great adventure of a society reaching out into the apparent void for the amenities, the consummations, after having earnestly gathered in so many of the preparations and necessities. . . . Never would be such a chance to see how the short-cut works, and if there be really any substitute for roundabout experience, for troublesome history, for the long, the immitigable process of time. It was a promise clearly of the highest entertainment."

Now this passage, maimed perforce by excision, shorn of its setting of description, and dulled by being disengaged from the text, which conveys in its flexible complexity the excitement of close animated talk, is still interesting to a reader on the brink of the book for two reasons. Firstly, it reminds him that Mr. James is here face to face with a familiar subject (only this time it is on a gigantic scale) which he has often treated in fiction in many subtle forms, namely " the match between the short cut and the long road." It may almost be said to be *his* subject, for no other author has treated it so often, so variously, or with such passionate discrimination. If one were to attempt to suggest the morality or philosophy behind his books in a sentence, " There are no short cuts to a good end " would serve the purpose. What are Maggie Verver and " Milly " but beautiful examples of " the long road," or Kate Croy and Charlotte Stant but instances of the disastrous " short cut " ? Where does the failure and vulgarity of the set in *The Awkward Age*, Mrs. Brookenham and her friends, lie ? Surely, in their attempt to take by storm the charms of refinement and the refinements of intimacy. In many short stories, recent and early, we find the same drama ; the contrast between the charms and superiorities (even the physical beauties) which have been won, paid for, as it were, by suffering, thought and sympathy, and those which have been appropriated by money, sheer brute brain, or self-assertion. Whether the contrast is between houses or manners or faces or minds, the same law is insisted on that *there is no short cut to beauty.* It is curious that just as no other author has noted so subtly the influence of wealth ; its liberating power, the aspects in which may be even symbolised by " the wings of a dove " bringing the inaccessible within reach, enabling a noble imagination to gratify itself, lending sometimes to a character, through . the consciousness of its possession, an intensified charm, making some virtues just what they ought to be by making them easy ; so no other author has insisted more subtly upon the beauty which wealth cannot buy, cannot add to, cannot diminish. How often in his books the failures are the successes, and the man or woman " who gets there " is, to the artist's eye, the one who fails ! The passage quoted above with its definition of the drama awaiting the analyst, will then interest the reader in the second place, by reminding him that of all the critics of modern life, Mr. James, by temperament and by philosophy, is most likely to be, apart from sentimental loyalties, America's severest judge. His book proves it. It is the criticism of a man who has found his sensibilities wounded, his discriminations ignored, and no reflection in the general scene of those qualities in men and women and their surroundings, which he has come, after much pondering, to prize most dearly. Sympathy, as is often the case, has but made the eye and mind of the observer more acutely sensitive to horrors and disappointments. He praises New York for its vehement life, for the appeal of dauntless power, for " the candour of its avidity, and the freshness of its audacity." But in the universal will " to move, move, move as an end in itself," as an appetite to be satisfied at any price, in " the will to grow, everywhere written large, and to grow at no matter what or whose expense," he, of all story-seekers, is likely to see least. Mr. James is a novelist and critic of wealth acquired, not of the gaining of wealth ; of emotions which are ends in themselves, not of qualities like energy and industry which are means. In no single case, though in other respects he has studied wealth more profoundly than Balzac, has he ever portrayed the emotions with which it is acquired. He is a critic of the results of riches ; of their romance when they are a possession, not of their romance when they are an aim. If he is on that account the most interesting critic of America, where getting and spending and hurry and effort are so generally regarded as ends in themselves; he must necessarily be also her most severe judge, since effort unconsecrated by fulfilment is unusually dyspathetic to him. When he thinks of New York under the figure of a child sprinkled with the sawdust of its broken dolls, "living but in the sense of its hour and in the immediacy of its want," with "its boundless liability to infection and boundless incapacity for attention, its ingenuous blankness to-day over the appetites and clamours of yesterday"—he can pity her. When he dwells on that air of asking for guidance, for corroboration, in the absence of tradition, which he reads in some bold flights of architectural taste and decoration, he sympathises still more ; the sky-scrapers forming for him "simply the most piercing notes in that concert of the expensively provisional into which your supreme sense of New York resolves itself." Waste, instability, a welter of objects and sounds in which detachment, dignity, meaning perishes and the individual seems to lose all rights, this, with the exception of a glow of richness and of innocent friendly gorgeousness, which hangs here and there over midnight restaurants or splendid hotels—this is the picture he leaves with us ; and we do not wonder to find "the restless analyst" pacing with relief the long cool corridors of the Presbyterian Hospital, where his last impression of what New York could indirectly achieve, was gathered in "the high, quiet, active wards, silvery dim with their whiteness and their shade, when the genius of the terrible city seemed to filter in with its energy sifted and softened, with its huge good nature refined."

It is impossible to follow him on his journeyings, or to quote here his happy evocations of the spirit of places. The object of this review is to indicate only the wide general criticisms to which his scrutiny of surfaces is always compelling him to return. The absence of privacy, of the respect for it, or even of the desire for it, was one of the characteristics he first noted, before which his analysis was destined to be brought up short again and again. He reads this characteristic in the domestic architecture, where as many rooms as possible lead into each other, in the great library at Boston, which, convenient and magnificent as it is, " has no room sufficiently withdrawn and consecrated not to constitute a thoroughfare; " but, above all, he sees it in the wonderful development of hotel life. When publicity is the vital medium, the hotel becomes the synonym of civilisation; in such institutions as the Waldorf-Astoria and in the costly caravansaries at Palm Beach, in Florida, he sees " the American spirit most seeking and most finding itself," " the gregarious state breaking down every barrier but two; " the barrier " consisting of the high pecuniary tax," and the qualification of presumable or plausible respectability, in the narrow sense of the word. He pays a tribute of astonishment to the magnificent organisation; but behind the lavish and, in a sense, even imaginative and educative entertainment, which the Hotel Spirit holds out to " the great, plastic public," he feels something which inspires misgiving.

> " The jealous cultivation of the common mean, the common mean only, the reduction of everything to an average of decent suitability, the gospel of precaution against the dangerous tendency latent in many things to become too good for their context, so that persons partaking of them may become too good for their company—the idealised form of all this glimmered for me, as an admonition or a betrayal, through the charming Florida radiance, constituting really the greatest interest of the lesson one had travelled so far to learn."

He laments again and again the little honour that is heaped on the art of discrimination. He complains of a " sense constantly fed, and from a hundred sources that as Nature abhors a vacuum, so it is of the genius of the American land and the American people to abhor, wherever it may be, a discrimination." The growing number of universities and libraries, scattered over the country, repeat to his imagination " the note of old thick-walled cloisters " in

Europe : they are sanctuaries, refuges, where disinterested sensibility and knowledge may be nourished and live. For the same reason his heart goes out to Washington, which he has named " the City of Conversation." " It might fairly have been that the charming place had on its conscience to make one forget for an hour the colossal greed of New York." Unlike Mr. Wells, who in his itinerary regretted the detachment of the universities and despised the aloofness of Washington and Boston, Mr. James welcomes everywhere with relief the votaries of " the ivory god whose name is leisure." They have at least time to form the critical habit, which is the faculty most wanted and most wanting, in a country " where the great black ebony god of business " counts so many worshippers.

One side—the cheerful one—of the triumph everywhere of the average and of the common mean is " the vivid general lift of poverty," the " pushed-up, promoted look of the poorer classes ; " but there is also the general tone of public manners to be considered. " The restless analyst " had noted early, firstly, the prevalence of the alien, " the Ethnic apparition sitting like a skeleton at the feast," and, secondly, the rapidity with which even the Italians loose, in the new atmosphere, that agreeable address and amenity of attitude which mark them in their own country. Later on, in connexion with the complaint that in casual business relations between people, the commonest is a " necessarily vicious circle of gross mutual endurance," he reaches what is perhaps the widest of his generalisations. The American postulate or basis for any successful accommodation of life is " that of active pecuniary gain, and of active pecuniary gain only— that of one's making the conditions so triumphantly pay that the prices, the manners, the other inconveniences take their place as a friction it is comparatively easy to salve, wounds directly treatable with a wash of gold. . . . To make so much money that you won't, that you don't ' mind,' don't mind anything—that is absolutely, I think, the main American formula. Thus, your making no money—or so little that it passes there for none—and being thereby distinctly reduced to minding, amounts to your being reduced to the knowledge that America is no place for you." As he goes on to point out, this is true of all the great countries. They are becoming more and more happy lands for the upper sort of person in the scale of wealth, who can "to their hearts' content build their own castles and move by their own motors," and, again, for the lower sort, who enjoy rushing about in promiscuous packs and hustled herds; but they are getting worse and worse for the middle sort of person, who has not the protections of the former class nor the tastes of the latter. But in Europe the pecuniary salve is, at any rate, sensibly less, and less also "the excoriation that makes it necessary, whether from above or below."

The "restless analyst" hits in one instance, after much searching, an explanation of the crudity of certain manners and types, which is, too, of the nature of an excuse. It is interesting also from the point of view of a reader of reviews because it illustrates the subtlety of his methods. Let us keep in mind "the smaller inherent accumulated resistance in the American air to any force that does not simplify," which, indirectly, will explain the explanation.

On his travels he had been jarred upon by the prominence everywhere of particularly gruesome examples of the commercial traveller. They seemed to him to form often one of the preponderating features in the social landscape, till it suddenly struck him that their prominence was not due to their own peculiar aggressiveness, but simply to the absence, in due proportion, of other professions and of the representatives of other interests; and that even their crudity might be explained in the following way: "Character is developed to visible fineness only by friction and discipline on a large scale, only by its having to reckon with a complexity of forces—a process which results, at the worst, in a certain amount of social training." It is just this complexity which is necessarily absent in America. The young people, too, who occasionally shocked the discriminating observer, by "the innocently immodest ventilation of their puerile privacies," were really in the same plight. They had the effect occasionally of a kind of blatancy, simply because they were not "shaded, embowered and protected," as it were, by a background and foreground of other social relations.

This account of a book so filled with intricate observations and vivid pictures, that the reviewer cannot do more than follow one or two threads of reflection which run through it, must not close without an indication of the points where his sympathy was met. We have mentioned the universities and the libraries; these, like the museums and art galleries, public and private, seem to him signs of an idealism, which not infrequently lurks, obscured but not to be mistaken, behind this American scene; signs of a good faith, hopefulness, and a hunger for what is beautiful, which are remarkable for their intensity.

> " The ground is so clear of preoccupation, the air so clear of prejudgement and doubt, that you wonder why the chance shouldn't be as great for the æsthetic revel as for the political and economic, why some great undaunted adventure of the arts, meeting in its path none of the aged lions of prescription, of proscription, of merely jealous tradition, should not take place in conditions unexampled."

It is apt to be a trying ordeal for both parties when a prophet returns to his own country. Mr. James, as a novelist, has excelled in representing the beauty of gentleness, of the affection which bears all things, and of the sympathy which understands. The sweetness and sanity of the most perfect refinement he has drawn best in conjunction with the tones and qualities of the American mind. This has been his artistic tribute to his country ; but the dense tangled forest, where these flowers sprang, has evidently seemed in its spirit so different from the specimens, which his art has culled, that it has filled him with dismay.

DESMOND MACCARTHY

₊ It is desirable that no contributions should be sent without previous communication with the Editor, who cannot undertake to return unsolicited MSS.

Address (for postal communications only), 7 Kennington Terrace, S.E. Stamped envelope for return should be enclosed in all cases.

THE

ALBANY REVIEW

CURRENT EVENTS

C AN the House of Lords be left alone with impunity ? Members of Parliament who dread the expense and risk involved in an early dissolution may convince themselves that it can. The progressive forces in the country have convinced themselves that it cannot.

The Lords and the Land And already, at the time of writing, there are many signs that the Government have recognised this fact, and are preparing for an avowed campaign, leading up to a definite conclusion. This means the introduction of measures which will either be accepted by the Lords outright, or, if rejected, will provide the best possible weapons for the inevitable conflict. Such measures are to be found, by the common consent of almost all schools of social reformers, in a series of bills dealing with the land. Mr. L. V. Harcourt has been raised to Cabinet rank and will take charge of the Small Holdings Bill. We can congratulate him the more warmly on this distinction because, if the forward policy is really to be adopted, this bill will probably take rank, when the session of 1907 is seen in retrospect, as the most memorable measure of the year. The speech of Dr. Macnamara, the Parliamentary Secretary to the Local Government Board, on Mr. Toulmin's resolution in favour of the purchase of land by local authorities, revealed a carefully-considered policy and a determination to press vigorously forward. Above all, the speeches of the

Prime Minister and Mr. Winston Churchill at the Land Demonstration on April 20, set the seal of official approval on the great programme—the Land Charter as it might fairly be called—which has brought practically every section of land reformers into line, and which marks the culminating point of many years of investigation and propaganda conducted along separate but converging lines. The occasion was a memorable moment in the history of land reform.

It is of the utmost importance that the Small Holdings Bill should follow the lines on which English progressive opinion has concentrated within recent years, and on which the Liberals and the Labour men, the town and the country members, are united. Mr. Sinclair's bill has been framed to meet the necessities of Scotland. The Crofter system and its administration, on which the bill is based, are well understood in that country ; while, on the other hand, less confidence is felt in the working of public bodies, especially in the country districts, than in England. This is precisely one of the points which illustrate the need of Home Rule for Scotland no less than for other parts of the United Kingdom. Small holding reformers in England have a somewhat different, but no less definite, programme. There the demand is, on the one hand, for the extension of existing powers possessed by local authorities—county, borough, district and parish councils : and on the other, for a body of national commissioners who shall have power to assist the small holdings movement both by stimulating the local authorities to action, and by taking their place if they fail. Both national and local authorities should have compulsory powers of purchase and of hire ; and the land thus acquired should be let to the small-holder. Provisions for encouraging co-operation, whether in the holding of land or in any of its other forms, should, if possible, be embodied in the bill. No small holdings legislation, of course, can have its full effect until public bodies are enabled to acquire land by a simple process and at a fair value. But this far-reaching reform, affecting all public purposes for which land is needed, will probably require a separate bill ; and it depends in its turn on a reform of the law of valuation and rating. Mr. Givskov's article, which we print below, shows how close is the connexion between land taxation and rural reform, and incidentally proves the great advantage of tenancy over freehold in the case of small-holders.

A genuinely national welcome, in which all parties have joined, has been given to the members of the Imperial
The Imperial Conference Conference ; and it bids fair to be remembered as the most successful of the series. The Prime Minister's introductory speech, laying stress on the unique character of an empire founded on independence, made a deep impression on the representatives of those daughter nations to whom independence means so much. It is only natural that General Botha, who stands for the latest application of the Liberal ideal of empire, should have attracted the largest share of attention. In the general satisfaction over the grant of self-government to the Transvaal, we are apt to forget the bitter animosity with which it was only recently opposed. It has become a commonplace to contrast the position of General Botha with that of Dr. Jameson. Yet even the colony over which Dr. Jameson presides was threatened, not so long since, with the suspension of its constitution, in obedience to a despotic impulse which was barely checked in time. Such things need to be remembered, if we are to avoid in years to come the evil features of the imperial policy of a decade ago. The comment of the *Times* on General Botha's speech at the Eighty Club—" what he said was admirable, and seems to show that the Government may be rewarded for their political generosity in a way few Englishmen had dared to hope "—is a notable sign of the changed spirit in which the nation looks out to-day upon imperial affairs. The case of the Transvaal is only one example of a principle to which we owe the presence, in their capacity as delegates from free communities, of all the colonial premiers. A Conference such as this appeals to the imagination, not only of England, but of the civilised world ; and, though its course is beset with difficulty, and the great problem of the

non-autonomous peoples of the Empire, in all its threatening magnitude, can hardly be touched by the deliberations now in progress, yet England can congratulate herself, with just pride, on an assemblage such as no other nation has ever welcomed to its capital.

The Protectionist party sees in the Imperial Conference an opportunity of recovering some of the credit which it lost at the last General Election. This is only natural, and no one need grudge it the pleasure of a brief recrudescence, especially as the Colonial premiers are far too well informed as to the state of opinion in England to allow themselves to be utilised as pawns in the party game. There are interesting differences of attitude among them, which correspond to some extent to the degree of national development attained by the nations they represent. The premiers of Australia and Cape Colony, though of course they studiously avoid the kind of threats which their self-constituted spokesmen in the English press are so fond of hurling at the head of the mother country, lose no opportunity of expressing their desire that the mother country should give a tariff preference to her colonies. They realise of course that England has not, any more than her partner States, any obligation to do so unless it is beneficial to herself ; but this part of the argument tends to appear in the later and less emphatic paragraphs of their speeches. The attitude of Canada, on the other hand, is that of a State which has travelled farther along the road of independent nationalism. Sir Wilfrid Laurier is more alive than any of his colleagues to the full bearing of the principle of independence which his country values so highly. He understands, with correctness and completeness, that England has the same right to internal freedom as Canada. He scrupulously avoids the slightest shade of dictation. The same conception of imperial policy inspires his views on the question of an Imperial Council. He accepts the excellent scheme of a permanent secretariat to the Conference, but he looks with distinct suspicion on the idea of a bureau of experts who, however subordinate in position and however purely

The Subjects of Discussion

consultative in name, might devise, behind their desks in London, schemes unfavourable to the freedom of one or more of the states of the Empire. The Preferentialists are so far right, that decisions on specific points, arrived at in concert by all the partner states, are a better means of promoting imperial union than any attempt at formal organisation. But there are plenty of points on which decisions can be reached besides that of Preference; and on most of these a Liberal Government, with its ideal of autonomy, must necessarily sympathise with the demand of the younger nations. To define the principles on which national defence forces should be organised in Canada, Australia, New Zealand and South Africa; to make it clear that we do not wish to restrict any of our sister nations in the policy of alien exclusion which they have come to consider vital to their national interests; to come to a more exact understanding as to the means by which England is to fulfil her direct responsibility towards the native races of South Africa; to help to improve communications within the Empire; to promote the policy of an all-British cable; to take joint measures against shipping rings, subject to the conclusions of the special conference for that purpose now sitting at the Board of Trade; all these are steps of the utmost importance in the path of a sound imperialism. The last two of these objects belong especially to the sphere of modern Liberalism; for in each case the public interest is being threatened by private monopolies, and there is a demand for that bold application of the collectivist principle which we have found to be so essential to social progress at home.

Europe is still echoing with the discussions of the proposals for reduction of armaments by common agreement. **The Prospects at the Hague** When Sir Henry Campbell-Bannerman wrote his famous article in the *Nation*, the whole subject was being cleverly hinted into the background as a deceiving and impossible Utopia. The Governments which wanted to exclude it from the Hague Conference were hoping to kill it not by violence but by suggestion. This process was sharply arrested by the Prime Minister's intervention. But the chances of a successful issue to the discussions are still doubtful. At one moment it looked as if Italy had decided to follow the lead of her ally rather than that of her friend, and to place her diplomatic alliance above her affinities of sympathy and politics. In short, there was a danger that Italy would reverse at the Hague the part she played at Algeciras. But this impression, which sprang up after the meeting of Prince von Bülow and Signor Tittoni, was in point of fact mistaken. Italy has not renounced the policy of reduction. Only she hopes to find a formula which will mediate between the rival desires of democracy and bureaucracy. Meanwhile it is important to remember that the chief successes of the first Hague Conference were due to unpremeditated discussions, and that the capital object of the friends of reform is to secure that the subject shall not be boycotted.

Lord Cromer's resignation closes the greatest administrative career of our generation, and leaves behind it the finest achievement in the annals of European imperialism. Within the limits of his own ideals Lord Cromer's success was as complete as it is likely to be enduring, and the prosperity, the security, and the solvency of Egypt will be to all time a monument to his genius. But the events of the past year have made it clear that his methods were those of a period of transition. The very success of his work had created a demand for a more liberal *régime*, which he was unwilling to satisfy. Relieved from the oppression of venal courts, crushing taxation, and a selfish official caste, even the peasantry has acquired a measure of self-respect and self-confidence, which has inevitably shaped itself into a demand for political rights and national autonomy. The result has been at length the emergence of a strong Nationalist movement which has assumed the character of an opposition. It is undoubtedly a mixed movement. There is in it some Pan-Islamic leaven, but there is a strong if unorganised tendency which owes everything to European culture, and also an older and more indigenous school of thought, which has its centre in a tolerant and liberal Mohamedan renaissance. The refusal to make any political concessions, the contempt for the Arabic language, and, above all, the disastrous Denshawai affair, have consolidated all these three tendencies against us. A more sympathetic policy ought to have won us the support of the two really Liberal movements against the Pan-Islamic agitators. Lord Cromer's last report, in an unfortunate tone of irony, offered the Nationalists, as a substitute for the increased control over Egyptian affairs which they claim for their own countrymen, a purely European council representing the interests of the foreign colony alone. Sir Eldon Gorst has a delicate task before him. There can be no sudden breach with the past, but his inclinations are believed to be towards a much franker sympathy with Egyptian aspirations. The maintenance of the army of occupation and of our financial control does not require us to anglicise education, to maintain direct foreign rule as opposed to foreign inspection, or to refuse the development—solemnly promised more than twenty years ago—of the national institutions.

The fate of the Duma is still in the balance. The Liberal centre has bent all its energies to the single task of avoiding any possible cause of conflict. It has **The Duma** agreed to work with a Ministry hopelessly defeated at the polls, abstained from raising such issues as the amnesty of political prisoners, and even agreed to vote the Budget practically unaltered. The limits of its rights are very narrow. It cannot, for example, refuse the estimates for such administrative services as the censorship or the political police. But for the moment it will make no attempt to overstep these limits. It argues that the risk of a second dissolution, followed by a second period of unmitigated repression, is grave enough to warrant almost any extreme of self-restraint. By struggling it could achieve nothing ; by merely existing it does at least impose a certain show of moderation on the Government, and keep intact the meagre rights of publicity and criticism which may in the long run be evolved into a real control. This almost excessive self-suppression has not, however, saved it from the constant menace of dissolution. It is possible that M. Stolypin himself does not intend to dissolve it. He can rule it by the mere threat of dissolution which others will always utter for him. But some of his colleagues are said to be determined to dissolve, and M. de Martens, in a remarkable letter to the *Times*, has declared that dissolution is a question only " of weeks or days," and urged that it must be followed by a restriction of the franchise. M. de Martens is too correct an official to have ventured on this blazing indiscretion without prompting, but it is impossible to say whether he spoke for the Tsar or for M. Stolypin, for the Grand Dukes or for the reactionary members of the Cabinet. There is no Russian Government ; there is a Court and there is a Ministry, and each is in turn the Government. The idea was presumably to sound Western opinion, for a *coup d'état* would more than ever compel the Tsar to rely on the money-markets of London and Paris. The reply has been decisive. English and French opinion is resolved to give the bureaucracy no help.

There is much that is good in the Budget of 1907. Mr. Asquith's determination to reduce the national indebtedness deserves the highest praise because **The Budget** such a measure, though of immense importance to the credit and therefore to the prosperity of the country, does not win the applause of the man in the street. The increased graduation of the death duties is a welcome step, though a small one, towards the limitation of privilege and the greater equalisation of opportunity. Every one must desire, again, that the small income-tax payer should be relieved, provided that his relief is not purchased at the expense of a much larger class. The proposal to discontinue, next year, the assignment to local authorities of the proceeds of certain national taxes, will make possible the revision of the licence duties, and the imposition of a tax on motors used for pleasure. And the promise of a fund which is to form the nucleus of an old age pension scheme must be hailed with satisfaction by social reformers. It must be said, however, that these promises, and these beginnings of reform, would have been more appropriate to 1906 than to 1907. Broadly speaking, the whole effect of Mr. Asquith's proposals is to leave the poor man's taxation almost precisely where it was when he came into office. He has given no direct relief whatever to the great bulk of the people—the 39,000,000 (out of 44,000,000) who do not pay income-tax. He has reduced that tax from 1s. to 9d. on all those with earned incomes up to £2,000 a year. That is to say, while a barrister with £1,800 a year has been granted a relief of over £22 a year, a working man with 30s. a week has been granted no relief at all. It is unfortunate that Mr. Asquith has refused to make a beginning with graduation, which is itself the best means of differentiating between earned and unearned income. Though he does not commit himself against the Income-Tax Committee's suggestions with regard to a super-tax and personal declarations of larger incomes, he has for the present ignored them. An income of £50,000 per annum and an income of £2,500 per annum are to pay at exactly the same rate, and that rate is scarcely higher than that which is to be paid by a hard-working tradesman or medical man making £800 a year. If the reduction had been confined to the lower middle classes, we should have heartily agreed with it, but we do not agree that the upper middle classes were overtaxed in the past year. With regard to old age pensions the sum of 2¼ millions, which Mr. Asquith will have available next year (if his estimates are realised) as the nucleus of an old age pension fund, is, of course, ludicrous when compared with the requirements of even a small scheme of pensions. There are about 1,300,000 people over seventy years of age, and to grant only one million of them a pension of 5s. per week would cost £13,000,000. Such a sum can only be obtained either by graduating the income-tax, or by great reductions in military expenditure, or (better still) by a combination of the two. It is fair to remember, however, the Chancellor's emphatic plea that this Budget is only the beginning of a series, and ought not to be judged by itself. If it were the last word of Liberal finance, it would bode ill for the future of the Liberal Party.

THE BISHOPS' DECLARATION OF JANUARY 1907

A SIGNIFICANT EPISODE IN THE STRUGGLE BETWEEN FRANCE AND THE HOLY SEE

TO shed light on the religious crisis in France is no easy matter. The question, in itself sufficiently complex, is rendered infinitely more so because it is inevitably bound up with a host of other considerations that must affect the judgement. The striking articles that have from time to time appeared in various foreign periodicals represent, rather than any profound study of the situation in France, an intense desire to prevent other countries from imitating her mistakes.

Apart from any question of interest there is one prejudice which, even if unconscious, is more deeply rooted than any other : what one may call the prejudice of the heart. To the Church most men owe some of their tenderest emotions. Her rites, her mysteries, her sacraments have opened for us the golden gate of dreams. We owe her an inexpressible debt of gratitude. To hear her spoken of solely as a political entity causes us pain, while most of our wives and sisters are unaware that she could be so regarded. Action by the Government which touches the Church wounds them ; it seems to them little less than an outrage, a desecration. To sentiments such as these, those who oppose the separation have of course appealed in their attempt to throw obstacles in the way of the new law; they have even gone so far as to accuse its supporters of being the party of force, the party of muskets !

To point out the worthlessness of this rhetorical plea is surely needless. Muskets apart, is any power comparable to the Church of Rome, with its universal organisation, its hierarchy, its discipline, its unity? It is obvious, then, that the task that lies before every one who believes in the truth, the righteousness, the success of the work which France has undertaken is more serious than might have been anticipated. Over and above the difficulties which are plain at a glance are others of which a word must be spoken. Half the witnesses of, and actors in, the crisis have been reduced to silence. Not only does the Holy See allow no word to transpire of the discussions which take place at the Vatican —if any do take place ; the public is kept in entire ignorance of the exact orders issued to the Episcopate, the most careful precautions being taken to ensure that nothing shall be known save the encyclicals. The bishops must obey ; but that is not all. They must not excuse themselves, while acting contrary to their conscience and their souls, by saying they obey the orders of Rome. On December 8, 1906, Monsignor Fuzet, Archbishop of Rouen, enjoined his clergy to make the annual declaration of the celebration of worship. On December 9 dispatches from Rome compelled him to issue a precisely contrary injunction: When his sense of honour, which he held sacred, compelled him to explain so remarkable a change of front and to free himself from responsibility for it by publishing the Papal order, he was accused of having violated Pontifical secrecy.

Tradition, perhaps, is in favour of such secrecy, but no policy could be less adapted to impress upon men's minds the idea of a power whose supremacy is moral, which goes on its way unswerving, with nothing to fear from the light.

The sole result is that the student of events can acquire accurate knowledge of one side only. As to the other he may feel a moral certainty, but that would be of no use to him, since refusal to give his authority would merely draw down upon him the charitable imputation of being an impudent liar, while disclosure of the names of his informants would expose them to exemplary chastisement.

These considerations have led me to believe that a description of one of the most recent incidents in the crisis might be of interest to the readers of the ALBANY REVIEW. Documents referring to it have already been made public in sufficient quantity to enable one to get to the bottom of the affair without dangerous citation of names ; and although the incident is complete in itself, it enables one to see in a nutshell the different, not to say opposing, points of view taken up since the beginning by the Pope and the bishops. Pius X, wrapped in a mysticism that vanishes away in the absolutism of revealed truth, inaccessible to reason, untouched by any shadow of doubt, utters with the tone and gesture of an exorcist liturgical formulæ decked out in the language of passion ; while the bishops, with endless precautions, maintain an attitude of trembling timidity before the sovereign Pontiff, striving meantime with unabated energy to save the external organisation of the Church of France.

Doctrinal Gallicanism is dead, but the Gallican Church is not to die ; it recognises its responsibility to its country. Even in its entire submission to the Roman See it retains patriotic feelings that do it honour.

In order to understand the Bishops' Declaration the preceding events must be briefly summarised.

The Separation Law of December 9, 1905, was solemnly condemned by the Bull " Vehementer" of February 11, 1906.

The French Episcopate meeting some months later—May and June 1906—by order of the Pope, refused, in spite of constant pressure, to let itself be drawn into definite conflict with the law, and took refuge in the old scholastic distinction of thesis and hypothesis. It placed itself in line with the Pontiff by declaring, by way of thesis, that the law was evil ; that having been done, however, it proceeded to devote a clear day's discussion to the details of a plan of accommodation. On the question of this *modus vivendi* the votes were 48 to 26 ; while the scheme itself, drawn up by Monsignor Fulbert Petit, Archbishop of Besançon, was carried by 56 to 18. The size of the majority came as a surprise to the bishops themselves ; and they all expected that Pius X would meet their desires by pronouncing the *tolerari posse*.

The Bull " Gravissimo " of August 10, 1906, was a severe blow to such hopes. The preamble, in which the bishops declared the law to be evil, was given an importance which they had been far from attributing to it ; nothing was said about the practical resolutions which followed ; finally, the Bull declared that no attempt to form legal and canonical associations was permitted. This Bull acted with paralysing effect upon the majority of the bishops, the more so as the Pope gave only the vaguest indication of the attitude to be taken up. " Your task, Reverend Brothers and Bishops, is to employ the means the law grants to all citizens to arrange and organise religious worship."

Every one believed that in future the Church of France would submit itself to the jurisdiction of the common law. The Government, far from throwing difficulties in the way of such recourse by insistence on troublesome formalities, did everything in its power to smooth the path and facilitate its use. For example, the Ministerial circular of December 1906 decided that in the case of the celebration of meetings for worship an annual declaration would suffice, whereas the law of June 30, 1881, had required, in the case of ordinary public assemblies, a declaration at each meeting.

In compliance with the terms of the Bull itself, the Archbishops of Rouen, Toulouse and Bordeaux on December 7, 1906, invited the clergy of their respective dioceses to make the annual declaration. On the very next day they received from Rome telegraphic orders to countermand the injunction. Thus on December 8 Pius X openly interdicted that recourse to the common law which he had enjoined on August 10.

This is not the place for a description of the third Convocation of the bishops, held between January 15 and 19, 1907, at the Castle of La Muette. In spite of the checks it had sustained in the last few months, the moderate majority did its best for the cause of reform. That the uncompromising attitude of the Pope had robbed the Church of its possessions [1] was subject for regret, but while the past

---

[1] It cannot be too often repeated that the Separation Law, far from robbing the Church of its property, assured it to it indefinitely through the associations for worship. Since the great majority of the Episcopate was willing to fall in with the law by forming these legal and canonical associations, the responsibility for the loss of the Church property must be laid at

was irrevocable, the majority was ready to make another effort to retain at least the legal right of using the sacred buildings. There was, however, an energetic minority which saw in the organisation of a conflict the prelude to a revival of religious faith and to a political restoration. Unable to agree, the two parties effected a kind of compromise. Two bishops, Monsignor Dadolle, Bishop of Dijon, and Monsignor Touchet, Bishop of Orleans, were delegated by their colleagues to lay before the Pope the minutes of the assembly, and to elucidate them where necessary by word of mouth. The former was more especially the representative of the moderate majority, the latter of the uncompromising minority. The special object of their mission was to lay before the Pope the text of a contract which, after it had been submitted to the mayor and prefect in each case, would give the clergy legal right to the use of their churches. Profiting by experience, the bishops, instead of coming to any definite decision themselves, submitted to Pius X schemes and proposals merely : laid on him the burden of responsibility which they did not venture to assume, and left to him who had hitherto so thoughtlessly directed everything the last decisive word. Rejection of the contract was a declaration of war on the law of France, and involved the organisation by the bishops of worship on a private basis. Acceptance was an indirect recognition of a section of the new law, a prelude to an understanding with the Government. The bishops were far from satisfied, but they at least believed that in their action they had shown due deference to the Holy See, and at the same time had avoided any betrayal of the interests of France.

Curiously enough, the Pope, who had once already, in the Bull " Gravissimo," acted in direct opposition to the manifest wishes of the Episcopate, found here a new opportunity of doing exactly the opposite of what was

the door of Pius X, and of Pius X alone. Those who try to stir up disturbance by declaring that the French Government has robbed the Church either have not read the law of December 1905—in which case they are guilty of culpable carelessness—or else they show their contempt for those who listen to them by the attempt to give historical currency to a lie.

expected of him. Although he decided to accept the formula of the contract, he caused the Episcopal delegates to prepare a preamble which lent it quite a new complexion. The contract had been a sort of olive branch ; but the preamble, aggressive and threatening in tone, was a veritable ultimatum.

Finally, instead of taking the responsibility of these decisions, the Pope managed to saddle the Episcopate with it.

The terms of the document had hardly been agreed upon before a number of copies were printed off by the Vatican press ; and Monsignors Dadolle and Touchet, returning hastily to France, had to communicate to their colleagues a document which fathered upon them a text of which they themselves were ignorant ![1]

It is not my purpose here to enter into the inner meaning of this document : this brief sketch of its history, origin, and nature is sufficient. The publication, bit by bit, of the facts which I have related was greeted by vehement denials on the part of the Catholic journals. Unfortunately there was more noise than accuracy about the denials, and some of them actually confirm what they attempt to disprove.

Perhaps the question is malicious, but one wonders whether the desire shown by the Cardinal-Archbishop of Bordeaux to anticipate a public exposure does not really conceal some anxiety to have the true history of the Declaration published. Anyhow, the explanations issued in the newspapers on February 22 afford a complete confirmation of the facts here set down.

From all this several important conclusions can be drawn. Firstly, the French Episcopate naturally imagined that after dispatching to Rome two of their most

[1] The text of the Declaration as published by the Catholic journals in Paris and communicated to them from the Archbishop had been corrected in several important particulars, and thereby considerably modified. The responsibility for these corrections was assigned to Monsignor Amette, Coadjutor-Archbishop of Paris, and a lively campaign against him ensued.

The authentic text, as issued from Rome, was published, among others, by the *Osservatore Romano* on January 31, and on February 29 by the *Nouvelliste* of Lyons.

distinguished representatives to express their views, while leaving all decisions to the Pontiff, they had shown all that could be expected from them in the matter of deference and submission. But even this did not satisfy Pius X. He was not satisfied even with forcing upon the bishops an attitude which nearly all of them personally regarded with profound regret. To issue commands and have commands obeyed was not enough for him ; he discovered a new mode of submission when he forced the Episcopate itself publicly to acknowledge the responsibility of acts of which its members disapproved, and documents published without their cognisance. Does not this in effect amount to the abdication of the Episcopate, and its absorption in Pontifical omnipotence ?

Some among my readers have perhaps studied the original documents bearing upon a particular epoch of the history of the Roman Church. What labour one devotes to that research! what joy when it is rewarded ! with what trembling fingers one turns over the precious leaves ! Innocently one regards a signature as a proof of genuineness. Facts such as these which I have here recounted are apt to make one rather sceptical of the most sacred documents of the Church.

What explanation is there of the Pope's behaviour ? His action is not the outcome of profound and painful thought ; but his intellectual bias is so entirely different from that of our own generation, and his abhorrence of the principles of the French Revolution is so great, that the resolutions at which he arrives by instinct harmonise with the ideas of the Middle Ages as much as they conflict with those of our own time. To credit him with machinations is to make as great a mistake as he does when he ascribes the overthrow of the Church to the satanic activity of a sect. His double manœuvre is therefore natural enough, and needs no malice prepense to explain it. On the one hand, he wanted to submit the French bishops, in whom he is very far from feeling complete confidence, to a further test, on the other, in approaching the public authorities he chose to mingle words of peace with threats and claims that he knew to be puerile, in the full knowledge that though a peace so proposed could not be accepted, he could at least declare that it had been offered.

Neither the Parliament nor the Government replied to the Papal document in the tone that was expected of them. Up to the present nothing has availed to make them deviate from the wise line of action that they have laid down for themselves.

PAUL SABATIER

Assisi, 13th April, 1907.

SOME ORATORS AT WESTMINSTER

A DISTINCTIVE feature of the twentieth century House of Commons is the disappearance of the orator. Time was, at and since the period of Pitt and Fox, when the House of Commons was a stage from which eminent men delivered elaborate discourses. Within my comparatively brief experience a great change has been wrought in this respect. There are many able men in the present Parliament ; there is not a single one who poses as an orator. New times, above all new Rules of Procedure, make new manners. There really isn't time now for a Member to lay himself out for a two hours' speech, as was a common custom even so recently as a quarter of a century ago. With the House meeting at the prosaic hour of a quarter to three o'clock and abruptly closing debate at eleven, there is no opening for such elaborate performance.

Moreover, habit in respect of debate is changed. In the good old days 660 Members were content to form an audience enraptured by the eloquence of eight or ten. Now, with special wires feeding local papers, every one feels called upon to deliver a certain quantum of remarks on important Bills or resolutions brought before the House. The average Member has more satisfaction in talking than in listening. This, combined with disposition to regard progress of legislative business as of more importance than flowers of oratory, has completed the change of fashion. In these prosaic days a Member, however eminent, rising with evident intent of delivering a set oration, would first be stared at, then left to discourse to himself, the Speaker, and an admiring family circle in the Ladies' Gallery.

I remember in days that are no more a quite different

state of things. In the Seventies, even in the Eighties, there were giants of oratory. Gladstone was the last survival. Even he towards the end of his career was influenced by the newer turn of thought which dominated Parliamentary debate. He could not help being eloquent when deeply moved ; but he was more direct in his methods, less voluminous in his speech.

His manner in speech-making was more strongly marked, by action than was that of his only rival, John Bright. He emphasised points by smiting the open palm of his left hand with sledge-hammer fist. Sometimes he, with gleaming eyes, pointed his forefinger straight at his adversary. In hottest moments he beat the brass-bound Box with clamorous hand that sometimes drowned the point he strove to make. Again, with both hands raised above his head ; often with left elbow leaning on the Box, right hand with closed fist shaken at the head of an unoffending country gentleman on the back bench opposite ; anon, standing half a step back from the Table, left hand hanging at his side, right uplifted, so that he might with thumb-nail lightly touch the shining crown of his head, he trampled his way through the argument he assailed as an elephant in an hour of aggravation rages through a jungle.

It is no new thing for great orators to indulge in extravagant gestures. Peel had none ; Pitt but few, these monotonous and mechanical. But Pitt's father, the great Chatham, knew how to flash his eagle eye, to flaunt his flannels and strike home with his crutch. Brougham once dropped on his knees in the House of Lords, and with outstretched hands implored the Peers not to reject the Reform Bill. Fox was sometimes moved to tears by his own eloquence. Burke on a historic occasion brought a dagger into debate, and at the proper cue flung it on the floor of the House of Commons. Sheridan, when nothing more effective was to be done, knew how to faint. Grattan used to scrape the ground with his knuckles as he bent his body and thanked God he had no peculiarities of gesture. In respect of originality, multiplicity and vehemence of gesture, Gladstone, as in some other things, beat the record of human achievement.

Disraeli lacked two qualities, failing which true eloquence is impossible. He was never quite in earnest, and was not troubled by dominating conviction. Only on the rarest occasions did he affect to be roused to righteous indignation, and then he was rather amusing than impressive. He was endowed with a lively fancy and cultivated the art of coining phrases, generally personal in their bearing. When these were flashed forth he delighted the House. For the rest, at the period I knew him, when he had grown respectable and was weighted with responsibility, he was often dull. There were, indeed, in the course of a session, few things more dreary than a long speech from Dizzy. At short, sharp replies to questions designed to be embarrassing he was effective. When it came to a long speech the lack of stamina was disclosed, and the House listened to something which, if not occasionally incomprehensible, was frequently involved.

When he rose to speak he rested his hand for a moment on the Box, only for a moment, for he invariably endeavoured to gain the ear of his audience by making a brilliant point in an opening sentence. The attitude he found most conducive to happy delivery was to stand balancing himself on heel and toe with hands in his coat-tail pocket. In this pose, with head hung down as if he were mentally debating how best to express a thought just born to him, he slowly uttered the polished and poisoned sentences over which he had spent laborious hours in his study.

Those familiar with his manner knew a full moment beforehand when he was approaching what he regarded as the most effective place for dropping the gem of phrase he made-believe to have just dug up from an unvisited corner of his mind. They saw him lead up to it. They noted the disappearance of the hand in the direction of the coat-tail pocket, sometimes in search of a pocket-handkerchief brought out and shaken with careless air, most often to extend the coat-tails whilst, with body gently rocked to and fro and an affected hesitancy of speech, the *bon mot* was flashed forth. Not being a born orator, but a keen observer recognising the necessity noted by Hamlet in his advice to the players of accompanying voice by action, he performed a series of bodily jerks as remote from the natural gestures of the true orator as the waddling of a duck across a stubble field is from the progress of a swan over the bosom of a lake.

John Bright, perhaps the finest orator known to the House of Commons in the last half of the nineteenth century, was morally and politically the antithesis of Disraeli. Before, in the closing years of a long life, he reached the unexpected haven of community with the Conservative Party on the question of Home Rule, political animosity passed by no ditch through the mire of which it might drag him. But it never accused him of speaking with uncertain sound, of denouncing to-day what yesterday he upheld.

To an orator this atmosphere of acknowledged sincerity and honest conviction is a mighty adjunct of power. To it Bright added airy graces of oratory. He kept himself well in hand throughout his speech, never losing his hold upon his audience. His gestures were of the fewest. Unlike Disraeli's, they were appropriate because natural. A simple wave of the right hand and the point of his sentence was emphasised. Nature gifted him with a fine presence and a voice the like of which has rarely rung through the classic chamber. " Like a bell " was the illustration commonly employed in endeavour to convey an impression of its music. I should say like a peal of bells, for a single one could not produce the varied tones in which Bright suited his voice to his theme.

On the whole, the dominant note was one of pathos. Probably because all his great speeches pleaded for the cause of the oppressed or denounced an accomplished wrong, a tone of melancholy ran through all. For the expression of pathos there were marvellously touching vibrations in his voice, carrying to the listener's heart the tender thoughts that came glowing from the speaker's, clad in simple words as they passed his tongue.

HENRY W. LUCY
(Toby, M.P., of " Punch ")

SMALL HOLDINGS AND LAND
TAXATION

BEFORE a Small-holdings Act is passed in England, it may be worth while to examine the workings of a similar system in another country, in order, if possible, to avoid those mistakes which in Denmark have almost entirely stultified the professed purpose of the Act. Although the peasant farmer produces from 50 per cent. to 100 per cent. more per acre than the large-holder, yet he nowhere retains nearly as great a proportion of what he produces ; and it is precisely in those countries where the production of the small-holders is most abundant that they themselves retain the smallest share. Their hours are excessively long, their lives dreary, their food of the plainest ; and when taxes and rent are paid, little is left them beyond a bare subsistence.

The seeds of Denmark's agricultural prosperity were sown in 1788, and began with the liberation of the peasant serfs. The same statesmen who freed the serfs also caused the land to be valued, and imposed a permanent tax. The standard of valuation was the old Danish Tax-unit, "a ton of hard corn." Not more than one "ton of hard corn" might be imposed as a tax on eight acres of prime land (being about one-fifth of the estimated yield). On land of inferior quality it would be charged on fifty or more acres. Not only State taxes, but also Commune and County rates, were levied on this valuation, and the public thus had a very considerable share in the value of all the Danish land. Every mortgage effected yielded precedence to the right of the State, whose income from this source was great enough to permit a system of almost entirely free trade. Very few other taxes were needed, and moreover the taxes on the value of the land, while preventing the farmers mortgaging their properties up to the chimney-pots, would always be capitalised, and the full capitalised value deducted from the purchase-price, every time a property changed hands. Consequently they ceased to wear the character of taxes, and became simply a first mortgage to the State, which needed therefore so much the less income from other sources.

The succeeding years saw enormous progress in national education; then it was that agricultural co-operation began to strike root among the well-to-do and enlightened yeomanry; and apace with the number of co-operative enterprises grew the number of small-holders.

The Government also took steps in 1899 to promote small holdings; and though the number thus established is under 2000, yet their action has stimulated the already existing desire among the labouring class for land. The Act does not provide the land : the labourer must himself procure the piece he wants, and then apply for Government aid. Often they do not obtain it, but having once bought the land, and perhaps started building, they stick to it and make the best of the bargain.

The Act bears clear traces of being a compromise between the conflicting demands of (1) the labourers, for sufficient land to make them independent, and (2) the farmers, for holdings such that the owners shall be unable to live on the proceeds, and have to supplement them by work on the farms. The farmers, however, had the stronger backing, and the Act became a half-way house considerably nearer to their views than to those of the peasants.

The applicant for a loan from Government must have been an agricultural labourer for five years previously, and possess not less than one-tenth of the value of the holding. He may then obtain a loan of the remaining nine-tenths, not exceeding £200. The interest on the loan is at 3 per cent., and no sinking fund for the first five years.

However, it was found impossible for the State-aided small-holder to make both ends meet, although he worked for six months in the year as a day-labourer on a larger farm ; and five years later (1904) the Act was revised, and the maximum Government grant raised to £275 (of which the small-holder has to find £27). Even this extension has proved insufficient. We will inquire presently why.

However unsatisfactory these results from the small-holder's point of view, the large farmers have certainly benefited in increased labour supply. The community has also benefited by the check on the migration of the agricultural labourers to the towns. During the last five years, the tide in Denmark has been, surprisingly but certainly, flowing from town to country, and though this is due largely to general economic conditions, the Act has unmistakably helped. From 1890 to 1901 three-quarters of the increase of the population took place in the towns. From 1901 to 1906, over one-half of the increase was in the country. The Act has also undoubtedly helped to increase the food production of the country. It is a notice-able fact that the smallest holdings have almost as much stock as the largest ones. The average number of animals on a State-aided small holding is far higher than the average of all the farms in the country, as is seen in the following table :—

No. of	State-aided holdings (average)	All holdings (average)	
Horses	134	127	per land value, as measured by 100 tons of hard corn
Horned Cattle	986	481	,,　,,　,,　,,
Pigs	1120	381	,,　,,　,,　,,
Sheep	151	229	,,　,,　,,　,,
Poultry	8020	3021	,,　,,　,,　,,

The State-aided holdings are therefore, with regard to productivity, a distinct advance on farming on a large scale ; more food being produced on any given area parcelled out into small farms than if farmed by a few large holders. And yet, since the small-holder cannot live without working half the year for others, one hesitates to pronounce small holdings to be really the more profitable. Something is evi-dently wrong. Either there is some economic disadvantage inherent in the nature of a small holding,—or the small-holder does not get his fair share of what he produces.

In *Danish Agriculture at the Beginning of the 20th Century*, a book published in 1904, the economist, Mr. N. P. Jensen, calculates that the net income of an average Danish peasant farmer with about 13 acres of land does not exceed £24 a year, after deducting the interest on the purchase-money. If so, it is not surprising that he has to eke out his living as a day-labourer. What is it that handicaps him?

Let us not assume, to start with, that the small-holder has to fight with difficulties of working inherent in the nature of such holdings. Practically no such difficulties exist. He may perhaps lay out proportionally more on his buildings than the large farmer, but in any case he must have his dwelling-house, and it need not, and rarely does, cost him more than if he were an ordinary labourer. If his cow-shed is bigger and better than that of the large-holder, he has more than a proportionally greater quantity of live-stock. He and his family have every inducement to pay the greatest possible attention to their agriculture, because they are working for their own profit. Thus, given sufficient land, he ought to prosper. Now, statistics show that the average size of the 1859 State-created holdings in Denmark is 7½ acres; 64 being above 16 acres, 605 above 8 acres, and only 71 less than 4 acres. A farm of from 4 to 16 acres, even though of poor quality, is certainly enough to fully occupy one family. It is therefore obvious that it is not insufficient area which prevents the small-holder from prospering.

But although it is not a question of area, it is very much a question of the price paid for the area. Mr. Jensen states in his book that, while the farmer of 13 acres of good land clears rather less than £24, he clears, on an average, £25 if the land be bad: and Mr. Jensen admits that the reason for this is the price he must pay for the land. For 13 acres of good holding he pays on an average £467—for the same amount of bad, only £182. The fact is, that the advantages which co-operation has given to the small-holder over the large-holder have enormously enhanced the price of land for such holdings. When then the State steps in and creates a steady and increasing demand for them, the price is forced up far in advance of the real economic value, all the more so, because the Danish Act suffers from certain serious defects.

It is, for instance, to be regretted that the Act leaves the labourers themselves to find the land. Not only are large farms bought and parcelled out at a profit of 100 per cent., but a whole system of swindling has been established. When a farm is bought by speculators for division into small holdings, these " farm-butchers " go touting to every likely young man. If he reply that he has not the sum required by the Act, they offer to supply the needful money on condition that he pays a higher price. If he has the money, they kindly offer him two sets of purchase-deeds, one showing a higher price, in case he obtains a Government loan, another a considerably lower one, in the event of his not getting it. In most cases, having no money at all, he stands to lose nothing by making any purchase at any price, while if the loan is obtained, the speculators get the whole of the excessive purchase-money in ready cash. The reason why the small-holder is ready to pay more for the land than its real value is very simple. He gets this loan from the Government at 3 per cent. interest. If he be a good business man, he will reason it out thus :—" My holding is worth 3,000 kroners. If I rented it, I must pay 150 kroners; *i.e.* 5 per cent. on the value ; if I purchase it outright with a Government loan for 5,000 kroners at 3 per cent. interest, I still pay only 150 kroners a year, for what is now my own." However, most of the aspirants for small holdings leave the farm-butcher to do their thinking for them. He tells them what others have paid, paints the glories of independence, and offers them the two sets of purchase-deeds. The poor labourer buys the land at the extravagant price, and obtains the loan. The farm-butcher pockets it, and the tax-payer pays it; but the State-created small-holder remains as poor as ever.

In fact, he is often worse off than before. The holding being the only object which he owns, he has absolutely nothing else to offer as security if he requires a small loan or credit. But the Act specially makes distraint on these small holdings illegal. He therefore finds it impossible to get credit. This, by the way, also leads to great loss to those builders who must be employed, and causes them to build for small-holders at a specially high rate. In fact, the small-holder sits in his little holding absolutely unassailable, but in the same sense as a pauper is unassailable ; and not infrequently one hears them wish that they were back again at the "secure" work of farm-labourers.

· Of course there are a large number who, by sheer hard work and privation, get on despite exorbitant prices. But the tendency is decidedly towards establishing a class of semi-paupers ; and already the name of "State-peasant" has a derogatory ring.

The crucial question is : How does the small-holder himself fare ? From outside, his house is pretty enough, newly built, with fine airy rooms. But inside, the furniture is too often poor, and the food poorer still. These peasant owners supply England with the greater part of her good butter, and with the eggs, bacon and poultry they raise. But they themselves never touch them. The price of the small-holder's butter must go to pay interest on his enormous loan and for the taxes, while he himself eats margarine. He and his family feed on what no one else will buy from them : skim milk, rye bread, and generally potatoes. His own pigs go abroad, and he eats American pork and bacon.

How far he can supplement his own produce by his work as a day-labourer may be seen in the following statistics. According to "*Dan. Stat.*" (1906), a labourer (not employed for the whole year) earns on the average 2*s.* 7*d.* in spring and autumn ; 3*s.* 2*d.* in harvest ; and 1*s.* 4*d.* in winter ; in all about £15 for the average 155 days spent away from his own holding. The amount varies a little in different parts of the country, wages being lowest where the land is best, and where therefore the peasant has less access to it.

The small-holders' difficulties have been greatly increased by a most unfortunate change in the system of taxation, which was made a few years ago when the yeoman class (the Danish "Liberals ") came into power. Almost their first act was to abolish those taxes and other charges on the land, which I mentioned at the beginning. Now such taxes, imposed on the value of the land, are amongst the most just of all. For they cannot be shifted, but must be borne by the landowners, who are thereby induced to make the best possible use of their land, or to sell it if they themselves cannot make it pay. It was to this system of taxation, more than to anything else, that the prosperity of Danish agriculture was due. But this the farmers did not recognise ; they only saw, that, if these charges were abolished, the selling and mortgaging value of their land would increase by an amount equal to the capitalised value of the charges taken off it—which up till then had always been deducted from the purchase price. The capitalised value of the abolished tax amounted to £16,000,000 for the whole country. That is to say, the nation at large had a first mortgage for this amount on all the land. Every individual living in the country was a co-owner of it, and the a nual revenue from this source decreased by so much the amount levied in other forms of taxation. The abolition of these land-taxes was an encroachment upon the equal right of every inhabitant. To those who owned no land it gave of course no relief, and was a clear injury, as it increased their other taxes. The landowners even did not benefit equally, but in proportion to the extent of their property. While it put about £550 into the pockets of each of 7000 large landowners, 47,000 yeoman farmers each received about £190, but 68,000 small-holders got only £19, and 70,000 smaller still benefited by £2 to £4 each.

The amount of taxes on land values thus repealed was in the aggregate about £555,000 a year. They were replaced partly by a tax on real estate, partly by a general property tax, and partly by an income tax. The communal and county rates on the land-values basis amounted annually to about £950,000 more. They too are being replaced gradually by a tax on real estate. When, a few years hence, the change has been completely effected, taxes and rates to a total capitalised value of £40,000,000 will have been taken off the land and placed on the shoulders of labour. This is a heavy sum for a small country. Moreover, the market value of land increases in proportion to the total taxation abolished. During the last two or three years it has increased by 25 per cent. to 40 per cent., and already for this reason the new legislation has greatly injured the small-holder. Besides this, it has made it possible for the wealthy landowner to retain his land, however unprofitably he may use it, and thus makes the land still harder to obtain.

Besides the direct damage done by repealing the old land-values tax, the new taxes which replace it (on real estate, general property and income) plunder the small-holder for the benefit of the large one, being mainly levied on the products of labour—on buildings, stock, improvements, etc., of which the small-holder possesses proportionally more per acre. Consequently his taxes amount to a larger sum per acre ; *i. e.* he must pay a much larger proportion of the fruits of his labour than the large-owner. Thus unfortunately, in "freeing the land," they have enslaved the men who live on it.

The consequences of this change of taxation are only just beginning to be felt, but they are already clearly foreshadowed. The aggregate mortgage debt is estimated by a Government Commission at £91,000,000 (55 per cent. of the market value of all the agricultural holdings in Denmark), and there is abundant evidence that it is increasing by leaps and bounds. This is one of the worst results of the short-sighted, selfish politics of the yeoman, and by no means the only one. The old land-taxes were paid by the landowner; he could not shift them. The new taxes can be thrown on to the shoulders of the consumer. Consequently prices increase all round, whilst wages tend to decline. The following tables will illustrate the general diminution in the well-being of the people after the old tax was removed in 1902.

Prices in Copenhagen of—

	in 1896	in 1903	in 1905
Beef per ½ kilo. (1·1 lbs.)	5d.	6d.	7½d.
Veal per ½ kilo.	5¼d.	6¾d.	7¾d.
Lamb per ½ kilo.	6d.	7¼d.	—
Pork per ½ kilo.	5¾d.	7¼d.	9d.[1]

The enlightened peasant farmers are keenly alive to the injustice they have suffered, and have no doubts whatever as to the right means of redressing it. At the three last annual meetings of the Danish Peasant Farmers' Associa-

[1] *Statistick Aarbok* (1905).

tions the following resolution was passed :—" The peasant farmers demand the earliest possible abolition of all duties and taxes levied upon articles of consumption, or assessed in proportion to the income of labour ; and in lieu thereof they demand, that a tax be imposed on that value of land which is not due to any individual effort, but is derived from the growth and development of the community."

The great flaw, then, in the Danish Acts is that the labourers, having to procure the land themselves, start with funds exhausted and under a heavy load of debt; and so long as the principle is maintained of making the small-holders proprietors of their own land, this difficulty is insuperable. The only possible way, in any country, of securing to them the fruits of their labour, is to make them tenants of the State. The rent should be periodically assessed, so as to preserve to the community that increase in the value of the land which is derived, not from the labour of the individual, but from the development of the community. The Government should also, of course, have power to enforce the compulsory sale of land suitable for small holdings. But the mere fact of the Government entering the market as a land purchaser on a large scale must immediately cause a great rise in the price of such land, and the small-holder would still have to pay too much in increased rent. The community may gain by him, but he himself will more often than not become the step-child of the community.

There is, however, one means, which, with the greatest certainty and ease, will do for every single person what Small-holding Acts can do for but a limited number and with uncertain results. This means is the Taxation of Land Values, by which access to the land will be thrown open, not to a favoured few, but to every willing worker. Small-holdings Acts very carefully contrived may benefit the community and create a certain number of more or less contented peasant farmers; but with the Taxation of Land Values there would be no need for any Small-holdings Acts, nor for any other measures for the protection of labour ;— for labour will then be quite able to protect itself.

ERIK GIVSKOV

A REBEL

MANY acquiescent : the few triumphant : the mass accepting with bewilderment, if without wonder, a routine which they think to be permanent and inevitable ; such is the attitude of modern man towards modern things. It seems so established and secure—this enormous construction of mechanical industry, business communication, and the heaped-up wealth of the world. It has brought into existence so many million superfluous lives. It has placed at the disposal of those who attain, such aggregations of riches and comfort and power over the bodies and the souls of men. So many who are inflamed to revolt in adolescence are found afterwards meekly bowing their necks to the burden, and identifying, in assured accents, civilisation with progress. In time of Order it stands for the forces which dominate and control; it refuses to believe that this time of Order will ever in the future be disturbed. It is impatient of the anarchic impulses which occasionally challenge its control ; the love of Beauty and the Arts which in past days has scourged and tortured humanity; the demand for social justice, and those "ancient earth's equalities" which stimulate such a demand : the callings of religious and supernatural impulses which may make all its professed prizes appear but as ashes and a little dust. Where it advances these are beaten down and presently disappear ; where it is triumphant, as at the mouth of the Hudson River, or on the southern shores of Lake Michigan, they have become (for the successful) but as idle dreams. And it is advancing always : civilising the Tropics and "educating the Equator"; pushing the missionary forward in remote forests and marshes, and following hard after him. It is transforming the ancient East, awakening China with rude blows, converting Japan into a huge factory. It is swinging steel bridges across the Zambesi, and flooding the markets of Burma and Cochin China with its stamped cottons. This is the white man's burden, which he must shoulder till he die ; changing the world, but finding no intelligible reason for the change ; destroying what he cannot understand, and despising it even in its destruction.

What is the aim of it all ? What is the end of it all ? These are just the questions none can answer. Dominance of individual or nation in a world-struggle, say some ; to which the query, " And when dominance is obtained ? " produces no reply. Happiness in wide commonalty spread, bravely assert others : to which an examination of those who are triumphant in the tumult would seem an even more convincing negative than investigation amongst those who have failed. The successful millionaire who seeks power, the son of the successful millionaire who seeks pleasure, have this link at least in common, that they both reveal human effort stranded in a kind of cosmic weariness. " He gave them their hearts' desire, and sent leanness withal into their souls," is written over all those gorgeous palaces, and evidences of a half-fabulous wealth, and effort by bizarre and frantic enjoyments to pass easier and quicker the impracticable hours. The "Will to Live," says the philosopher, blind and unconscious, seeking residence and a home in that human energy which is accomplishing all these things ; indifferent to the welfare of the individual, like some wild beast that has captured control of intelligent machinery, and is directing it in all ruinous courses. Accumulation and Acceleration, affirms the observer who is content with the vision of actual things without a theory behind them ; Accumulation for the sake of Acceleration, and Acceleration for the sake of Accumulation : that is the unending end of " progress." It's worth while, says President Roosevelt to Mr. Wells. " Suppose after all that it ends in your butterflies and morlocks. The effort's worth it. It's worth it, even then." It's worth while. What " it " is worth whose " while " remains conjectural. " This is the Law,"—so chant in pitiful asseveration Mr. Wells' deformed monsters, half brute, half men. " This is the Law. There are none that escape."

There are a few who escape. Their freedom is only bought at a price. The most of them bear to the day's ending the marks and scars of that conflict. They are rebels against the accepted order of the world. That accepted order, animated by the instinct of self-preservation, is committed to their destruction. The Spirit of the Hive raises against them the Inhabitants of the Hive. In one of Lewis Carroll's later books he pictures the lunatics having become so numerous that they outnumber the sane people, combining against the sane people, clapping them into asylums. Sane people, discovered hiding in remote villages, are dragged before the courts, certified by lunatic doctors as indubitably sane, promptly placed under lock and key as a menace to a lunatic society. Modern life has scarcely yet attained this organised apprehension of the dangers of the " sin of witchcraft." Its attitude to its rebels is in part tolerant, in part contemptuous, only occasionally afraid. It is so secure in its own power. It cannot conceive that these few, clever persons can have behind them the " great allies " which may one day bring all its edifice tumbling to the ground. So the rebels write plays impeaching its whole scheme of existence, and it crowds to the theatres where these are performed, laughing heartily at their whimsical humours. And the rebels deliver their hearts' bitterness in speech and song, and it purchases " Leaves of Grass " and patronises a " Pathetic Symphony." And the rebels die, worn out by the long struggle against its serene insolence and satisfaction ; and their lives are written in two large expensive volumes, and applauded as biographies of singular interest.

Lafcadio Hearn was a rebel. He did not merely revolt (as so many) against the obvious flaws and deficiencies in modern civilisation—the monstrous inequalities of fortune, the arrogance of its wealthy, the bleak, starved life of the poor. He rejected with a kind of terror and a kind of disdain, the whole scheme and system of modern civilisation —life directed to such unimaginable ends. He fled from it as men flee from a city struck with the plague. He fled from it first into the South, where Nature and the languorous air themselves conspire against its supremacy ; then Westward, into a land always of afternoon. But it pursued him into his new home, and would not let him rest; laying its firm, cold hand upon his adopted country, darkening its skies with industrial development and the preparation of war, transforming Japan in a decade into an ugly thing. To the last he cherished schemes of further escape into remoter regions : down to the Philippines, to Java and Borneo, to those Tropics that still " pulled at his heart-strings "; or with a resolution " to haunt old crumbling Portuguese and Spanish cities, and steam up the Amazon and the Orinoco, and get romances which nobody else could find." But his escape was contrived by death, which came to him, in fashion similar to the death of Stevenson, quite sudden and unexpected one evening in Tokyo, on the 20th of September, 1904. He possessed a curious and restless mind, a capacity of deep, sensitive feeling, and a magic splendour of style. His work has that particular quality of distinction which is the guarantee of literature. Both his published volumes of sketches and stories, of the South and of Japan, and these intimate and generous letters [1] will be reckoned among the stuff of this time that will endure.

His father was Irish, his mother was Greek. There was not a drop of blood in him that was not rebel blood from the beginning. He was born in Santa Maura, set in the blue Ionian sea under the blue sky. That love of the blue and desire for it became incorporated in his being— " The holiness of the sky-colour," he was to write later, " the divinity of Blue. Blue is the World-Soul." He is described as a dark, passionate child, with gold rings in his ears, dwelling amongst strangers, away from father and mother, in a land of the North which at best could be for him but a land of exile ; full of the spirit of mutiny.

As a child he rejected the creed of success and the orthodox Catholic religion in which he was reared. He turned instinctively to Beauty and the love of it, which still possesses a power over the few to torment and to inspire.

[1] *The Life and Letters of Lafcadio Hearn.* By Elizabeth Bisland. 2 vols. Constable & Co.

The story of these days is curiously similar to that of Richard Jeffreys in *The Story of My Heart.* " Colour is to me a sort of food," is the confession of the one ; colour " that used to make me hungry and thirsty " is the description by the other. Both were excited to sudden almost intoxicating emotion, which they could in no way explain, by introduction to the Greek mythology, and the pictures of Greek statues, and the old beautiful things. " I adored them ! " confesses Hearn, " I loved them ! I promised to detest for ever all who refused them reverence."

Less fortunate than the youthful Shelley, who sought for ghosts and sought in vain, this child was troubled by grim ghosts who came unsought, and all his life was darkened by the vision. He refused a worship to the God of his foster-parents, and would pray to the Devils, thinking them strong and placable. " To the Devils," he writes, " because I supposed them stronger than the rest, I had often prayed for help and friendship : very humbly at first, and in great fear of being too grimly answered—but afterwards with words of reproach on finding that my condescensions had been ignored."

At school an accident deprived him of the sight of one eye, and produced a disfigurement to which he was always sensitive. He passed through Ushaw aloof and solitary, not understanding his companions, not caring to be understood. From thence he escaped into the dim underworld of England's subterranean cities, suffering the last extremities of indignity and privation. At the age of nineteen he left England for ever, and sailed for the West. In America also he lived in poverty ; until at last he found a vocation as sensational reporter of murder and outrage on a Cincinnati paper. " Grievously wounded by realities," he hated the grey North, the tumult, the confusion, the faces, all hard and white and eager, all set upon gain. The nostalgia of the Tropics was upon him : he came down one day to New Orleans, then an old tranquil Spanish city set in a Southern air ; and was filled with the sudden sense of coming home.

He obtained a living there, serving Admetus in rather desultory journalism. Outside this labour he occupied himself with investigations in the music of the various peoples of mankind, in original composition, and in issuing translations of Gautier and other modern French novelists, which excited the fury of Puritan America. Here he discovered a scheme of the universe which he could accept, in the philosophy of Herbert Spencer. It came to him as a large revelation transforming his world. It provided a great and tragic vision full of pathos and poetry ; of the Cosmic Process travelling from its commencement to its close. Philosophers to-day have ceased to regard the synthetic philosophy as a serious and intelligible system. But its power as a poetic drama is unquestioned. The " First Principles " furnishes a Lucretian scheme of the making and unmaking of all material things. It is an attempt to express in philosophy the declaration of the poet—

> Worlds on worlds are rolling ever
> From creation to decay,
> Like the bubbles on a river,
> Sparkling, bursting, borne away.

The Time Process is here revealed in alternate elaboration and dissolution. The first ripple upon the boundless deep of the Primitive Quiet is pictured as breaking up, like the ripples on the seashore, into ever increasing complexity. Until the primeval movement has originated all the immense and variegated world ; the colour and form of animals, the play of human intelligence, the cataract, through illimitable spaces, of sun and star. Nor is the reverse process unheeded ; the replacement of energy by weariness and development by death. Until the multiplicity passes back into unity again ; and the noise of the last ripple on the boundless Deep finds its rest again in a universal Quiet, when all the tale is told.

This sombre and magnificent vision which embraced within its horizon the infinitely great and infinitely little, the life of the midge and the gnat equally with the clash and fusion of worlds, exercised over Lafcadio Hearn a lifelong fascination. Sometimes he found Spencer's " Oceanic Philosophy " (as he called it) a vision to dizzy and appall :

in which all human ardours and affections vanished at last into nothingness and cold. At such times he thinks that the apprehension by mankind of the truth of their being and destiny will be the beginning of the end. " I fancy the era *must* come," he writes, "when the superior intelligences will ask themselves, of what avail are the noblest heroisms and self-denials, since even the constellations are surely burning out, and all forms are destined to melt back into that infinite darkness of death and of life." Sometimes he found a relief and welcome in the escape to this wise Agnosticism concerning the Unknown from the dogmas of the historic creeds of Christendom. " Worlds are but dreams of God and evanescent," he cries in a kind of ecstasy ; " the galaxies of suns burn out, the heavens wither : even time and space are only relative : and the civilisation of a planet but an incident of its growth." He came to amalgamate this scientific philosophy interpreted in terms of mysticism with the Buddhist religion of the East, finding an explanation of the Chain of Life, a place for Nemesis and the Furies, in that doctrine of heredity which reveals the individuals but as flowers on a continuous stem ; finding also, despite this vision of a darkening sky, a place in his human scheme for gentleness and kindness, and love for all gentle and kindly things.

After a time the Wander-thirst came upon him again. New Orleans failed to satisfy the home-sickness for the South; and " he cast himself back into the arms of the Tropics, for which," says his biographer, " he suffered a life-long and unappeasable nostalgia." He wandered into sunny seas, and finally came to rest at St. Pierre in Martinique, abiding there so content beneath the shadow of the great volcano which was to effect its destruction. In this languid and tropical town, where all the shadows were blue, and the sun shines always, and the ten commandments were abrogated, and existence passed in an enchantment of scent and strong colours, he found a realisation of his heart's desire. " The sweetest, queerest, darlingest little city in the Antilles," he called it ; " I love it as if it were a human being."

Here he first realised his great literary gifts. Here he tolerated and enjoyed the life around him. These were the

happiest hours of a life not rich in happiness. Long afterwards he mourned with a kind of personal affection over
the ruin which had come upon it all. " All this was—and
is not ! . . . Never again will sun or moon shine upon the
streets of that city: never again will its ways be trodden :—
never again will its gardens blossom . . . except in dreams."

In 1889 he was back in America, in severe distress for
lack of funds. He came to New York, and was filled with
terror and revolt at the life he saw there. " New York in
winter signifieth for such as me—Dissolution—Eternal darkness and worms." The rush and clamour of business, the
feverish fight for fortune, the squalor and confusion of its
unregulated individualism, afflicted him with a kind of
obsession, like hideous dreams.

Long afterwards, when it seemed possible that he would
be compelled to return, " the great nightmare of it," he
confessed, " always dwells with me—moos at me in the
night." He caught at the first chance of escape: the offer
of a newspaper to send him to Japan. In Japan thus
casually entered he was to spend the remainder of his
days, teaching in the schools, marrying a Japanese wife,
becoming a naturalised citizen of his new country, inter-
preting the " soul of Japan " to the Western world.

It was not his beloved Tropics with the heat and magic
of Nature, and the hues and dyes of Paradise. It was a world
" chromatically spectral," made up of faded tints and shades
of blue and grey. It was a land like the Garden of Proser-
pine " where the world is quiet," and where " even the seasons
are feeble, ghostly things." But it was so delicate, so child-
like, so fantastic and unreal, above all so remote from the
harsh and violent universe which he hated, that he fell in
love with it from the first. He saw it as a kind of fairy-
land of little peoples—courteous, serene, simple, passionless.
Later he came to lament the coldness which accompanied
the fascination of its outward show, and the iron grip
which lay behind the velvet glove.

"This is a domesticated nature," he wrote, " which
loves man and makes itself beautiful for him in a
quiet grey-and-blue way like the Japanese women,

and the trees seem to know what people say about them—seem to have little human souls. What I love in Japan is the Japanese—the poor, simple humanity of the country. It is divine. There is nothing in this world approaching the naïve, natural charm of them."

" We are the barbarians. These are the civilised," was his deliberate verdict. " A people," he called them, " the most lovable in the world."

He came to Japan in the time of the great change : when the nation was hurrying in one generation from the thirteenth to the twentieth century, and consuming its vital energies in so terrific a process. He saw his pupils " torn to pieces," in Lamennais' phrase, " not by four horses but by two worlds." He regarded the change with the profoundest regret. It was a change from the charm of childhood to the harshness and raw impatience of adolescence. The " great tenderness " of old Japan was giving place to a new ugly thing; which would have no time to spare for the cherry blossom and the children, music and happy laughter. He attempted what was possible in preserving the best of the past ; giving most serious and wise advice to his pupils in the confusion of this hurrying change, to cling to all that was best in the old, to maintain their old truths and traditions, at least to reject the insolences and vulgarities of the new age. He waged a fierce warfare with the missionaries, whom he accused of being " pioneers of destruction": representing everywhere " the edge—the *acies*—of Occidental aggression "; and never able to replace what they destroy.

He was angry with the facile attempts to interpret this people by the average traveller—sometimes as a doll's house, sometimes as a kind of barbaric race. " I have learnt about Japan," he confessed to the end, " only enough to convince me that I know nothing about Japan." Yet he wrote of what he knew, and his books probably represent the truest interpretation of this bewildering people which has ever been recorded. It was the secret door of knowledge unlocked by the key of sympathy. When he died in the midst of the high heroisms of war, "Surely we could lose two or three battleships at Port Arthur," wrote one of them, "rather than Lafcadio Hearn."

This man possessed a genius for friendship. His affections were as violent and sometimes as wilful and capricious as those of a child. These letters are full of the evidence of the tenderness and compassion which was in him, which he extended especially to all weak and suffering things. And as in so many of the Southern people, all this tenderness and compassion was especially concentrated upon his children. The acceptance of Fatherhood was the sudden kindling of a flame. "Don't have children," he wrote to a friend, "unless you wish to discover new Americas." As these children grew older, he was tortured with anxiety when he thought of the world to which they would be committed, and what that world might make of them. He contemplated with a kind of terror these little white souls obtaining the desperate knowledge of good and evil in the same chequered experience which he had suffered and enjoyed. "I am worried about my boy," he writes, "how to save him out of this strange world of cruelty and intrigue." "If anything were to happen to him, the sun would go out." "A being entirely innocent of evil, what chance for him in such a world as this of Japan?" And this child inspired in that last paper on "Illusion," one of the tenderest and most haunting passages of modern English prose, musical with the tears and sadness of all human change :—

> "Quickly as he runs," is the ending, "the child will come no nearer to me—the slim brown hand will never cling to mine. For this light is the light of a Japanese sun that set long years ago. . . . Never, dearest!—never shall we meet—not even when the stars are dead!
>
> "And yet—can it be possible that I shall not remember?—that I shall not still see, in other million summers, the same sea-wall under the same white noon,—the same shadows of grasses and of little stones,—the running of the same little sandalled feet, that will never, never reach my side?"

The letters are full of a certain richness of imagery—a searching and defiant examination of the modern world and the impulses which move the hearts of men : a judgement by a mind curiously detached and simple, of a world absorbed in irrelevant things. He regards with a grave surprise the foreigners in Japan. He is astonished at "the extraordinary wastefulness" of it all. "Men work like slaves for no other earthly reason than that conventions require them to live beyond their means, and those who are free to live as they wish, live on a scale that seems extravagant in the extreme. All goes right in the end, but I have not yet escaped the sensation of imagining one life devouring a hundred for mere amusement." Born, like De Musset, too late, in a world too old, he found the accepted conduct of life becoming not so much wicked as foolish: so frantic a waste of possibilities of happiness and kindness, in those who so soon will be gone. Lafcadio Hearn was a Pagan from heel to crown. He eagerly applied the confession of Gautier to his own condition. "Never have I been to Golgotha to gather passion-flowers; and the deep river flowing from the side of the Crucified, and making a crimson girdle about the world, has never bathed me with its waves." Yet the Christian centuries could not thus leave him unmoved. The serenity and assurance of the Pagan world, its indifference to the less fortunate, its absorption in an ideal of individual perfection, was troubled and often transformed by the new spirit of pity. He was disturbed by the demands of the Christian ethics even when he was desirous of repudiating them. Uplifted always by the magic of Beauty, he was oppressed also by that sadness which to-day accompanies her manifestations. The medieval singer wept "because love is not loved." This man mourned because Beauty was despised by the multitude and trampled under foot of men. And he recognised a deeper sorrow, also, in the transitory and hazardous nature of all earthly Beauty, with the moan of the autumn wind beneath the spring sunshine, and the seeds of death lying in the heart of the flowers. "She dwells with Beauty," wrote the poet of Melancholy, "Beauty that must die." That Beauty "must die" seems an intolerable outrage, to a mind which has apprehended the present as merely the dividing line between an unborn future and a dead past. The Pagan acceptance of the moment in its fulness was impossible to one in whose blood flowed the inheritance of nineteen Christian centuries. So he was troubled with the vision of the days to come—the inevitable drift of society towards abyss. He could see no light behind the cloud. He feared Socialism, and industrialism, and a hard, cruel, pitiless competition for unsatisfying pleasure. He felt "an unutterable weariness of the aggressive characteristics of existence in a highly-organised society." The "Western business man" he found "a very terrible and wonderful person" : an answer to a wish : the product of the insensate thirst for power : trampling under, not cruelly, but carelessly, cruel in his carelessness, all weak and gentle and pitiful things. He refused to believe that the existing state of things could continue indefinitely. "There must be social smashings, earthquakes, chaos—breakings-up, recrystallisations, to lighten the burden. And what will these be?"

He died too early to see, his prophecy either fulfilled or disproved. "What shall it profit?" is the challenge of his work and experience. What shall a man—or a nation—give in exchange for his soul? It is a plea sometimes tranquil, sometimes passionate, for the things of enduring excellence ; for Beauty, and the love of it, in the common ways of men ; for quietness and a contentment with little material display ; for those elements of courtesy and tenderness and simplicity which to-day are in danger of disappearance before the aggression of noisier ambitions. His work embodies a question and an appeal. The question is one which should be directed towards any civilisation whose wealth and power are blinding it to the ultimate object of human energy. The appeal can never be superfluous until love and loss and longing have altogether vanished from the world.

C. F. G. Masterman

THE CONSERVATISM OF WOMAN

WOMEN are not voters to-day. But it requires no gift of prophecy to state that in a very short time they will be. The insurgent section of women suffragists, by tactics which have revivified a dead cause, and persuaded even the politician that women are in deadly earnest, has visibly shortened the period of waiting. There can be no doubt that this is the last stage. As in all movements towards freedom, after rebellion comes victory. Women will soon be enfranchised citizens.

It is well therefore to turn inquiring eyes upon the future voters and their conditions. From thoughtful investigation, we should be able to deduce some idea of the forces which their enfranchisement will introduce into the political world. Much has been said and written upon this subject during the last forty years. But the greater part of what is said and written on every subject, is mere statement coloured by assumption, and on this subject assumption and prejudice have run riot. There has been some recent improvement, one must admit, due probably to a stirring of deep waters by rebellion among women, and to a demand on the part of readers for something more than crude rehashes of old masculine " philosophy." But one of the most vital problems of any time—that of the position and power of woman in civilised society—has been supposed generally to be sufficiently met by vague generalisations and prejudiced dogma, served up in floods of ridicule.

Among the assumptions presented as conclusive arguments and reliable prophecies, perhaps the most harmful are those embodying the opposition of progressive politicians to women's suffrage. Every section of the progressive army has voiced them—Whig, Liberal, Radical, and Socialist. Whatever the extent of their other differences, they are alike pledged to the principle of women's enfranchisement, and they have alike sought excuse and delay in doleful prognostications of its results.

This, of course, is a most illogical and short-sighted attitude. ʻIt could be equalled only by women, who suffer to-day under the unjust and retrogressive legislation passed by men, demanding the immediate disfranchisement of the whole male sex. Those who believe in the right of the people to self-rule, cut a sorry figure indeed when, themselves free, they attempt to justify the denial of freedom to others. But this excuse of political expediency, that the influence of women in politics would be anti-progressive or even retrogressive, is in itself totally unsound.

Woman is undoubtedly conservative. And a cheap and nasty pseudo-science has turned this fact into an argument against women's political liberty ! Perhaps our educational establishments are somewhat to blame for this. A more general teaching of the *exact* sciences—of logic and mathematics—may ultimately improve the national capacity for reasoning. But meanwhile, it is necessary to prove that there is nothing in the racial conservatism of women to justify the assumption that they would be any more retrogressive or " stand-still " in politics than men are.

Our current carelessness in the use of words is appalling. Most Liberals in using the word " conservative " read into it, influenced by long political habit, the meaning of retrogressive, inert, narrow, and afraid of change. Then on vague, unsubstantial grounds they apply these meanings to the conservatism of women. But the etymology of the word embodies the meaning of preserving, holding together, keeping from harm. Woman acts in this capacity in the racial life : through her the race passes onward to the coming years ; in her the qualities and powers born of new life-conditions are knit into the new generations. Hers is a mission of building up and protecting. However gross the misuse of the word in the political life of the past and the present, there is urgent need for some of the protective tendencies of woman's conservatism in our future legislation.

To woman, the mother, has fallen the burden of reproduction and of the preservation of child-life. In the early days of savagery this burden tamed her, and taught her love and industry, while her mate was still unawakened.

While the man fought, hunted, fed, and forgot, the woman learned to remember and to foresee—not for herself, or by the stress of her own individual needs, but under the spur of wondering maternal love for the small weak being that she fed at her breast.

Man, the hunter, was essentially a destroyer. His share in continuing the life of the race placed no burden upon him such as that under which woman was earlier civilised. From his hands we have all the engines of that international murder which is called war ; while from hers we have the implements of industry. In the main woman has not been a destructive, but a protective and life-continuing power. But where she has become a destroyer it has been no light matter to meet her. When her natural tendency to preserve has been thwarted, where danger has threatened, or harm overtaken, the weak and young to whom she has devoted herself, her wrath has been pitiless and overwhelming.

The natural object of production is consumption. The desire to consume, the need of consumption, preceded and instigated the first act of production. This was a woman's act. In order to preserve the life of her child, she had to provide necessaries for its consumption, and she became a producer under the stress of its needs. The whole process was directed and developed for the consumer, with the natural object of life-preservation. It was from the point of view of the consumer, for a consumer, and as a consumer, that woman produced necessaries and invented industry.

As a producer woman became a more desirable object to man than she had been as a fellow consumer only. The cunning of her hands—their stores, their handiwork—revealed possibilities of comfort and indulgence which otherwise would not have suggested themselves to his intelligence. Thus was instituted the long age of economic and sex-slavery to which woman has been subjected. The necessity of protecting her child, even from her mate, made her submissive under the domination of the fiercer sex, to whom she was desirable both as a woman and as a worker.

Through the uncounted ages that have followed until to-day, there has been a gradual shifting of production into the hands of men, and a gradual distortion of productive industry from its natural object. Slowly woman has become the consumer of society, the final user and preparer of the things necessary to our physical existence. Not this solely at any time. There has always been a certain percentage of productive work done by women, varying with time, condition, and place. Though we have an increasing band of these women workers in the industrial market of to-day, the majority of them are only temporarily employed there. The period between school-life and marriage is generally passed in such economic independence as women's wages make possible. But the great majority of adult women are not engaged in productive work at all. They are the final purchasers, preparers, and distributors, of the wealth products made in the world's manufactories. They are the world's consumers. Even if women to a far greater extent than at present come to engage in productive work, they will always remain essentially consumers. They will always judge production from the consumer's point of view. It is not merely a matter of age-long habit and environment, it is an essential condition of their very nature, consequent upon their share in race-reproduction.

But while the purpose of industry, during this long period, has been debased into self-aggrandisement and unrighteous profit, the extent and nature of production have developed immensely, under the impetus of man's fiercer spirit and more restless direction. The industrial world—its products, its possibilities—have loomed large over the other things of life. The world has been ruled according to the creed of the producer. Provided that production had been subordinated to the needs of the consumer, this looming large of the economic issues of life would have been no evil. But with woman, the essential conserver and consumer of the community, shut out from all political and industrial direction, evil came apace. To exchange at a profit, over and above the value of labour expended, material used, and expense of transit, became the object of production. Invention and discovery quickened the rate of the struggle. It roused the fighting spirit of men, until, in the competitive chaos which ensued, the consumer, the product, and finally the rank-and-file producer, were sacrificed to the directors of industry. The reign of low wages and high profits, of adulterated products, shoddy, and short weight, of gilt and crinkled-paper imitations, of shams and shames, is the result. In it lies racial destruction and decay; from it spring immorality and death.

With the enfranchisement of women the consumer will come into politics, and will share that legislative control of industry which is growing every year. The individual purchaser for the household, the collective purchasers of the State, will begin to look upon shopping with the eyes of law-makers. The consumer's demand for a pure and clean product, for a cheap product, for a sufficient variety of products, will acquire a new strength. It will be the demand of citizens—of the directors of the world's affairs; it will be the woman's primal demand for life-protection and life-nourishment brought down to modern days and backed by modern weapons. The highest price and the least valuable product are the objectives of to-day's productive methods, and both are alike anathema to the consumer. Thus the new women-voters will be thrown into direct fundamental opposition to those methods of ruthless commercialism which underlie the many industrial evils of the day.

Men in increasing numbers see and deplore these evils, and many of them toil persistently, if ineffectually, to remove them. The long-continued and now regrettable economic dependence of women upon men, has produced at least one racial benefit in the growth towards gentleness and the great widening of human sympathy among men. The chivalrous code of duty and protection, so often misplaced and harmful, has a beautiful side in its practical efforts towards national redress and reform. But while the balance is weighted heavily on one side, no tinkering adjustment of the fulcrum will produce equilibrium. The weight must be balanced by an equal weight; the pull in one direction must be neutralised by a pull in the other. Men find their chief economic interest in production. By inheritance and environment they tend to consider their own direct profit from production as the most important matter. It is ultimately the same both with the single producer and the capitalist. Each seeks a high price for the commodity he sells; each seeks to part with the smallest possible portion of that commodity for the fixed price. Thus both these forces tend to the detriment of the consumer, by the adulteration or increased price of the product. In spite of the stress of competition, in spite of trade-union organisations, and of the inspection of weights and measures, and the analysis of food-stuffs, the consumer is robbed and preyed upon on all sides. The worst burden of our present industrial system lies on the consumer's shoulders, and the clearest and straightest way to re-adjustment and reform is to be found in the new powers to be wielded by the overburdened woman.

It is to the consumer's interest to have commodities cheap and good; it is to the consumer's interest to have choice and variety. Therefore it will be to the interest of the consumer, newly enfranchised, to reduce the cost of production in every possible way. Such items as the cost of transit, the additional charges due to taxation, will be scrutinised from a new standpoint. The unequal taxation of necessaries, purchased chiefly by women, which has been fulminated against for at least a generation, will most probably be effectively dealt with. The burden imposed upon the consumer by the present railway freights will assume that importance it deserves, and State control or State ownership will follow. In like manner a new impetus will be given to inventive genius in the realm of industry, especially with regard to the development of natural advantages, and side by side with it will grow a powerful crusade against shoddy and adulteration, such as never can be experienced until the consumer is aroused.

With regard to wages, a second vital factor in woman's

environment must be considered. Practically all other costs of production are likely to be reduced by her legislative power. But the first cost of production, the wages of the worker, are, speaking generally, the woman's capital. She is economically dependent upon the productive worker. Therefore, while she will come into the political arena as the champion of the consumer's right to a good product, she will also come as the champion of the worker's right to a sufficient wage. She will learn, and teach, that a good product can only be produced by a well-paid worker, and that shoddy and sham are the accompaniments of sweated labour. So that while production will receive through her the hope of purification, while in her hands it will again be directed to its true purpose, the supply of a sufficiency of good products for the consumer, the conditions of the real producer are likely to benefit from her activity—not only because of the fact that not otherwise can she obtain a good product for consumption, but because her work of protection and preservation does not, in these days, end with infancy. The preservation of the upgrown is necessary for the good of the race.

The growth of humane spirit and of knowledge has gone on apace for half-a-century. The woman's rise to the status of citizenship is coming. Armed with these greater powers, she will come back to a work from which she has long been painfully divorced—the work of turning the energies of the nation towards the preservation of itself, towards the nourishment, welfare, and happiness of its units. All those social evils which deprave and destroy the children of the nation, which, though lying close at her feet to-day, she cannot touch, will be her charge and burden when she rises to her true status as mother of the nation, equal in right and power with the father. There is no vital reform which she does not need, more perhaps than man needs it ; there is no evil which does not spatter her with its mud. As the conservative life-force, she is needed to influence, initiate, and hasten, the social and economic reforms of the world.

TERESA BILLINGTON-GREIG

MR. ARTHUR SYMONS AS A CRITIC[1]

MR. ARTHUR SYMONS is one of the subtlest critics now writing, here or abroad, for a public anxious to acquire or to test opinions upon works of art. As a critic he is remarkable for wide sensibilities, for connoisseurship in music and painting and acting, as well as in literature, and for his willingness to judge a particular work of art on its own lines, " generously expanding it to the full measure of its intention." He can also transmit the emotions which a work of art has stirred in him, and he writes of these things like one possessed with the idea that the beauty which artists ` create and discover is as important as anything in the world. In fact, so far as any philosophy appears in his writings that is what it amounts to. His defence of certain poets and painters often leads him to the verge of a mysticism, which implies that of any experience whatever the aspect which possesses some beauty must be the most important one. In consequence of this belief, which is a mystical philosophy or nothing, he will never be a widely-influential critic, since this is not the view of common-sense ; and, secondly, it is not surprising to find him in consequence interpreting with the most patient sympathy those artists and poets whose choice of subjects have been aspects of things often regarded by the public as either trivial or immoral. He is the one interpreter of the " decadents " worth reading in the English language. In his preface to a reprint of a volume of his own poems, *Silhouettes*, which fell under this ban, he says :

" Nor do I affect to doubt that the creation of this supreme emotion is a higher form of art than the reflection of the most exquisite sensation, the evocation of

[1] *Studies in Seven Arts.* Constable & Co.

the most magical impression. I claim only an equal liberty for the rendering of every mood of that variable and inexplicable and contradictory creature which we call ourselves, of every aspect under which we are gifted or condemned to apprehend the beauty and strangeness and curiosity of the visible world."

Here we have an admission on the general question of values in art, which does not sufficiently influence him in judging those poets and artists, whose talent lies in expressing moods and perceptions which have no great emotional value. In self-defence this claim would not blind him to his own limitations as a poet; but when he makes it on behalf of others, the very fact that they require this particular defence disposes him to greater leniency towards their faults and to an intenser appreciation of their merits. Like every other critic, Mr. Symons tends to be more than just in some directions. His bias as a critic is to be too appreciative of those who look for beauty curiously, sadly, and even perversely, in moods and perceptions which are generally regarded as trivial or base. The ordinary reader is inclined to judge the poem by the mood from which it sprung. Is it one which he would wish to shake off from himself? Then, though for the *poet* many things may glimmer through that mood with a peculiar charm, he will have nothing to do- with the poem which expresses it. Mr. Symons contends that if such moods lead on to perceptions which have some beauty of their own, there is no reason why an artist, who can express this beauty better than others, should not do so. Certainly, there is no reason why he should not; but the reader who, missing " the creation of supreme emotion " in such work, refuses to put a high value on such work is also right. The emotional quality of much of the work which is called " decadent " is poor, and this fact is one which Mr. Symons, partly from the peculiar susceptibility of his imagination to certain beauties, and partly, no doubt, because he appears as the interpreter of writers who are frequently dismissed with crass contempt by the public, does not often take into account. It is curious to see how justly he holds the balance in such a case as that of Ernest Dowson,[1] where he is on his guard against the bias of friendship, a study which is at the same time an admirable criticism and an admirable portrait ; but when this subject is not so near him personally, he is not equally on his guard against a sentimental artistic bias in favour of a mysticism which has after all inspired very little work not open to the criticism of being freakish and too slight. His book upon *The Symbolist Movement* [2] is written too exclusively from within that movement. It contains many comments of excellent precision, for instance that upon Villiers de l'Isle Adam : " Satire with him is the revenge of beauty upon ugliness, the persecution of the ugly ; it is not merely social satire, it is a satire on the material universe by one who believes in a spiritual universe. Thus it is the only laughter of our time which is fundamental, as fundamental as that of Swift and of Rabelais."

But since behind the æsthetic theories of the symbolists (of De l'Isle Adam, Verlaine, Rimbaud, Mallarmé, and others) lay a kind of mystical philosophy, he is compelled to write about these ideas ; and it is here that he often fails to satisfy readers, who have followed with admiration his analysis of each author's quality. We want these ideas focused in the world and in the history of thought ; we want them treated with detachment by the critic, however sympathetic he may be to this mysticism himself, and to the works of art founded upon it, and this we do not get.

The result is that his criticism, where such authors are concerned, is apt to lose the breadth, which should include a survey of ideas different from or hostile to those which underlie the work of these authors. He does not meet, for instance, the objections which are vaguely condemned in the term " decadent." Decadence, he says, is a term which only has a meaning when applied to style or form, and in *Studies in Prose and Verse* he proceeds with a consistency which revenges itself to prove that Meredith is a " decadent."

" What decadence in literature really means·is that

[1] *Studies in Prose and Verse.* J. M. Dent & Co.
[2] *The Symbolist Movement.* Heinemann.

learned corruption of language by which style *ceases to be organic* and becomes, in the pursuit of some new expressiveness or beauty, deliberately abnormal. Meredith's style is as self-conscious as Mallarmé's. But unlike many self-conscious styles it is *alive in every fibre.* Not since the Elizabethans have we had so flame-like a life possessing the wanton body of a style. And with this fantastic, poetic, learned, passionate, intellectual style, a style which might have lent itself so well to the making of Elizabethan drama, Meredith has set himself to the task of writing novels of contemporary life, in which the English society of to-day is to be shown to us in the habit and manners of our time."

This passage is instructive as an illustration of the vagueness of the words usually employed in criticism. What does "*organic*" mean (the italics are not the author's) if not "*alive in every fibre*"? And if style, as he so often, in common with other critics, asserts, be a quality of the matter and inseparable from it, is then the substance of Meredith's writing "decadent"? No one will be brought to agree to this. It is clear that when people use the word they must mean something more than abnormality of expression and a keen, conscious relish of words. They mean different things at different times; but perhaps the writers to whom they most consistently apply the term, are those who seem to cut life up into little separate moments of emotion, who dwell curiously upon each as if its true significance lay in being regarded by itself, when a greater vigour of mind or strength of feeling would have contemplated the experience in wider relations. Such writers, by narrowing their intention, may find beauty in objects and emotions which on the whole are ugly or disagreeable. The elaboration of style which often accompanies such exercises of the imagination is the natural result of having to make much out of little.

Those who do not already sympathise with æsthetic mysticism will be made impatient by Mr. Symons' uncritical attitude towards it; and they will value far more his criticism of writers, whom he does not attempt to judge from that point of view. His *Studies in Prose and Verse*, which is about to be reprinted, contains much excellent criticism, uncoloured by such philosophisings.

Here is a good comment on Maupassant:

"The man of the world is perfectly willing to admit that he is no better than you, because he takes it for granted that you will admit yourself to be no better than he. It is a way of avoiding comparisons. To Maupassant this cynical point of view was invaluable for his purpose. He wanted to tell stories just for the pleasure of telling them; he wanted to concern himself with his story simply as a story, and he wanted every incident to be immediately effective. Now cynicism in France supplied a sufficient basis for all these requirements; it is the equivalent, for popular purposes, of that appeal to the average, which in England is sentimentality."

Of Russia, *à propos* of Gorki, he says:

"It has lost none of its instincts and it has just discovered the soul. And it is ceaselessly perturbed by that strange inner companion; it listens to a voice which is not the voice of the blood; it listens to both voices, saying contrary things; and it is astonished, melancholy, questioning. Other novelists tell us of society; tell us, that is, what we are when we are not ourselves. The Russian novelists show us the soul when it is alone with itself, unconscious, or morbidly conscious, gay, uneasy, confident, suspicious, agonised with duty, a tyrannous slave or a devout and humble master. . . . The English novelist shows us an idea coming into a man's head; when he has got the idea he sometimes proceeds to feel as the idea suggests to him. The French novelist shows us a sensation, tempered or directed by will, coming into a man's consciousness; even his instincts wait on the instinctive criticism of the intelligence; so that passion, for instance, cools into sensuality while it waits. But to the Russian there is nothing in the world except the feeling which invades him like an atmosphere, or grows up within him like a plant putting out its leaves, or crushes him under it like a great weight falling from above."

Studies in Seven Arts [1] was published almost at the same time as a reprint of Mr. Symons' first book of criticism, *An Introduction to the Study of Browning*.[2]   There is hardly a quality in common between the two books to show they are by the same writer.   The *Study of Browning* is a simple commentary upon the poems taken one by one, which draws attention to certain qualities psychological and æsthetic, and states these as clearly as possible.   It is perhaps the best primer on the subject written for those who are studying poets as part of their education.   *Studies in the Seven Arts*, on the other hand, is written with greater elaboration than any of his other critical books.   It is filled with attempts to transmit the emotions which the author has experienced in front of pictures, on hearing certain pieces of music, while watching dancing or looking at statues.   It is full of æsthetic philosophy, and it comes under the class of criticism which is written not only to convey ideas, but also the temperament of the critic himself. That is to say, it is the kind of criticism which aims at being a work of art in itself.   The danger of this kind of criticism is that the writer is liable to become more absorbed in his own ideas than in the object itself.   Mr. Symons does not always escape this fault ; and since his weakness lies chiefly in reflection and his strength in acute perception, this is to be particularly regretted.   For instance, he begins a passage upon Rodin with an excellent analysis, and ends it in a very weak vein of epithalamic meditation.

" All Rodin's work is founded on a conception of force; first, the force of the earth, then the two conflicting forces, man and woman; with, always, behind and beyond, the secret, unseizable, inexplicable force of that mystery which surrounds the vital energy of the earth itself, as it surrounds us in our existence on

[1] Constable & Co.   [2] J. M. Dent & Co.

earth. Out of these forces he has chosen for the most part the universal, vivifying force of sex. In man he represents the obvious energy of nature, thews and muscles, bones, strength of limb; in the woman, the exquisite strength of weakness, the subtler energy of the senses. They fight the eternal battle of sex, they seek each other that they may overcome each other. And the woman, softly, overcomes, to her perdition. The man holds her in the hollow of his hand, as God holds both man and woman" (a reference to the great sculptured hand which holds a lump of earth with two little figures cuddled up inside it); "he could close his hand upon the fragile thing that nestles there and crush it; but something paralyses his muscles in a tender inaction. The hand will never close over her, she will always have the slave's conquest."

Now there is nothing in the sentiment of the statue, "Le Baiser," for instance, which the passage recalls, to suggest "overcomes to her own perdition," etc. : the critic is interested in this sentiment and has simply gone off along that line. Few will agree with him that the sculptured hand grasping the lump of earth, with the man and woman inside it, is one of Rodin's finest creations; though, as the reader follows the critic's sympathetic description of it, he may begin to waver in this opinion. Still, there is much to be said for the opinion that this work appeals more through conveying a philosophic idea than through its intrinsic beauty.

The essay on Watts is perhaps the best in the book. As a portrait painter he contrasts him with most modern painters in his power of painting the intimate individuality of his sitters and in his abstention from seizing on some momentary or accidental effect. "Whistler with his unerring 'science of beauty,' in his unerring sense of the painter's opportunity, poises his figures on the turn of a heel, in the act of buttoning a long glove, the hand resting jauntily on a cane, the child's feet grasping the floor, the aged man or woman outlined against a dim grey wall with the immobility of the wall itself. Sargent pours the crude light of the studio roof upon all in a man that would most escape that interrogation, crying to him roughly to speak out, stripping off some of his shyest and most honest disguises, and giving us, as the truth, whatever remains over after the soul has been frightened out of sight. Manet is not more tender, but he is more complete in his capture, giving us life as well as the moment, and the whole sensitive intelligence of the flesh, which to him is the whole of life. All these will have things their own way, will snatch the beauty or the energy which they desire, like a thing possessed wilfully, only Watts is content to wait, disinterested, humble, incurious, sure that the secret, if not the meaning of the secret, will come to him." Admirable criticism ! though "the secret, if not the meaning of the secret " is an obscure saying—perhaps it is meant to remind us of the absence of anything, which suggests the wand of a physiognomic lecturer in the touch of Watts' brush. He praises Whistler with an intimate fervour, which leads him into using far-fetched fancies to express what he wishes to say, and thanks to unusual literary skill he succeeds in capturing many a flying perception, though the literal reader will find himself continually exclaiming "What next ! " His interpretation of the portrait of Sarasate, which he contrasts with Watts' portrait of Joachim, is an example of the ingenious tenacity with which he will follow out his idea. It forms part of the argument that in Whistler's portraits the pose itself is as much a part of the interpretation as the painting. Now Sarasate is a genuine but not a profound artist ; his tone is wonderful ; but he has nothing but his temperament and his technique. " He is seen (in the picture) making his astonishing appearance, violin in hand, out of darkness upon a stage, where he is to be the virtuoso. . . . The man who holds the violin in his hands is a child, pleased to please ; not a student or a diviner. And Whistler has rendered all this, as truthfully as Watts has rendered the very different problem of Joachim, in perhaps the greatest of his portraits. Joachim is in the act of playing, he bends his brows over the music which he is studying, not reading ; if there is any platform or any audience, he is unconscious

of them ; he is conscious only of Beethoven. Note how
Sarasate dandles the violin. It is a child, a jewel. He is
already thinking of the sound, the flawless tone, not of
Beethoven. Whistler has caught him, posed him, another
butterfly and alive." This is a piece of criticism which
will make the reader, when he is next in front of the
picture, look at it with fresh interest. Mr. Symons
studies Whistler with the peculiar sympathy that he has
for all artists, whether they are " symbolists " or impres-
sionists, who work in the belief that art must never be a
statement, but always an evocation. But in comparing
him with Velasquez who made a beauty up from "a very
carefully studied vision of reality ", he recognises Whistler's
limitations. He " tricks life and the world into beauty by
excepting in them only what suits his purpose, as indeed
every artist must do, but also by narrowing his purpose till
it is indeed for the most part symbolised by the butterfly of
his signature." If Mr. Symons had submitted Verlaine
and the Symbolists to such stern tests of comparison there
would have been no serious fault to find with his criticism
of them. There is another criticism of Whistler so good
in itself as to be well worth quotation, which might also
apply to a great deal of the literature to which he tends to
be too indulgent : " Whistler begins by building his world
after nature's, with supports as solid and as visible. Gradually
he knocks away support after support, expecting the
structure to support itself by its own consciousness, so to
speak. At the perfect moment he gives to the eye just
enough to catch in the outlines of things that it may be able
to complete them by that imaginative sympathy which is
part of the seeing of works of art. But he can never be
content with that service, and demands more and more
of it, in his challenge with things, with himself. And
he comes finally to suppose that all eyes have the sight and
sensitiveness of his own ; which is as if one were to expect
the A B C class to read Euclid off the black-board."

In his essay on Richard Strauss Mr. Symons has no
difficulty in proving that the attempt to convey ideas or
facts through music is to ignore the characteristic of that
art, which is to convey emotion directly without the

medium of ideas. The essay on the ideas of Wagner is not so clear ; in it ˙he seems to have taken more trouble to please himself than to make the exposition easy to the reader. In his description of the personality of Duse in private life, his literary power fails him as it rarely does. His article on Gustave Moreau is excellent : " Beauty, to him, is bounded on the one side by prettiness, on the other by the fantastic and the unnatural. At a touch of nature his whole world of cold excitement would drop to pieces, scatter into coloured fragments of broken glass." As an example of that sensibility which makes Mr. Symons so interesting a critic we may point to the description of Cologne Cathedral : he complains of the vast nakedness of space " frugal and fruitless, out of which nothing grows in the luxuriant way of the great French Gothic cathedrals." It reminds him of Bach's bare-stone work in music, " its ornamentation is certainly his also, with its harpsichord trills and Italian flourishes." . . . " Mystery no longer envelops the sacred rites ; there is no shadow from divine things ; here is a daylight church through which the air blows freely. If there is any mysticism built up into these stones, it is the icy Flemish mysticism of Ruysbroeck, whose name one sees on a station not far from Cologne." " How reasonable is God ! " one says sitting here among these cold, ascending pillars ; and not, as in Chartres or Barcelona, in that dimness touched with fire : " How terrible is God ! " " This cathedral is one of the unconsoling images of eternity. . . . I can find in it neither ecstasy nor any passionate kind of hope. It shelters no dreams, only a calm certainty, as of a mind which has reasoned itself sure." Perhaps this passage marks better than any other the limit of his sympathies ; perhaps he should feel more and find more beauty in " a daylight church through which the air blows freely " : but how well he has expressed an impression to which he does not respond ! Can we ask more of a critic, than that he should describe his impressions so that others, while understanding what he feels, may guess what they would have felt themselves ?

DESMOND MACCARTHY

THE TERRITORIAL ARMY

THE central feature of Mr. Haldane's army scheme is the reorganisation of the auxiliary forces, and the creation of what he terms the territorial army. The changes in the regular army are matters of detail, and though of great importance have not the far-reaching possibilities of the other half of his scheme. An endeavour will be made in this article to examine in broad outline the objects of this scheme, its advantages, and its drawbacks ; and then to consider the only other alternative presented to us—conscription.

First, as to the scheme itself. It may be asked whether, seeing that we now have militia and volunteer artillery, militia and volunteer infantry, and yeomanry cavalry, there will be any very great change in calling these old forces by the new name of a territorial army. The change will be this. At present all these different forces are on different engagements, with different liabilities, with no unity of command, and with some of their most important commanders belonging to the foreign service branch of the army, who must inevitably be withdrawn at the first menace of war ; but, worst of all, with practically the whole of their artillery immobile. The whole force is therefore incapable of rapid movement, and would in consequence suffer defeat from a far smaller force with mobile artillery and unity of command, even if this latter force were inferior, man for man, in physique, morale, and training. Under the new plan the whole would be as homogeneous and as mobile as any army in the ordinary accepted meaning of the term, ready to take the field in divisions with its proper comple-ments of the three arms, horse, foot, and artillery, and under its own commanders. Thus, if the regular army were entirely removed from this country, the efficiency of the territorial force would not be affected in the slightest. The present writer has insistently urged the desirability of creating such a force, on the ground that only by this means can any real reform of the army and any sensible economy be effected. And indeed this must be the case. Whenever an attempt has been made to reduce the numbers of the regular forces of the crown, and it will not be denied that no real economy can be accomplished by any other means, the objection has always been raised that this country would be inadequately defended in the event of any such reductions taking place. If it be urged that the primary duty of the regular forces is service oversea, and that all that are redundant to that purpose should be cut off, we are told that the defence of these shores from invasion cannot be left to a disorganised force. We are reminded of the striking episode of the summer of 1900, when, owing to the apprehension in the public mind created by the absence of regular troops, costly expedients were resorted to in order to create fresh battalions, called royal reserve regiments. Unless, therefore, a force can be created which can preserve this country from the danger of invasion, and in which the public will have confidence, all hope of economy must be abandoned.

It may be asked why the new territorial force, which will admittedly be built up from materials already existing, will be so much more effective for the purpose of national defence than the auxiliary forces as we see them to-day. It would seem to have two advantages, one ideal, the other real. If the idea be once firmly planted in the minds of the public, and of the territorial force, that the citizen army, and the citizen army alone, is responsible for the safety of this country from invasion, the whole thing will be taken seriously, and efforts will be made by all classes of society to make the thing a success. The actual advantage will be the mobility of the territorial force. It is not sufficiently realised that the defence of any territory against attack from the sea involves the necessity of far greater mobility on the part of the defenders than if the attack be threatened by land. The force that attacks by sea can move at least four times as fast as a force attacking by land, and its opportunity for feints which will successfully draw off large parts of the defending force in a wrong direction, are well-nigh unlimited. If this country were invaded to-day in the absence of the regular army, the most immense confusion would prevail. With the territorial force in working order, one, two, or three divisions could be ordered to the threatened point, and would immediately move towards it, to be further reinforced by divisions as required. Sedentary defence is always necessary for some few places in the United Kingdom ; the great government dockyards, the great private ship-building yards, and other places near the coast where warlike material is manufactured must be scientifically defended by a special branch of the territorial army. For the rest what is required is mobility, mobility, mobility.

The one thing that is essential for the creation of this mobile territorial army is an administrative power not dependent upon the administration of the foreign service army. This separate administration is provided for in two ways, firstly by the creation of county associations, which, although they have none of the powers of command or training, will in every other way exercise control over the territorial force within the county. Opinion seems to be generally favourable to the creation of such county associations, although the details of the composition of each association cannot be supposed to commend themselves to extremists on either side. The extreme democrat is horrified at the proposal to make the lord-lieutenant the *ex officio* chairman ; the martinet is aghast at the mayor and corporation, county aldermen and county councillors having any share in military matters. It is probably wise to found these association committees, for it is certain that the territorial forces, as we know them at present, have always been at loggerheads with the War Office. Nor has the situation been improved in this respect in any sensible measure by the decentralising reforms carried out under the Esher scheme. There would therefore seem to be no alternative to some kind of local control, combining both the military and the civil authorities within the county.

The second method proposed under the scheme of giving a separate administration to the territorial force is the creation of a separate department at the War Office to deal with the territorial army. Of the desirability of this separate department there can be no question in the minds of all those who are acquainted with the opinion of the auxiliary forces. The present system, under which every matter not settled locally is passed through the various channels at the War Office, none of which have any knowledge of the facts at issue, has failed, and must fail to be either efficient or satisfactory.

Such being, in very broad outline, the objects of the creation of the territorial force, let us examine the objections which have been brought against it. The first is that it is not wanted at all, since the invasion of this country is rendered impossible by a preponderating navy. This argument seems fortunately to have lost much of its force during the last two years. The extreme difficulty of blockade, as shown in all our naval manœuvres, and in the Russo-Japanese war, has convinced most thoughtful students of war that the evasion of even a most powerful naval force by a flotilla of transports must always be possible. The same argument disposes of the " starving out " theory ; for just as the invading force may elude our own naval blockade, so can the ships carrying our food supplies evade the hostile naval blockade. The royal commission on food supplies in time of war seems finally to have disposed of the theory that this country can easily be starved out. From what is known of the views of foreign powers it is reasonable to assume that they share this opinion, and realise that if this country is ever to be brought to its knees it must be by a hostile force landing on our shores, and not by a naval blockade. Even if invasion were extremely improbable it would still have to be guarded against, for the penalty of failing to provide against it would be national annihilation. The pedestrian is especially warned to " beware of the steam roller," not because the steam roller is particularly likely to run over him, for it is certainly the most easily eluded of all forms of traffic, but because the penalty of failure to avoid it would be so utterly fatal.

The second objection urged is that, granted a force must be maintained at home to repel a sudden invasion, the proposed new territorial army will be inadequate to the task, since though its numbers may be sufficient, its training will be so short that it will be unfit to meet the invader's troops who have had a longer period of training. This school of critics regards the value of the soldier as depending solely, or mainly, on his length of service ; a force trained for a fortnight will be hopelessly defeated by a force trained for six weeks ; a force trained for one year must succumb to a force trained for two years ; and so on. But these critics have overlooked the fact that they are " hoist by their own petard." If the value of the soldier depends on his length of service, our own regular troops must be far superior to those of all other nations, for our regular soldiers are trained for seven years, as compared with the two years of most continental armies. Now the first onslaught of the surprise invasion can only take place when the 120,000 regular troops of the expeditionary force are still in this country. Long before these 120,000 are embarked for foreign service the territorial force will be embodied, and will immediately begin to pile up that length of training which this class of critic considers so essential. Indeed the whole theory that the value of the soldier is dependent on his length of training must be regarded with great suspicion. Every improvement of modern weapons has continued to make length of training of less importance, character of more importance. Thus, in the days of the long bow it took a man ten years to become thoroughly proficient with his weapon ; now-a-days a man can become a first-rate rifle shot in a few months. The same phenomenon is observable in civil life. Improvements in machinery often render manual dexterity less essential. On the other hand, character becomes of greater importance. The wide field covered by modern battles, the distance of each man, not only from his fellows, but from his officers, makes it more important than ever that he should have his heart in his job. No amount of training, and training only, will make a man prefer death to surrender ; for this is the problem which each man in a modern battle has often to think out for himself and by

himself. It is not suggested that training is of little importance ; it is of first-rate importance of course, but courage,
character, common-sense, confidence in the leader, these are
of greater importance still.

The third objection is that on the terms offered the
territorial force cannot be formed, for the men will not join.
This is the most formidable line of opposition, and only
time can show whether it is well founded ; but it falls to
be said that it largely depends upon the loudness of this
criticism whether it succeeds or fails.. It would be an evil
thing to ruin the chances of a great national reform in order
to secure a dialectical advantage. Still it is probable that
concessions will have to be made. The estimate of the cost
of the territorial force is extremely low. All forces in
England that have been successful have been expensive.
Cromwell's cavalry troopers received about the same rate of
pay as a lieutenant of cavalry does to-day, his commanding
officers received more than the corresponding ranks at the
present time. But though the territorial force may cost
more money than is at present anticipated, it will still, if
successfully created, be a step in the direction of economy
for the reason already given. To maintain regular troops
costing anything from £80 to £130 a man to defend this
country from invasion, when the same function can be
equally well performed by citizen soldiers costing from £7
to £10 per man, is plainly a most extravagant method.

The fourth, and an interesting objection, is that of the
extreme democratic section. Mr. Robert Blatchford in a
recent article feared that the formation of the territorial
army meant the creation of a huge police force, with power
to over-ride the wishes of the democracy. All armies have
this danger, but the proposed territorial force would
presumably have it in a less degree than any other form of
army. Being based on a voluntary system of enlistment, the
executive could not employ the force on tasks distasteful
to the national sentiment, without running the risk of the
immediate disappearance of the whole by resignation. It
may be said that this force will be recruited from a special
class, and that it will be an armed and triumphant
bourgeoisie ; but it would seem that the argument is really

the other way. They will be less likely to run the risk of exasperating the people than a corresponding number of men with less to lose. In fact, the surest way to prevent the bureaucracy and the bourgeoisie from becoming an arrogant governing caste is to put them into the territorial force. But it must be admitted that the system of officering the territorial force, and, for that matter, all existing branches of the various imperial forces, is to the last degree undemocratic ; it is far less democratic than the system prevailing in many other armies ; fortunately there is nothing in the composition of the territorial force to render reform impossible.

The last objection, the most insistent, and the most loudly voiced, is that no force can be adequate or successful that is not based upon conscription. This seems to the present writer to be a fallacy. He believes that it can be proved that conscription for home service, even if it were possible, far from rendering our imperial position more secure, would render it far more difficult. If the population be conscripted for home service it will be less likely to volunteer in large numbers for foreign service, and no one has suggested that conscription for foreign service would for one moment be tolerated by the people of this country. Many cogent reasons can be urged for the view just enunciated that conscription for home service renders foreign service more difficult of attainment. During the great war with France a century ago under the militia ballot we had, in fact, conscription. No doubt the militia ballot was a bad form of compulsory service, for it allowed substitution, but it was conscription all the same. What was its effect ? Our difficulties in finding sufficient men to fight our battles on land or sea were overwhelming. The man who had served in the militia considered he had fulfilled his whole duty to the State. This article would stretch to unreasonable limits were the whole history of this movement to be traced, but it can be confidently asserted that the more study given to this subject during the period between 1797 and 1815, the more apparent will it become that in spite of the element of compulsion for home service being then in active operation, the difficulty of finding men for service abroad was far greater than it is at the present day.

Let us see how compulsory service for home defence affects nations with imperial obligations for oversea service. France has a colonial empire which is small by comparison with our own, and the number of men required, whether in peace or war, is but a tithe of what is required by England. Yet in Tonkin and Madagascar, to take only the most recent instances, the difficulty of providing a sufficient number of good white troops was very considerable. So great was the difficulty that in one part of the Madagascar campaign, *i. e.* 1894-5, the Government managed to get the people to assent to the employment of ordinary conscripts for service in that country ; for various reasons, notably the youth of the conscripts, the experiment was so dire a failure that it will probably never be repeated.

Germany has even less necessity for white troops to serve oversea than France, and yet her difficulties have been very great both in finding men for the international expeditionary force sent to China in 1900, and for the war against the Hereros in South West Africa. The difficulty experienced by Germany in providing a sufficient number of white troops for her small necessities for war oversea is particularly instructive. In Germany, if anywhere, the conscript army has been brought to the highest point of efficiency ; the greatest minds have been directed to its perfection ; the whole nation, from the emperor to the peasant, has joined in creating and maintaining it, and it is to-day 'the concrete expression of the national will and national ideal. But yet, when it comes to sending five or ten thousand men to a war across the sea, the men are not forthcoming, indeed the disinclination of the people to serve abroad has been such as to cause the Government quite recently the gravest embarrassment.

If we compare this state of affairs with our own case we have some reason for gratification. Every year in peace time we send an expeditionary force of close upon 20,000 men for oversea service, and in time of war there appears to be no limit to the numbers that are prepared to serve. First and last we sent over 400 000 men to fight in South Africa.

What the reason for this phenomenon may be it is difficult to say. Perhaps it is that there is only a certain amount of military ardour in each man, and that the element of compulsion destroys this spark of patriotism with extraordinary rapidity. Compulsory service for home defence may be compared to inoculation with an antitoxin, which acts as a prophylactic against any further attacks of martial zeal or national self-sacrifice.

It may be argued that the theory just enunciated is disproved by the military achievements of Japan oversea, whose army is based upon universal compulsory service. But readers of Sir Ian Hamilton's second volume on the Russo-Japanese war will not need to be reminded of the exceptional features of this war. The Japanese are a strange people, wholly different in ideas and methods to the peoples of Western Europe. Again, every Japanese man and woman had learnt to regard Russia as their one great enemy, and the defeat of Russia in Manchuria and the seizure of Port Arthur as the one great end to be pursued at all costs. Every Japanese man, therefore, knew full well the purpose for which he was compelled to join the army, and since that purpose was one on which his heart was set, the element of compulsion had no drawbacks, and indeed entirely disappeared.

We, as a nation, have fortunately no such definite objective, no insult to be wiped out only by ruthless war. It would seem then to be true that voluntary service is the only method of defending our widely scattered empire with its indefinite obligations and indefinite future hostilities. Compulsion, far from being a help, may be a hindrance, as it was to our own country in the past, and as it is to other European countries to-day. Surely it is better, then, to concentrate upon what is not only possible, but even desirable, namely, the creation of a great volunteer army appealing to all classes of the King's subjects, in sympathy with similar forces in every great self-governing colony, and itself forming a sure defence and a link of empire.

JOHN SEELY

DAUGHTERS OF JOY

1

LONG, subtle-floating, the choir
Of strings—soft floods of tone—
In pleading dance-measured invades
Cloud-like the pavement, where
With the night-wind's vast lament in mine ears, I am
walking alone.

2

You, from the dance, I cried,
In tears, at this street-corner ?
" I am going home, my friend.
(Strange, that you knew me !)
Dances are not for the sore heart, nor lights for the scorner."

3

How came you to live so, sister ?
" Jealous was he I cared for—
False, but jealous—he died—
Flung himself into the river ;
And then a child . . . no matter!   What should the child
be spared for ?

4

" What mattered ?   What matters in London
But the play of the iron mill ?
It is full of women who smile
And heroes live upon them.
There, if a love rise in your heart, 'tis that that you must kill.

5

" Smile under the lamp-glare—
To laugh cracks your painting—
There's no place to weep in there
Or bow the head in silence :
Under an archway the clever children ˌmock at a woman
fainting.

189

"Sick, hie to the almshouse—
Lie in your shroud, thinking ;
Soiled before you have loved,
When you have loved, betrayed ;
And is there, once betrayed, a better end than drinking ?

"Yes, wiser ones will save—
And then there may be marriage ;
After precipitous years
Settling down (with your past
Always to take the opposite seat) in a well-padded carriage ! "

Through Asia sweeps that voice,
Through Christendom and Jewry ;
Look up at the tavern door—
See !   A phantom peering in,
The smile of a daughter of joy on the drawn face of a fury.

Down the dark tremendous vale
Whirling like leaves, O Daughters
Of Joy, O gash'd priestesses
Night-bound, hectic, marred,
Ye that were lovely once as clouds mirrored in waters,

To what dominion dire
Flag your fierce wings, till they
Glide through the dense realms lit
Only by eyes of prey ?
Whither, O sister-spirits eternal, sink ye away ?

Back to the Past we sink,
Whence the human would be soaring,
To deep-pent Chaos back,—
Hold out no hand to us—
Rushing disharmonies, lost, lost past deploring !

So the blazing rout shall coil
Unnumbered down for ever,
And the foul shall breed the foul
And the heavenly heights be far
While man knows not of love, and cannot curb his fever.

HERBERT TRENCH

THE AMERICAN AND HIS HOLIDAY

A DISTINGUISHED American wit once said that all good Americans go to Paris when they die. That represented the acme of aspiration of the sixties and seventies. In those days we took in England by the way, and in passing did homage to Shakspeare, the Crystal Palace, Westminster Abbey and Madame Tussaud's. We yawned our way through a British Sunday in those relentless lodging-houses of the Bloomsbury district, where the economical of our nation congregated. Even supposing we had it in our unregenerate hearts to demand to be entertained on Sundays, the British sense of propriety nipped that in the bud. We were not entertained, unless staring through tears of fatigue at vagrant cats prowling about the trees of Bloomsbury on a godless quest after sparrows may be called being entertained.

In those days we were given over to an orgie of church going, and in a liberal way we patronised all creeds. We also went on Dickens pilgrimages, as no one else did. The London we adored was Dickens' London with a few churches and historical names thrown in, for even then London was fast becoming a city of reminiscences. Finally, having seen all the churches and all the imaginary haunts of the famous people who never existed, having eaten more vegetable-marrow—that national vegetable of England—than we wanted, as well as that other national asset, a heavy, bilious kind of plum-cake, we finally escaped from the British Sabbath, and fled to that gay city on the Seine, in whose deplorable vocabulary there is no such word as " home." There, instead, we became acquainted with that French national institution, the " café chantant," which for a

191

traveller does quite as well, and which made our respectable
American souls thrill with the consciousness of seeing
" life."

Since then the wheel of change has swung round ; Paris
has sobered down and London has cheered up. Divine
Providence is with the nation that has " home " in its
vocabulary, and these summers the sun positively shines in
London, and, encouraged by nature, London has annexed
some of that gaiety on the Sabbath which the Continent is
fast losing. To be sure, if we are a hungry and homeless
wayfarer, it is still rather difficult to get anything to eat on
Sundays in London, but we are permitted to listen to music,
and certain picture-galleries are open to us. In fact, the
Americans have taught the British the first rudiments of
enjoyment. The new British gaiety is England's concession
to her best transatlantic customer. Years ago it was
only artistic heathens who were " at home " on Sundays,
but now everybody is at home on Sundays, and the only
wonder is that, when everybody is at home, they ever get
any one to come to see them. However, the travelling
American is always to be relied on, especially the feminine
American, well-dressed with the national figure, enthusiastic,
keenly intelligent, and eager for information which is stuffed
into that other national institution—the side bag. The
truth is, if it had not been for Americans, Europe as a
summer resort would never have been discovered. Next to
the original discovery of Columbus that is the greatest. Why
grumble over the engaging peculiarities of the American
tariff, when America yearly exports that tremendous output
of brave American citizens on whom in a modest way England
also puts on a little import duty ? There is no question but
that they pay their way, to the joy of others besides the English
shopkeeper. Even those higher in the social scale get their
little welcome pickings. I remember an astute American,
after studying English methods, saying with bated breath,
" An American has to get up early to get ahead of an
Englishman, and even then he's sure to find him there
already." Yes, it is the American dollars, that bulge British
pockets, which have given the English their new gaiety !

To say in America that you are going abroad puts you

at once on a superior social footing. It is a kind of self-bestowed order of knighthood without a title, but which gives you a keen sense of superiority. The American who goes abroad never returns exactly the same. His outlook has immeasurably broadened, and though he may believe more than ever in his national eagle he will find that there are other formidable heraldic birds and beasts on earth besides that great bird who spreads his wings across the national shield and occasionally favours the world with an ear-splitting shriek. It gives the patriotic American a wrong estimate of values if he only hears his own eagle scream, and it is necessary for him to hear the screams and roars of Europe. Hence the educational value of European travel.

The travelling Americans can be divided into the extravagant and the stingy ; there is no medium. They either overpay their way, or they underpay their way. It is a mistake to think that the travelling American is rich. He mostly has to count his pennies to make them meet. But it is this wrong estimate of Americans that is responsible for the increased cost of travelling. We are not all Vander-bilts and things ! It is not the Vanderbilts nor the Rockefellers who help to circulate the American dollar abroad, but rather the shoals of modest students, teachers, tourists, and town and country folks who come over here to spend what they have saved up for this event of their lives. They say it is the steerage that pays on the ocean liners, and so it is the modestly "comfortably off" who make the effete countries prosperous. The necessity of European travel for the American is amply testified by its ever-increasing tide, in spite also of the ever-increasing cost. But go he must, in spite of an expense which years ago would have appalled a rich man.

Americans who feel that "Urup" is banded against them come across by way of Cook's Tours and other per-sonally conducted parties, and pay a round sum for which they take part in a frenzied flight across the Continent, while Europe passes before their dazed sight like a kaleido-scope. Their time is limited to the summer, and Europe is large, so they have to step lively. A kind of nightmare of travel begins, and they see the sights in a race against time. They shoot through picture galleries, churches, public buildings, and past monuments ; in fact, they are not spared a single one of all those free entertainments to which the personally conducted are liable, and until exhausted nature gives up. Who has not strayed across worn-out American tourists stranded in hotel parlours, hollow-eyed, sallow, haggard of cheek, straight-fronted though exhausted, shirt-waisted, side-bagged, loathing sights, hating churches, hating pictures ? An American was overheard to ask a porter in a Geneva hotel, " Is there a museum in this town ? " " No, sir," said the porter, humiliated by this disgraceful confession. " Thank God," the young American cried fervently, and shook the astonished man's hand.

The American, like his English cousin, is limited in his expressions of rapture. I remember a divine night in Venice. The Grand Canal lay bathed in moonlight, and from a passing gondola, gay with lanterns, a song floated softly upwards. Suddenly through the stillness of this City of Dreams I heard a compatriot, a wide-awake, red-headed youth from Maine, exclaim with sincere conviction, "I say, a gondola does beat a buggy all hollow, don't it ! "

The rapture with which the American goes to Europe is only equalled by the rapture with which he returns home. Europe is a hard nut to crack even in three months. It is only as he finds himself gradually recovering on his homeward journey from a physical and mental collapse, the result of a chaotic multitude of impressions on a perfectly exhausted brain, that he begins to enjoy himself in retrospection. But he would enjoy himself more did there not loom before him then the prospect of that fateful interview with the keeper of the national conscience, the custom-house inspector. Who of us has been able to look into the inspector's suspicious eye without quailing ? No woman, of that I am sure ! Men are much more scrupulous as minor criminals. A dear friend of mine smuggled a silver tea-service under her petticoats, where a tea-pot, the milk jug, and a sugar basin thumped her most cruelly. She had bought them in Paris, where a guileless " antique dealer " swore by all the gods—and offered to give it to her in writing—that this particular service had been the private property of Louis XVI. Having escaped the argus-eyed but guileless inspectors, whose wistful orbs she had disdained to blind even with a five dollar bill, and at the cost of a few bruises, she reached home with that sense of satisfaction which a woman always feels when she has smuggled successfully. She divested herself of the private property of Louis XVI, and took a few days to let the bruises heal, and then she went on a shopping expedition just to prove to herself how cheap Europe really is. Fate took her, she told me afterwards, to a huge establishment built along the soaring fancy of a Whiteley, and just as she looked into the interior of what Americans call a "dumb salesman," and which far from an impropriety is merely the name of an electrically lighted glass-case, she stared aghast and petrified, for there in the "dumb salesman's" interior stood the exact copy of her own Louis XVI tea-set which she had imperilled her immortal soul to smuggle over, and on inquiry she found the price which, of course, included the duty she had not paid, as well as a handsome profit, to be ten dollars less than she had paid for it in Paris. She did say that it seemed funny of Louis XVI to have two tea-sets just alike, but she supposed he had forgotten.

"However," and my friend spoke as one registering a solemn vow, " I'll never buy anything in France again ! A country," and words cannot do justice to her withering scorn, "that doesn't know the meaning of 'home.'"

Though I did not quite follow her reasoning, I was more than ever convinced of the wisdom of having a good conscience, and buying one's Old Masters, Lowestoft china, Chippendale, and old silver in America. Why not give the American workman a chance!

Though all Americans may want to go to Europe, fortunately for the National Exchequer there are millions who can't. The only class that doesn't need or want a change in summer is the lowest class. It is change and refreshment enough for them to have the streets watered occasionally, whereupon they can bask luxuriously in the resulting steam, while they watch the closed ice-carts roll stolidly by, for the trusts won't sell ice except at famine prices, for even trusts must live. And your sweltering householder and his white-faced children gasping hot air, a whole panting family hanging out of each dingy window, are not profitable customers. It would be rather pleasant to hope that some day the gentlemen of the ice trusts may realise the drawback of having no ice. There are commercial crimes that make one regret a rational religion which is fast doing away with that particular form of future punishment in which the world wisely believed for so many centuries, and which is so simple and yet so effective.

Apart from these forlorn waifs and strays, every American tries by hook or by crook to get a little holiday in summer. The relentless climate makes it a sheer necessity. The only saving grace the cruel heat has, is that it is dry, and not damp like the English. In New England the cities pour themselves into the country and the sea-shore, while the West crowds to the sea-bound Eastern towns as to havens of bliss. The American summer sojourner of towns is for this reason quite a different kind from the native. By the blessed 4th of July, which American patriotism celebrates in a manner calculated to be most destructive to life and property, whoever can afford it flees from town, and offers up a silent prayer that the ardent patriotism of the citizens who are left will not prove fatally destructive. For, without any exaggeration, what between fires, accidents, and deaths, the United States may be said to offer up every 4th of July, in the aggregate, a good-sized town and its inhabitants as a thank-offering for the many blessings only the free enjoy. Still, one can't pay too much for real liberty.

Of the people who desert the towns, some of the frivolous go to summer hotels—curious American products bereft of men but prolific of boys, little boys too youthful even to flirt with. Only at the week's end do the grown men arrive in trains, whereupon animation is restored to the lovely but deserted creatures who, dressed in the last " cry " of fashion, have to rock forsaken on the hotel piazzas through most of the week. On Saturday nights there is a kind of thanksgiving " hop," and such young feminine things as can't find a masculine creature to hop with, hop with each other. But it is sad to see two girls dance together—the real salt and savour of dancing quite disappears. The truth is, the dancing man is fast vanishing from the face of the earth. The modern young man won't dance, and he hates summer hotels, so he growls and plunges his way into the primæval forests, and in his bungling fashion tries to escape the piazza girl, but he can't. For she plunges after him into the primæval forest, and for his sake she dares many things: gets spiders in her hair, ear-wigs down her back, and ants and grasshoppers up her spine. Still, the young man is destined to be captured whether on a hotel piazza or in the Adirondacks, for though ornamented with freckles and mosquito-bites, and with her nose peeling, the new six feet American girl has been found to be quite as dangerous as the five feet three inches kind in a ball room. You really never can tell.

The American man has a perfectly beautiful reputation as a husband. To such an extent indeed that when future generations demand the description of a martyr, then will the biography of the American husband be produced as a sample of what a real martyr is. His reputation as a martyr rests on his willingness to let his wife go away without him, while he, in company with the family cat, guards his home, and without the cat, earns his daily cake, for the necessaries of life are not so necessary to the American as the luxuries. He is also cited as sweltering in town while his dearest rocks on hotel piazzas, and arduously constructs bits of needle-work for the dust to settle on. His claim to domestic martyrdom has not only resulted in a universal disparagement of the foreign brand of husbands but in a doubt, occasionally expressed, as to whether he really exists. At any rate, an Englishwoman was heard to remark, " I wonder if American women really have any husbands ? "

Far be it from any one to disparage the American husband, for he is good and dutiful, and well-trained. All one ventures to question is whether he is such a real, out and out martyr as foreigners have been led to believe ? Does the American husband really dislike to consort with the family cat ? Is it a fearful sacrifice for him to have the run of the house ? Must it not be a real solace for him to put his feet on the Ormolu table, or on the drawing-room chairs, or his hat on the bust of Clytie—it always is the bust of Clytie!—in the bay-window? Are there not ameliorations to his martyrdom? Does he not take this opportunity to invite to his deserted home his most undesirable bachelor friends, and refresh them with those sacred drinks for which the American husband is so justly celebrated? Is it an awful agony to stay at the Club until hours whose smallness would cause comment, if indulged in at other times? As for going to Europe, what American husband would not much rather pay untold bills than trot behind the insatiable partner of his joys through those awful picture galleries, not one of which is spared him? With what concentrated regret many an American husband, lured across the water, and tugging after his charming tyrant in a toque, thinks of that happy, deserted family cat, licking its face, or toying with a mouse, or sleeping the sleep of the unbothered just. Or of those dear friends having a " gin-cocktail " at the Club in peace, while he works like a slave seeing things he doesn't want to see! Far be it from any one to disparage American husbands, only in the cause of justice and fair play they really should not be made out to be martyrs of the very first class, because they are left at home. Martyrs of the third class one might call them, with an occasional day off.

In America, apart from the piazza rockers, hotel hoppers, and the select who retire into Newport palaces, country-houses, bungalows, and the primæval forests, as well as the elect who go abroad, there is a tremendous, serious-minded contingent whose object in life is to improve their minds, and they always take the summer in which to do it. Now a nation which makes of learning a summer entertainment, of that much may be expected. The more unsophisticated Americans are nothing if not conscientious. The less they know of the world, the more seriously they are inclined to take their own minds, especially the New Englanders. England has no idea what good stock she lost when she lost her New Englanders.

To be perfectly just the American never does anything by half, though he probably does things in too much of a hurry. So in summer there is a feverish demand for instruction by what, in default of other description, we must call the middle classes.   As a national asset, these are of vastly more importance than the multi-millionaires.   The American middle classes are in the throes of a tremendous educational movement of incalculable importance, as it is absolutely voluntary, serious and sincere; a movement that has produced among others that extraordinary system of which "Chatauqua" is the most familiar.   Thousands of men, women, and even children, come to this New York village, from which the system takes its name, every summer to receive instruction.   It is amazing to study the curriculum of a day's lectures at Chatauqua, and to watch the eager thousands ready to undertake this mental toil for the sake of learning.   It is study for study's sake.   What in its modest way can be more ennobling ?   And in what other country in the world could such a spontaneous and serious effort be possible except in America ?   As a factor in the future greatness of the country, one is inclined to think that this is overlooked when in the discouragement of recent revelations the world is tempted to apply the adjective " decadent " to the youngest and possibly the greatest of the nations.

When all schools and universities are closed, except such as have University extension lectures to offer, the summer schools open their rather shabby portals to an eager multitude, who long to be taught with a longing that partakes of the solemnity of a religious rite, and there is no doubt that the summer school, voluntarily attended, has a tremendous and far-reaching influence among those who form the backbone of the nation.

Perhaps the Americans are given over to too much of an orgie of information.   Perhaps they do try to inform themselves with too much of a frantic and unhumorous haste.   Granted !   It is also possible that with a greater sense of humour they might know more, while they learned less.   But a sense of humour is not always safe nor desirable for the eager aspirant.   It sometimes acts as an icy douche to young ideals.   Life is probably made easier by a dash of humour, but it is never an ingredient in great national movements.   Martyrs, pioneers, discoverers, and other epoch-making human beings are not usually gifted with much humour.   It is therefore a fine unhumorous stock that takes its learning by way of summer amusement, and the information so acquired by the first generation will probably reappear as wisdom in the second. The only time when one deplores the wisdom of this electric system is when summer empties its hordes of conscientious and eager teachers into the cities, who flock there to give their tired brains an extra polish, instead of letting them lie fallow. But every great movement has its martyrs.

Here is another American expedient in this longing to get an education. Many young men and girls — with the perfect republican right to be called ladies and gentlemen—do what can only be described as menial service in summer to earn enough money to pay for their schooling in winter. I myself have come across two head-waiters in summer hotels who were trying to earn enough money to study for the ministry. In another summer hotel, quite a large proportion of the waitresses were earning money to become school teachers, or to go to commercial schools. I remember a young man who saved the wages he earned during his holidays by being a tram-car conductor, to pay his way through the University in winter. Much can be expected of a nation which is made of such stuff!

The endeavour of Cecil Rhodes to transplant young foreigners into England is probably not that they should study the wisdom of books, but rather that they should become acquainted with that other important branch of education, the knowledge of men, so that the barrier of ignorance shall for ever, even if slowly, fall between the great nations, as it is bound to do if their young men in their impressionable youth are brought together. One cannot but wonder when men shake their heads and question the wisdom of the Rhodes scheme. Cecil Rhodes was the only great modern epic poet, and he, instead of putting his aspirations for his country into verse, made them into a splendid and generous deed, with an imagination worthy of an inarticulate Milton. Palaces of Peace are of no earthly use for the purposes of arbitration, if the people who meet there have no common sympathy.

It must be confessed that there is something very engaging in the way the American encourages the most heterodox creeds. He is surprised at no man's religion; no established church has the power to make one sinner more fashionable before God than any other. That is a mercy! Because of this singular independence of belief, and the impossibility of becoming a social martyr because of belonging to an unfashionable sect—such as Dissenters in England—therefore all religions over there flourish merrily side by side. New England, apart from Utah, where the Mormons still prosper though curbed as to their matrimonial proclivities, is the fruitful ground for all creeds new and old. Boston, famous for many a great philosopher, boasts of a magnificent spiritualistic temple, whose Egyptian style of architecture declines to harmonise with the architecture of the rest of the neighbourhood. It was built by a faithful and inspired grocer. As for the Christian Science churches, they flourish like the green bay-tree. Here this great modern cult had its beginning, and from here ten thousand pilgrims went to Concord, N.H., to do homage to the great Mrs. Eddy, who, a realistic newspaper reporter informed us, received her faithful in a purple velvet dress, and wearing a purple velvet bonnet. One is inclined to think that the mention of a bonnet is both disrespectful and irreligious. We in Boston also sat at the feet of Eastern pundits in "parlors," and the only time we rebelled was when our prophet from the East —that he was a prophet was evident from the cut of his brown frock-coat—with downcast eyes and profound learning which few of us understood, was found to be—it leaked out at an unregenerate masculine Club—a young German whose father manufactured velvet in the Fatherland. That was a little too much for us! So we ceased to sit at his feet.

For a time we also revelled in theosophy. We had over a real theosophist from India, and for a whole season we had him instead of teas and musicales, and other frivolous amusements. There was no mistaking him, for he had Eastern legs, as well as Eastern eyes. We understood that he was a martyr for the sake of his religion. Men at the Club scoffed at him, but they couldn't say he wasn't Oriental! Finally he and his crinkly hair, and his Oriental eyes and his Oriental legs, vanished, and years after we heard that he had settled in Bombay, and that he had given up martyrdom —at least of that kind—and had married, and that there were now eight little martyrs, also probably with Oriental eyes and Oriental legs.

A small and select group of us also investigated spiritualism, and saw uncanny sights, and were pelted with mysterious flowers, and I remember a guitar floating in black space that hit an unbeliever on the head with a spite that was distinctly earthly. The only trouble with this ardent hospitality to all forms of belief was that we got so dreadfully tired of them in no time. And so, after this digression, one comes back naturally to one of the most curious of summer gatherings I ever saw, and that was a spiritualistic camp-meeting.

The tendency of birds of a feather is to flock together. Hence in America those other queer summer gatherings where besides education one pursues the cheerful creeds which, like the Methodist, flourish in the open air. If the conscientious American is not improving his mind, he loves to improve his soul, and he loves to do it in a crowd. This spiritualistic camp-meeting, of which I speak, stood on the sloping pine-clad shores of a little New England lake. It consisted of shabby, gim-crack, two-roomed cottages, built between the aromatic pine-trees, along straggling woodland paths soft with pine needles. The domestic arrangements were much in evidence, and the name and spiritualistic speciality of each occupier were set forth on a modest placard fastened to the shabby front door, and sometimes one caught sight of the occupier, when not in a trance, in black broad-cloth and long hair, helping strange, sallow ladies with short hair in their simple housekeeping duties, and both had that curious detached look characteristic of ardent spiritualists. Séances were the order of the day, and one could choose one's favourite brand of manifestation by studying the placard first, as one would the dishes in a modest eating-house. Slate-writing, trance mediums, materialisation mediums, and those that foretold the future, or, most unnecessarily, retold the past, all were at the service of the wayfarer at any price, from twenty-five cents up. Here believers and unbelievers trod on each other's heels in their frantic desire to penetrate into the yonder. A thoughtful woman once said to me, " If we could be sure of the happy future we are promised, we should all commit suicide ; so it is the greatest proof of divine wisdom that we don't know." As for unbelievers, they were as common as the other kind, for your true un-believer is quite prepared to believe anything—no matter how foolish. So there was a positive rush and crush to commune with the tired spirits of the dead. This spiritualistic camp-meeting flourished for years in this out-at-elbow, uncanny village, inhabited only during summer by hundreds of mis-cellaneous human beings collected together for converse with the departed, and stamped with the unmistakable stamp of those who meddle with the unseen. In the Autumn they scattered like ghosts at midnight.

It was such a beautiful, dingy spot, and in its midst a rickety spiritualistic temple, while over all there was a generally unkempt appearance, as if the presiding elders had too much to do to devote their attention to picking up the banana- and orange-peels, the peanut- and egg-shells, the empty gingerbeer bottles, and an occasional celluloid collar, of the pilgrims to the Infinite.

The American people's motto of life is unquestionably " Get your money's worth, and don't waste time," and it permeates their pleasure as well as their toil. They make a pleasure of business, and that is the reason they are so shrewd and so successful. On the other hand, it retaliates on them by creating those countless men who beyond their business have no resource whatever in life.

The serious danger to the American is that he loves his business too much ; if he does not die in harness, he often enough is confronted by a dreary old age utterly devoid of interest. If one were permitted to give a word of advice to the American man, it would be, " Learn to enjoy some-thing besides your business." If, on the other hand, one were to offer advice to the American woman, it would be, " Do not work so hard for your pleasure." While to the nation at large one would venture to say, " It sometimes pays to waste money, while a judicious waste of time has, in the long run, proved to be a valuable investment."

ANNIE E. LANE

POSITIVISM

EVERY year the papers devote soon after the first of January a few short paragraphs to the Positivist Church whose great festival falls on that day. But the paragraphs grow shorter year by year. This does not in itself show that the Comtist Church of Humanity is declining : it only shows that it has lost its novelty. We who lie outside the communion can only guess its present state. It used to be said—but that was twenty years agone —that while the French members of it would require an omnibus or even a break to carry them all, the English, with a little squeezing, could be got into a four-wheeled cab. What has been the history of the Positivist Church here since then ? Has it grown to the break or has it shrunk to a hansom ? For when Mr. Frederic Harrison speaks as high-priest, we need not suppose that the audience to so attractive a lecturer are all or any "joined members" of the body which he addresses.

This religious side of Comte's teaching, which Huxley called Catholicism *minus* Christianity, and Mr. Harrison (in reply) Catholicism *plus* Science, has never been reckoned here an integral or an important part of Comte's message to the world. It was certainly not that part of it which attracted John Stuart Mill and drew from him his appreciative notice of Auguste Comte. Moreover, the very word "positivist," though it was an invention of Comte's, and though it is used by him and his disciples alike for the philosophical and the religious side of his doctrine, is now claimed by or bestowed on a much wider school of thought and on many who will have naught at all to do with Comte's system of religion and morals. The

POSITIVISM

French are always great at systematising ; greater still at *naming*. The word Positivism came at as happy a moment or happier than Zola's Naturalism. In the latter case it seems almost beside the mark to urge touching Zola's characters (these at any rate) that if they are "naturalistic," they are certainly very often not natural. Even so, though an English philosopher may think there is nothing less positive than the idea of regenerating the world through the Worship of Humanity, or through the peculiar place assigned by Comte to woman in the scheme, he will yet be apt to confess that in the root of the matter Comte was still in the right. For the root of the matter, our philosopher will probably say, lay in this, that Comte did understand and set forth as none before had done the true nature of positive knowledge, or if you like of scientific evidence concerning the truth of things, and did, by this very act (which he clenched through his classification of the sciences, and still more by his famous theory of the three stages of human inquiry and knowledge), establish the positive attitude of mind upon eternal foundations. This is exactly what Mill recognises or believes. "The foundation of M. Comte's philosophy is by no means peculiar to him, but is the general property of the age, however far as yet from being universally accepted, even by thoughtful minds." So says Mill. But he recognises that this floating spirit of modern thought has, by Comte's system, received so to say a local habitation and a name, which were lacking to it before. Spencer disputes that last proposition, but on a personal issue only : he thinks he has done more to crystallise or materialise this *Zeit-Geist* than has Comte. That is no matter. On the fundamental solidity of Comte's system (in philosophy) Spencer and Mill and Huxley and Haeckel, even Fiske, would or should be agreed. This is the Positivism which survives and will survive.

Or will it ? It is strange how the fable of Columbus' egg is for ever being re-enacted in the history of mankind. Historically, as a phase in the evolution of human thought, the enthusiasm which greeted Comte's doctrine of positive knowledge (enforced, it has been said, by his theory of the three stages, theological, metaphysic, and positive, through which knowledge is supposed to have passed) is comprehensible enough. But within the province of Pure Reason it is not comprehensible. For the truth is, all this doctrine of Positive Knowledge, all Mill's, Huxley's, Spencer's and of the others not less than Comte's, reposes upon a simple and rather elementary confusion of ideas.

Let us pause for a moment before the historical aspect of the matter. If there be any parallelism between the laws of mind and the laws of physics—and who can question that there is ?—if, therefore, action and reaction is an essential condition of the former as of the latter, then historically the " positivist " standpoint is wholly reasonable. When human thought has been told for centuries that, under penalties in two worlds, it must accept the metaphysics of (say) the *Quicunque vult* and utter a hearty Amen to Tertullian's famous *Est impossibile ? Certum est ;* when, in a word, it had been compelled for those hundreds of years to breathe the highly æsthetic but " stuffy " atmosphere of an incense-filled cathedral, then it was obvious that whatever afforded most prospect or appearance of daylight and champain, it would greet with the greatest delight and accept with the fullest acceptation ; and out of the delight and acceptation would inevitably spring the glorification of physical science, its clarity, its exactitude, all in it which affords the completest contrast conceivable to the *Est impossibile ? Certum est* before spoken of. This enthusiasm for science, this glorification *is* Positivism. By the same law of reaction, metaphysic is reckoned a half-way house to the daylight and champain, between the pure unreason of Tertullian and the only complete reason which is Science. All this I say is natural enough in the historical aspect of the matter : and being natural, κατὰ φύσιν, it is right.

But the historical aspect of a doctrine in no way affects the doctrine as it stands in the eye of Pure Reason. It is one of the paradoxes of life that these two points of view may lie far apart. And so it still remains the fact that judged in that way, in the way of Reason simply, Positivism resolves itself, as I have said, into not much more than a rather simple confusion of ideas.

The confusion is between Reason and Demonstration.

POSITIVISM

That clarity of Science, so much vaunted, proves upon a close examination to be no more than this, that its results are more easily demonstrable than are other results. The advantages which the truths of science (understanding thereby physical science) have over the truths of metaphysic (understanding thereby Ontology or Epistemology, the study of the human mind or the theory of knowledge) is not that the former are *more true* than the latter—in truth there is not a more or less—but that they are more demonstrable. And from the point of view of Pure Reason it is easy to see that facility or difficulty in demonstration do not and cannot add or subtract one iota to or from the value of a truth in itself ; seeing that they are no part nor parcel of the truth they deal with. " A thing," says Marcus Antoninus, " that is any wise beautiful is beautiful in itself, and because of itself, and praise is no part of itself." Just in the same way we may speak in respect of truth : a proposition is either true or false in itself and because of itself ; and demonstrability is no part of itself. If then it can be shown that positive truth and positive knowledge (in the Positivist's sense of these phrases, I mean) are necessarily more easily demonstrable than what we may call ontological truths, it follows that, from the historical point of view described anon they have an advantage and a sort of extra claim on our attention, but that within the sphere of pure reason they have no advantage and no special claims. In one word, the fact remains that truth is truth whether of the mind or matter, and that it cannot become anything more than true by increasing the number of people who accept it.

" If it can be shown " I have said. No doubt demonstration is always an advantage. I take it the proposition would need no showing to a person who was familiar with both kinds of truth, the scientific and the metaphysical. But such folk are few ; and fortunately this proposition may be demonstrated likewise to those who are not of a metaphysical turn.

It follows directly from a consideration of the relationship of words to thoughts, and the necessary fact that all words which describe parts of the non-self, the outer world, must be more exact in their significance than the words which describe parts (phases or aspects) of the self or *ego*.

(1) In the first place, the former class of words must have been the earliest in any language, by the simple reason that for a word to gain currency it must express what is in the minds of two people, an A and a B (two at least), at the same time, and must be known by A to be in the mind of B and by B to be in the mind of A at the same time. Now the chances of this happening in the case of an impression from without (one of Mr. Spencer's "vivid" impressions) is out of all proportion to the chances of it happening in the case of thoughts within (Mr. Spencer's " faint " impressions).

It militates nothing against this truth, that language itself very likely took its rise rather from the emotions than from the impressions : because the *currency* of language depended on the parts of it remaining when the emotion had passed away. Take the following supposititious illustration. Imagine in some remote ancestral settlement a child carried off by a cave-bear, and the horror of the sight evoking from the parents of the child a cry, which becomes the first name ever given to the cave-bear. In order that the cry may become a part of language, it must be evoked again by the sight of a second cave-bear; and the bystanders must perceive the thing that has called it forth, though they themselves feel none of the emotion which called it forth.

(2) We know too, of course, as a fact that, if we follow back the words we to-day use for thoughts and emotions— for our metaphysical world—they are all found to have first served for some object or sensation of the physical world. " Grief " is that which is heavy (*gravis*) ; " Sorrow " is a sore or wound; "Attention " is derived from tension (*tendere*), a physical stretching ; the Greek μανθάνω, " I understand," " I think," is from a root " to measure "; and " reason " (*ratio*) derives from the same idea. There is no need to multiply examples, which one might multiply indefinitely. Sometimes a word still essentially physical is used symbolically for thought or emotion, as " brain," " head," " heart" are used. No one doubts that in such cases the physical meaning came the first.

Wherefore it follows in a double measure—first, it follows from the reason itself (given above) which caused the original words of currency to be names of physical phenomena ; secondly, it follows from the much greater antiquity of the names for physical phenomena—that in every language to-day all the words of this class are much more exact in their significance than are the words which relate to the world of thought. The conclusion from this is equally inevitable—*It is much easier to demonstrate the truths (or facts) of the world of sensation than it is to demonstrate the truths (or facts) of the world of thought.*

Facility of demonstration and nothing else is the hall-mark of all the truths of physical science : and it is only through a confusion of ideas that this quality which is external to the truths themselves should have been mistaken for a quality inherent in the truths themselves. For of course facility of demonstration includes the facility of demonstration to oneself. When people talk of verification as a property of scientific truths, they mean the same thing— " demonstration " (to themselves if to no other). All the terms which are used to designate the truths of science, " positive," " exact,"[1] " verifiable," etc., resolve into this one quality—capacity for demonstration.

Take the proposition "Shakespeare is a greater poet than Longfellow." Here clearly we have something which is not demonstrable. Yet like every other proposition it must be either true or false. In what relation does it stand to the proposition "Water is compounded of hydrogen and oxygen"? By the Positivist school, though they would not deny the first proposition, yet the second would be reckoned the more true. But there cannot be a more true or a less true in the case of either : each is either true or it is false. In what then do they differ ? In demonstrability and nothing else.

Our sociability and the growth of democracy have been contributory causes, second to the reaction against obscurantism, towards the acceptance of the positivist standpoint : the first, because it makes us apt to distrust our individual judgement and our private thoughts ; the second, because it makes us fancy that that which not many minds can quite

---

[1] Yes, even "exact." It is true that we have only one form of an exact mental science—Pure mathematics. But the only reason why metaphysics cannot be made into one is the want of an exact terminology. With such, synthetic *a priori* judgements would be as easy in metaphysics as in mathematics.

grasp cannot be wholly true. Who is not familiar with the appeals from the obscurity of metaphysicians to the clarity of science? The inference in such always is that what cannot be expressed with perfect clearness (clearness, that is, not to the mind of the thinker, but to all and sundry of his audience) cannot be thought with accuracy.

I know that this will seem a hard saying to many, that there are problems on which it is possible for a man to reason correctly to himself, yet not in words, and on which, for lack of words, he cannot reason correctly (*i. e.* demonstrate) for the benefit of the crowd. Some philologists have maintained that no thought was possible without words. Max Müller was one who did so. I doubt that no one who has frequented the society of painters or of musicians could sustain this thesis. For such an one must come to see that painters and musicians habitually think in *media* which are not words. Some of their thoughts are demonstrable propositions—demonstrable in their own language, and even capable of translation into ours. Such are the laws of perspective, to which we may add the laws of "values" or atmospheric effects, which are almost as strict as the laws of perspective : these two for the painters; and the law of harmony for the composers. But there are many other facts and truths which the painter knows, or the musician knows, that he can express only in his own medium and "demonstrate" only by his achievement. Nor is it any wise different with language, when that is used as an art, as the medium for an art. Words now have other than a purely intellectual value, and there are truths which they express that are not demonstrable truths. There are laws of verse in virtue of which Shakespeare is a greater poet than Longfellow : and if it is a fact that he is so, then all the laws upon which that fact depends must be facts or truths likewise. A person who has the critical sense, and who has studied both authors, may be perfectly conscious of and yet unable to demonstrate them.

This I believe to be the real truth of the relation of "positive" knowledge to other knowledge. And against it it is of no effect to argue, that the notion of a human being being responsible to himself alone for his reason opens the door to a new medieval obscurantism. Because, in dealing with truth, you cannot be concerned with the consequences of truth : or rather, if you hold that truth in itself may lead to error, you abolish the function of reason altogether. " O Callicles," Socrates says in the *Gorgias*, " if there were not some community of feeling among mankind, however varying in different persons—I mean to say if every man's feelings were peculiar to himself and were not shared by the rest of the species—I do not see how we could ever communicate our impressions to each other." But the function of reason requires the same assumption for itself that it makes for the impressions. If our faculty of tracing effects to causes were not really the same faculty in all mankind, no reasoning, no argument, no demonstration would be possible. Obscurantism is an act of will : it is the refusal to use one's reason. And the proverbial person convinced against his will uses this obscurantism just as much as he would do in matters where demonstration is not possible. You cannot of course make every man use his reason. But the simple test of demonstration will not make him do that either. And as a fact Positivism, being itself opposed to or defective in pure reason, has produced an obscurantism of its own.

The confusion of ideas which I have tried to expose between demonstration and reason is so inveterate (almost incidental to the fashion in which we receive all knowledge), and has especially so entered into the very flesh and bones of the Positivist philosophy, that I am quite sure that this paper will seem, to most readers of it, no more than a tissue of paradoxes. You cannot read John Stuart Mill, you cannot read Huxley or Spencer or Auguste Comte himself without seeing that it is impossible for any of these philosophers to carry on a sustained process of thought, but *in terms of* physical phenomena. Huxley indeed, the most metaphysical of all men of science, drops into the sceptical philosophy of Hume when writing as a metaphysician. But you see that this way of thinking has no real influence on the ordering of his ideas : he emerges immediately whole and unsinged, not even like Dante with the smell of those obscure regions on his clothes. Mill, when he is setting forth the fundamental thesis of Comte's system that " we have no knowledge of anything but phenomena, and our knowledge of phenomena is relative, not absolute. We know not the essence nor the mode of production of any fact, but only its relations to other facts," etc., goes on to say that this fundamental thesis is accepted by all modern philosophy, by Kant not less than by Comte. And verbally this is of course true : but Comte (and Mill with him) is thinking always in terms of physical phenomena. Kant is not : and so the word phenomenon has not the same significance to the German as to the other two. So again in Mill's proposition (in his Logic) that in another sort of world it would be possible for two and two to make five, you see how impossible it is for this thinker to think in terms of metaphysics, and how Kant's demonstration to the contrary has passed over his mind like water over a duck's back. Herbert Spencer's classification of phenomena as " vivid " and " faint " is just another instance in point : the very words " vivid " and " faint " are referred instinctively to physical *impressions*, never referred to thoughts as such. Herbert Spencer would not see, for instance, that the pleasure a man has in listening to music or contemplating the harmony of a picture is a process of thought in itself, and not a sort of echo or function of the sounds which his ears, the colours which his eyes, receive at the time. Elsewhere Spencer uses the identical argument whereby Kant demonstrates the non-externality of space to prove the indestructibility of matter. This is a still stronger proof of his inability to think otherwise than in terms of physical phenomena.

The whole of Comte's system rests upon the same inability to think in what I may call terms of thought. In his system, the positive knowledge at which we have arrived now is exact knowledge of physical phenomena : his famous three stages are reckoned only in *terms of* that. He imagines mankind always being concerned only to find out the nature of physical phenomena, and that the theological, metaphysical stages which human thought is by Comte supposed to have passed through, were simply imperfect guesses at physical phenomena and nothing else. Plato's doctrine of ideas is (for Comte) an example of the metaphysical stage of thought. Comte is so utterly imbued with the first principles of positivism, that he understands Plato's theories as guesses touching the cause of physical phenomena as such, not what they are, viz. guesses on the cause or nature of mental phenomena as such. And of course the average man, who has not so much accepted the positivist philosophy as absorbed it, would find it still more impossible to think as I have expressed it in *terms of thought*.

For instance, to the metaphysician the proposition that " Thought is not in Time or Space " expresses a truth which is almost elementary. With the positivist it is a truth which it would be impossible to demonstrate to conviction. Even if you demonstrated it to his reason, his mind would refuse to assimilate it ; it would in fact be rejected the next moment.

It will be almost as difficult to get any one to accept the theory of undemonstrable reason ; and yet I maintain that we have shown infallibly anon that demonstrability can be no portion of a truth in itself. I will now add one more illustration which may serve to make clearer the function of reason even when engaged with non-demonstrable propositions. Imagine the case of a widow, against the advice of her brother-in-law or of her lawyer, paying the debts of an extravagant son. Of course to the brother-in-law or the lawyer she is simply acting against reason. But (1) the advice of the brother-in-law or the lawyer is—probably—founded upon general considerations of the character of extravagant young men, whereas (2) the widow may think or she may know that her extravagant son is not an average extravagant young man. The question whether she is acting according to reason or against reason hangs upon the alternative (*a*) whether she is merely *choosing* to think her son better than the average, or (*b*) whether she has a real knowledge of his character and knows him to be better than the average. But how can she know it ? it will be asked. Why, by the same faculty whereby a man may know that Shakespeare is a greater poet than Longfellow. She cannot demonstrate her knowledge even to herself. But it may be real knowledge, for all that.

C. F. KEARY

A RUSSIAN MOTHER: A PERSONAL NARRATIVE (1897–1905)[1]

(*Conclusion*)

I TOOK out the Procurator's card, on which he had written, "Shall be obliged if you will assist Madame S——" On Semyonov's return, I handed him this card, and asked him to give it to the General. He went away, and did not return for a long while.

" Well ? " I asked.

He made a vague motion with his head, and gazed out of the window. The time dragged on, the General gave no sign of life. I slipped half-a-rouble into Semyonov's hand. He let it drop into his pocket without a word, and went off. On his return, he shook his head again, and again gazed out of the window.

I began to grow impatient. I had imagined that nothing could be simpler than for the General to come out to see me, to hear my story and to let me have an interview with my son.

I approached Semyonov again.

" What about the General ? "

Semyonov looked at me with condescending compassion.

" The General again ! " he said ; then added firmly : " The lieutenant will see you ! "

" But I want to see the General ! "

Semyonov shook his head and turned away.

I went back and sat down. Every moment I felt more dejected. . . . At last, after waiting what seemed to me an

---

[1] *The following narrative is a record of actual fact. The writer is still living.* TRANSLATOR'S NOTE.

eternity, an officer came into the entry with my card in his hand.

"You are S—— ? " he asked, mentioning my surname with no " Madame " before it.

" Yes."

" What do you want ? "

" I want to see the General."

" What for ? "

" About my son's case."

" You can explain that to me."

" No," I said firmly. " The procurator gave me an introduction to the General, and not to you. And it is the General I want to see ! "

The officer eyed me up and down, shrugged his shoulders and walked away.

Again the weary time dragged on. I got up and peeped into the next room, where the officers were sitting. Seeing me, they looked at one another, and one of them shouted :

" Semyonov ! what are you about ? "

Semyonov came up to me.

" You sit still," he said impressively.

After a brief interval another officer came out.

" You want to see the General ? "

" Yes, I do."

" But you can tell me what you want."

" No ; I want to see the General."

I realised afterwards how absurd this desire on my part was. But I imagined that the Procurator's card would have some effect, that the General would listen to me : from what I had seen and heard in the entry I felt that I must appeal to some one else, not to these unfeeling officers.

After another half-hour a third officer at last appeared in the doorway.

" This way ! " he said.

Overjoyed I rushed to the door. He hurriedly barred my way.

" There's no hurry ! Follow me ! "

We walked through two rooms. At the further end of a third room, a grey-headed general with bushy eyebrows was sitting with my card in his hand. It was General Schramm. A group of officers stood round him, like a bodyguard. My escort stopped me in the doorway, so that there was the whole length of the room between me and the General.

"Speak from here!" said the officer, keeping his eye steadily on me and watching every movement I made.

It was only when I thought over these strange proceedings afterwards that I realised that they looked upon me as a dangerous woman. I had hoped to be able to tell the whole story of my son's arrest and to show the peculiar cruelty of the case. But I was quite disconcerted by the strange position I found myself in. The General, too, was looking me up and down.

"What do you want?" he asked me harshly.

"You have arrested my son. You are keeping him in prison, and we, his parents, are in complete ignorance of the reason . . ." I faltered.

He interrupted me at once.

"Yes, we have arrested him! Yes, we are keeping him in prison! and we are not obliged to explain the reason to his parents!"

"But my son could not have committed any political offence on the journey. He has been living with us for the last nine months. We know every detail of his life, and all at once, when he was permitted to go to the Ural, you pounce on him here in Moscow, and arrest him? What for?"

"I repeat, madam, I have no intention of explaining what for. We have arrested him, so you may be sure there is good reason to do so!"

"But it is illegal!" I said.

He simply grinned.

"It's not for you to decide that. I have the honour to wish you good-morning!"

"But at least let me see my son!" I cried.

"Lieutenant Ortchinsky, you will talk to this lady."

And that was all I got by seeing the General.

My son's fate seemed to be in the hands of two lieutenants, one of whom bore the inappropriate name of

Angelo. He was quite young, had not long worn the gendarmes' uniform, and still had something human left in him. His companion, Ortchinsky, was a gendarme in the most repellent meaning of the word, a gendarme by vocation, and possessed of a genuine talent for driving people to hopelessness and despair. Whether he had taken a special dislike to me, or for some reason hated my son, I cannot say, but he seemed to take a delight in torturing us both.

As a rule he kept me waiting for over an hour before he deigned to see me. Then he would summon me to a room where he was sitting at a table, and though a chair might be standing near as though set there on purpose, he would never ask me to sit down however long our interview lasted. He would sit back in his easy-chair with his legs crossed and with a spiteful look in his eyes would refuse the simplest request I made him. I was always reminded of a cat with a mouse in its claws.

Lieutenant Ortchinsky only let me see my son once in ten days, though I knew for a fact that as a mother coming from a distance I was legally entitled to an interview twice a week. But to whom could I complain? Not to the General! I realised that would be useless.

Ortchinsky had, moreover, dozens of pretexts for refusing me. There was not an officer to be spared to preside at an interview; the room was being whitewashed; there were fears of an epidemic; or the visit of a high official was expected, and so on endlessly.

" My son is ill ! " I would say, trying to touch him.

" The doctor will see to him ! " was his laconic reply.

" But I should like to see him," I persisted.

" A visit from his tender mamma may upset him when he is ill ! " was the reply with a malignant laugh.

All this ill-nature was inexplicable. Was it a sort of professional spite ? Was it by way of punishing my son for his obstinate silence at the examinations ? I cannot tell, but I suffered horribly at his hands.

It happened more than once that after Ortchinsky had refused me, Angelo came out into the entry and murmured in an undertone : " Come at seven. I shall be here and will let you see him ! "

But he seemed only to venture to be human when he was out of Ortchinsky's sight.

This time my son was not in prison : all the prisons were full. Plehve's iron hand was felt everywhere. Arrests were a daily occurrence, whole parties were despatched to Siberia, and the slightest manifestation of independent thought was sternly repressed. My son was confined in the Srietensky police station. The first time I walked into the yard, I saw his face at a grating window, looking towards the gate. It was some comfort to find him there. It was June, the window was open and he could see through the grating what was going on outside. It is true there was nothing particularly cheering to see in the yard. The police were continually bringing in drunken men by the dozen and knocking them about with genuine zeal. Still it was not a real prison. And how delighted he was at seeing me from the window! His position was comparatively tolerable. He had air, and the prisoners were able to talk to one another, which means a great deal in prison. I took him books, good food, flowers, and did all I could to brighten his existence. . . . But to discover why he had been arrested seemed impossible. When I asked my boy himself, I heard Angelo's voice at once: "Talking about the case is forbidden!" My son could only shrug his shoulders and submit. To all my inquiries, messieurs les gendarmes replied in such a way as to lead me to suppose the worst. Yet I knew that my son could have committed no new offence, and I knew too the gendarmes' amiable propensity for exaggerating the guilt of their political prisoners.

August had come. My younger children were going to the gymnasium, and the approach of term made my presence at home imperatively necessary to prepare them.

My heart ached at the thought of leaving my son alone in Moscow, yet I could not neglect my younger children.

I resolved to find out if possible about what date we might expect my son's release, so that I might return then. I spoke of this to Lieutenant Ortchinsky. He seemed pleased and I caught a strange expression in his eyes. He grew affable and talkative all at once.

" By all means, go by all means ! " he advised. " We have still to make a few inquiries, to obtain some evidence, probably in a month's time we shall let your son proceed on his way to the Ural ! "

I was overjoyed at this hope. How could I suspect that a trap was being prepared for me ?

Before going home, I set off to St. Petersburg hoping I might do something for my son there. The Chief of Police, Lopuhin, received me at once, but, to my amazement, it appeared that he knew nothing of my son's detention in Moscow. He heard my story gravely, promised to inquire at once what was the reason of it, and said to me at parting:

" I imagine that there must be some misunderstanding in the matter, or we should have known something about it in our department."

" A nice misunderstanding ! " I could not help saying. " To keep a man locked up for three months through a misunderstanding ! "

Lopuhin was a little disconcerted, and said that if it should turn out to be so, he would allow my son to return to St. Petersburg to go up for his examination at the Mining School before his sentence was carried out.

Buoyed up with this hope, I was able to take some comfort home to my anxious and worried husband. The case seemed, after all, not so serious and our anxieties might soon be over.

While I was busy with my younger children, I got several letters from my son, but very brief ones. He simply wrote that he was well and wanted nothing. This brevity began to alarm me : he usually wrote so fully.

And so soon as I had after a fashion prepared my children for the term, I hastened back to Moscow at the beginning of September. I went at once to the Gendarmerie Department and asked for Ortchinsky.

After the usual weary waiting, he came out at last to see me. There was a malignant expression on his face and he smiled ironically.

" So you're back again ! " he said scoffingly, and in answer to my inquiry about my son's release he answered carelessly:

" Oh not so soon ! Another three months ! "

"What?" I cried. "You told me yourself September!"

"I dare say! Fresh facts have come to light. . . . We have had to transfer your son to prison," and his eyes shone with the malignant catlike expression.

"To prison? Again! To solitary confinement?" I screamed.

"Yes, solitary confinement!" was the answer.

I could hardly stand. . . . But I did not want to let him enjoy the spectacle of my despair. I struggled to control myself and said:

"Kindly give me a permit to see my son!"

"But it's an awfully long way off!" said Lieutenant Ortchinsky, with undisguised mirth. "It's at the Butyrsky Gate, it's a long way to go!"

I saw he was jeering at me.

"I ask for an interview with my son to which I am legally entitled as a mother coming from a distance" I said.

He jingled his spurs.

"To-morrow at two o'clock!"

But I did not defer my visit to the prison till then. I was met there by Angelo. He seemed ill at ease and I soon saw why, when he led me into a little cupboard of a room, where through two gratings as close-meshed as sieves, I could just distinguish the figure of a man. It was only on looking closely that I recognised with horror and despair that it was my son! Yes, behind a double grating as though he were a wild beast, thin as a skeleton, deadly pale, with sunken eyes, he had not strength even to rejoice at seeing me. Slowly and apathetically he said:

"You have come to me again!"

"But what is wrong? You are ill! You can scarcely stand!" I cried.

"They are keeping me in the dark!" he answered brokenly. "I could have borne anything but that! I am in a tomb!"

I turned to Angelo, who was standing beside me.

"This is infamous!" I cried, beside myself. "And you allowed it? You could!" He did not speak. I turned to my son.

"Be brave!" I said resolutely, "I will get you out from

here. Put an end to the interview ! " I said to Angelo, feeling that I might faint. . . .

I drove back in a frenzy. I felt one thing, that I would never go to the gendarmes again. Every appeal to them was an unspeakable humiliation. Now I understood Ortchinsky's desire to get me out of Moscow.

It appeared that the very day after I left, my son was transferred to the prison and put in the dark. This torture was devised to force him to answer the questions put to him. Later on, my son told me that in his cell not a sound was audible, he could not even hear the steps of sentinels. A screen was put up outside the window so that he could not see the sky and the cell was always in darkness. He used to sit for hours together gazing at a tiny hole in the screen through which a ray of light penetrated.

When I made a complaint later on, it appeared that no one was responsible. The gendarmes referred the matter to the Prison Department, the latter put it down to the Office of Public Security, they referred it to the Procurator's Superintendence, the latter passed it on to the Police Department, and the Police Department referred it back to the Gendarmerie. From the prison I went straight to the Procurator of the Palace. In the strongest terms I protested against the torture inflicted on my son. I warned the Procurator that I would not let the matter rest, that if I could not learn the reason why my son was being tortured like this, I should set off that night to St. Petersburg to put the matter before the highest authorities and to agitate for my son's release on bail. I was resolved to get at the truth.

" If my son had assassinated the Tsar," I said, " you could not have treated him worse. . . . And yet the Chief of the Police Department obviously does not consider him such an important political prisoner, since he found it possible to promise me that on his release he should be allowed to return to St. Petersburg for his examination."

It afterwards appeared that the Chief of the Police had made the inquiries he had promised, but the Gendarmerie had reported that a new plot had been discovered in which my son was implicated, and Lopuhin could do nothing but accept their statement.

My despairing protest had some effect. The Procurator sent for his Secretary for Political Cases, Dobrynin, and they were for a long time talking together in the next room.

At last the Secretary came to me.

"You are positive that your son is kept in the dark?" he asked.

"I have come straight from him," I replied. "He is in a state bordering on insanity, and if you do not take steps at once, I must set off to-night for St. Petersburg."

The Secretary soothed me by promising to go to the prison at once, and he suggested that I should put off going to St. Petersburg at least till the next day, when he would see the General of Gendarmerie about the case. I was in great agitation and did not know what to decide. They persuaded me to go to my hotel to rest, promising to let me hear the result next day.

I had only just got up next morning, when I got a telephone message that the Procurator begged me to be at the Gendarmerie Department at one o'clock.

Hateful as this was to me, there was no help for it; I had to go.

I was met by Semyonov, who had acquired a great liking for my half roubles.

"Your son is here!" he whispered to me. I had barely time to recover from this astounding piece of news, when the Procurator's Secretary, Dobrynin, came out to me.

"Well," he said with a beaming countenance, "you have had a wonderful stroke of luck. Last night they obtained some important information which they had been hoping for a long while, and which throws light on your son's case, and enables us to release him!"

I could not believe my ears! Yesterday torture—to-day release! I saw that the Secretary's story was not true; no information had been received; simply, they saw that I would not hold my tongue, and to shut my mouth they released my son.

My son was summoned to me; how thin and white and weak he was! But now there was a smile on his lips and he held out his hands to me. . . .

A RUSSIAN MOTHER

We had still to go to the Office of Public Security to receive the formal ticket of discharge. I was afraid to leave my boy's side, afraid to let go of his hand for fear that he should be snatched from me by some new trick.

In the Public Security Office we had a veritable torture to go through. We were kept from one to four, we were for some mysterious reason separated, he was sent to one room while I was kept in another. We were told that we could not travel together, we were forbidden to remain the night in Moscow, and after prolonged protests on our part, we received permission for me to accompany my son and for my son to go to Vologda to take leave of his brother. It was made an absolute condition of this permission that we should leave by the nine o'clock train the same evening.

I will not describe the desperate haste we had to drive to my hotel, to pack, to dine, to buy a few indispensable things, to telegraph to my husband. . . . It was only when we were sitting in the railway-carriage and the train had started that we breathed freely as though waking up from a fearful nightmare.

Only then I learned from my son the cause of his arrest. The matter was so simple. He wanted to see his betrothed from whom he had long been separated. She was an " illegal," and had been living abroad. They corresponded and she came to Moscow, of course under an assumed name, hoping in that great city they might escape notice.

But their correspondence had been intercepted by the gendarmes, and my son had received permission to go to Moscow on purpose to enable them to catch his betrothed there. They had scarcely met when they were both arrested ; they had barely had time to say a few words to each other. Then being afraid of making the poor girl's position worse, my son had obstinately refused to answer when he was questioned about her, and the gendarmes had punished him for it. . . . He had paid dearly indeed for those few moments with the woman he loved.

It was in the deepest dejection that my son left Moscow, and no wonder. His betrothed was left behind in prison there. They met once again . . . in the Irkutsk forwarding prison.

My son sank into a troubled sleep and I gazed at his wasted face, his sunken eyes, and the greenish pallor of his cheeks. . . . What awful sufferings had fallen to his lot ! . . . And why ? Because his convictions were not those required by the Government. . . .

The three days in Vologda passed quickly. . . . Those days have remained in my memory as one of the few bright spots in my life. I had both my boys with me, and though it was in exile, at least they were out of prison. We had much to talk of. . . .

My younger son was living in exile with his wife and children, and his life was for the time a comparatively happy one. . . . But his sentence was of course hanging over his head like the sword of Damocles. . . . It was then he told me that if they were to send him to Eastern Siberia he would not go. I did not understand. . . . I tried to persuade him that such an inhuman punishment was out of the question ; but he shook his head, Plehve's savage cruelty was notorious. . . . With heavy hearts we parted. . . The brothers never saw each other again. . . .

I accompanied my elder son down the Volga as far as Nizhni Novgorod, and a long, long while I stood on the quay till I lost sight of the white handkerchief fluttering in the air and the steamer itself had disappeared.

That winter passed more calmly. . . . Though my sons were in exile, they were at least free, and their letters were a great comfort to us.

But the spring brought us fresh troubles. First came the news of the sentence on my younger son—exile to the Yakutsk Region. And immediately his letters from Vologda ceased. . . . In vain I sent letter upon letter and telegram after telegram. Then followed a time of agonising suspense and apprehension. At last to my joy I got a postcard from Norway with the single word " Greeting ! " And so our younger son had become an emigrant—a voluntary exile from Russia for ever.

The whole summer had been spent in great anxiety about our younger son. In August a fresh blow fell upon us. Our elder son too was exiled to Yakutsk. As though that were not punishment enough, he was condemned to perform the journey to his destination by étape. In vain I appealed to the authorities, in vain I sent in a petition. I received an unqualified refusal.

Bitter as my own sorrow was, my first thought had to be to conceal this awful blow from my husband, whose health was completely shattered by our troubles. I had to invent a whole story ; I managed to write letters in my son's name and to read them to my husband. Happily he was deceived by them !

At last after another long agonising time of suspense, a letter reached me from our son, telling us that he had arrived at Irkutsk.

The tone of the letter was cheerful and calculated to soothe us. He wrote that as the winter was at hand, he was to remain till spring in the Alexandrovsky forwarding prison. He described his life there. . . . . Compared with his past experiences, as a prison, it was one of the best. The governor was humane, my son lived with his comrades, and could move about freely within the prison grounds.

" If you could see the numbers of exiles here," he wrote to us once, "you would be horrified ! Every Monday, Wednesday and Friday, politicals arrive in batches of seventy to eighty. All young, and for the most part of the intellectual class ! But their poverty ! Most of them have nothing but what they have on. Some have no warm clothing but the scarf round their necks and they are going to the most awful cold. It is fortunate that we have our own organisation for aid to the exiles or they would all be frozen. We are providing them with sheepskins, shubas, gloves and so on. And what splendid young people they are ! Not one of them loses heart, they all go forward full of pride and courage ! Each one feels that it is in the cause of liberty that he is being sacrificed and will not give in. But there are such masses, such masses of exiles, that one might think Plehve had determined to deport all the thought and enlightenment of Russia here ! "

From my son's letters we expected him to start for Yakutsk in May. The first party that started that spring were the victims of the hideous crime, known as the " Yakutsk tragedy " ! The unbearable and brutal tyranny of the soldiers in charge of the party led to a desperate protest. . . . Vague rumours of the torture and murder of exiles on the journey reached the Russian public. I was in an agony of apprehension for my son, I feared the worst! By a lucky chance he was not included in that doomed party. On the 15th of May we received the telegram : "To-morrow start for my destination."

The journey was easier in the spring than in the winter. The exiles travelled by barge up the river Lena and reached Yakutsk in three weeks. My son promised to write at every landing stage where there was a post, and declared that he was delighted to be leaving prison.

We breathed more freely again, and began eagerly tracing his supposed journey on the map.

The days went by, no letter came. One week passed, and another, and a month. . . . We grew more and more anxious. . . . By this time we reckoned he ought to have reached Yakutsk! And still he did not write! . . . . Six weeks passed, still the same sinister silence. . . . My husband was beside himself with alarm. . . . At last, I sent, without my husband's knowledge, a telegram to the Irkutsk prison authorities, inquiring where my son was.

I cannot describe my despair when the prepaid reply reached me : "Son not forwarded, confined Irkutsk prison."

I must explain that the Irkutsk prison is quite different from the Alexandrovsky forwarding prison, and I had often heard that the conditions in the former were awful! My despair was unbounded . . . again prison, again solitary confinement, sentinels, gendarmes . . . and all this thousands of miles away with no possibility of helping, no hope of seeing him, of alleviating his lot!

I had the greatest trouble to hide this fresh calamity from my husband. I succeeded in making him believe that our son was ill, and was staying on at Irkutsk till he had recovered strength for the journey.

The day after the telegram there reached me by a roundabout route the following note from my son, scribbled in pencil on a scrap of paper : "On the 15th of May, on the pretence of forwarding us to our place of exile, I was taken away with three comrades and brought here to Irkutsk. We have all been placed in solitary confinement. We are not given books or tobacco, nor allowed to write letters. We know nothing of what is in store for us. If this letter reaches you, help me. I send it on the chance."

I need not say that I set off the same day to St. Petersburg. In the Police Department Lopuhin received me at once. My surname was only too familiar to him. When I showed him my son's note, he seemed taken aback, in spite of his habitual sangfroid. He held the note in his hand and read it through more than once. Then he sent at once for the Captain of the Division and in my presence instructed him to telegraph immediately to the Governor of Eastern Siberia to inquire why my son had been detained. A few days later the following reply arrived : " Despatched yesterday to place of exile."

God only knows how much longer he might have suffered the agonies of solitary confinement but for the inquiry made by the Chief of the Police !

I seized the opportunity to discover where my son was being sent, and learned to my horror that it was to Kolymsk! I knew something about that awful place. Luckily I heard that the Governor of Eastern Siberia was expected in St. Petersburg, and I determined to obtain an interview with him.

It was the latter half of July, so that I was in St. Petersburg shortly after the assassination of Plehve. How many a mother must have crossed herself in thanksgiving at the news of his death ! . . .

At the end of July Count Kutaissov, the Governor of Eastern Siberia, arrived. Fortunately, he happened to be staying in the very street in which I had taken furnished rooms.

Then my sufferings began. Day after day I presented myself at his porter's lodge, and day after day I was refused admittance.

Ten days passed like this. On coming back to my room on the eleventh I wrote the following letter :

" Count ! For ten days in succession I have been refused admittance to you. Yet it is essential for me to see you about my son's case. My son, who was in the Alexandrovsky forwarding prison awaiting his despatch to his place of exile, was, on the 15th of May, quite illegally placed by the authorities in solitary confinement, and there his health, weakened by his previous sufferings, has been so seriously affected that he is in a condition of nervous collapse. I desire to have a personal explanation with you on this subject, and I venture to warn you, Count, that if I am not admitted to see you within the next three days, I will lay a petition before His Most Gracious Majesty, making known to him the circumstances mentioned above."

It was simply despair that induced me to send such a letter, and had it not been for Plehve's death, it would have been of course fruitless.

But under the influence of the changes in the political horizon, of the so-called " spring-time " of Liberalism, it produced an effect sooner than I had anticipated.

At eight o'clock next morning I was waked by a tap at my door, and heard the solemn announcement : " From his Excellency the Governor of Eastern Siberia. The Count summons you immediately to his presence."

Of course I dressed instantly, and within half-an-hour I was at the porter's lodge which I had hitherto found so inhospitable.

My conversation with Count Kutaissov was so curious that on returning I wrote it down word for word.

I was shown into the drawing-room, and had not long to wait. I heard the jingle of spurs, and there walked in a burly old general, close-shaven, with bushy overhanging eyebrows. I stood up.

So this was he, this was the man in whose hands our children's fate lay, the man whose first act on reaching Eastern Siberia was to deprive the exiles of the right of seeing their comrades on the march !

I looked at him with curiosity, trying to discover signs of cruelty in his face. But I could not detect them. I saw facing me a genial countenance, smiling affably.

" Pray come into my study ! "

He motioned me to an easy-chair. I sat down.

" May I smoke ? "

I bowed without speaking.

After the invariable custom of the gendarmes, he had put me facing the light, while he sat in the shade.

" You wrote to me ? "

" Yes."

" Your letter contained a threat ! "

" An entreaty, Count ! "

" No, a threat ! "

" No, an entreaty that you would see me, Count."

He shrugged his shoulders impatiently.

" We won't quarrel over words. You write of a supposed illegal action regarding your son. . . ."

I liked that " supposed."

" Yes, Count, a flagrantly illegal action. . . . My son was condemned to exile in a settlement ; and no one had the right to put him in prison and so inflict a fresh punishment without a revision of his sentence. It is an act of cruel tyranny."

The Count smiled ironically.

" Your son has not been put in prison at all ; he fell ill, could not continue his journey, and so was taken to the hospital."

I answered indignantly :

" Excuse me, Count, I know every detail of this affair. My son was not ill at that time. He was put in a cart with all his belongings, he took leave of his comrades, supposing that he was going to Yakutsk, but he was taken to Irkutsk and straight to prison, where he was put in solitary confinement. Afterwards he fell ill in prison, but he has none the less been kept all the while in his cell. He has not been taken to the hospital."

" Yes, yes, yes, to be sure," said the Count, " I recollect now ; it happened through a misunderstanding, it was the mistake of a clerk in my department."

" What?" I cried. " Then the fate of our children does not depend only on the higher authorities, but is at the mercy of any department clerk ! We were not aware of that before ! "

The Count threw away his cigarette angrily.

" Well," he said, " I did not mean to tell you, as these

are private matters. . . . But as you are his mother, I will tell you in strict secrecy, your son was arrested by the orders of the Chief of the Police Department."

It was a lie from beginning to end.

"Count, that cannot be so," I said. "I have been to the Chief of the Police Department, and I saw with my own eyes the telegram sent by him to the Governor of Eastern Siberia, inquiring the reason of my son's arrest. I read the reply too, which stated that my son was proceeding on his journey, but only after the inquiry had been made. . . ."

The Governor's face grew purple.

"In any case," he said angrily, "it has nothing to do with me. I had left before your son was arrested."

The more entangled in falsehood he became, the stronger I felt my position. Fortunately I had made careful inquiries and was well posted up in the facts.

"My son," I answered, "was thrown into prison on the 15th of May. You, Count, left Irkutsk on the 26th of June."

The smile vanished completely from the Governor's face, his menacing eyebrows scowled malignantly, and his whole countenance became suddenly ferocious.

"And what may you be pleased to desire of me, madam?" he almost shouted.

I plucked up my courage and came to a rapid decision.

"Considering that my son's health has suffered seriously from his illegal" (I emphasised the word) "detention in solitary confinement for six weeks, I beg you to fix a place of exile for him where there is a doctor, and where he may have the advantage of medical treatment. I beg you to leave him at Yakutsk."

"Never!" cried the Governor, "never! You would like him settled in St. Petersburg, I dare say?"

"But why not, Count, surely the Yakutsk tragedy——"

The Governor almost jumped out of his chair. He had come to St. Petersburg to give an explanation of this very affair, and had supposed that no rumours on the subject had reached the public there, that it was still a secret.

"What do you know of the Yakutsk tragedy? What

tragedy ? " he interrupted me. " There has been no tragedy ! "

I tried to speak quite calmly.

" Has there really been no tragedy ? Why, they are talking of all sorts of horrors here ; I have been told the unhappy exiles were bound to posts, flogged with cords and sticks. . . . They do talk even of murder. . . ."

" Nonsense, nonsense, nonsense ! " cried the Governor, " you have been reading ' Emancipation ! ' ' Emancipation ' is full of lies. Nothing but lies ! "

I was silent, seeing that I had touched upon the tender spot. Suddenly the Governor changed his tone.

" They make me out a brute, a hangman ! While I . . . I only carry out the orders of my superiors. . . . That scoundrel Plehve . . ."

Yes, my ears did not deceive me. . . . The Governor uttered that word, " scoundrel." Only three weeks earlier, before Plehve was in his grave, for no price in the world could one have heard it ! Then the Governor would have bitten his tongue off before he would have applied to the all-powerful Minister of the Interior the epithet that fitted him. Now when Plehve could not hear, could never know, his champion, the follower who had slavishly carried out his schemes, denounced him to the first chance comer, a person utterly unknown to him. I listened with curiosity.

" That scoundrel Plehve was always sending confidential instructions of the most revolting character, and the subordinates who had to carry them out were responsible to the public for them ! Could I help carrying them out ? People might take that into consideration . . . how could I help carrying them out ? It was not my desire to oppress the unhappy exiles ; on the contrary, I would most gladly have done all I could to alleviate their lot. But I am not in control. . . . I am under orders myself . . ."

I listened with indignation. I thought of all the misery, the tears, the suffering this autocrat, all-powerful in his far-away dominion, had caused by his inhuman rule, and now that the tide had turned he was throwing all this on the dead . . . I felt sickened, and longed to get away. "Count," I said insistently, "if you cannot possibly allow my son to remain at Yakutsk, at least let him stay at Olekminsk. There is a doctor and a chemist there. . . . Simple human justice requires that something should be done to make up for the wrong he has suffered in his illegal detention. And if it is true that you don't wish to aggravate the sufferings of the unhappy exiles, show it in this."

The Governor paused as though considering. ·

" I know your son," he said at last, " he is not one of the accommodating sort ; he ought to have been sent further. But perhaps he has been treated with excessive severity. . . . Very well, I consent. He shall be sent to Olekminsk ! "

" Excuse me, I am his mother and it is for my son I am acting. . . . And so forgive my lack of faith ; what guarantee have I of this ? " I asked distrustfully.

The Governor frowned.

" My word ! " he said haughtily.

Alas ! bitter experience had taught me to put little faith in the words of the higher officials !

" You may forget. . . . My son is not the only one . . . . there are thousands in your keeping. I beg you simply for my peace of mind to give me an official confirmation."

" Very good," said the Governor. " You shall have it."

I got up.

" And when you write to your son, tell him what you have heard here ; I do not act against them, I act for them."

He uttered this phrase with peculiar impressiveness. I smiled bitterly and went out.

Soon afterwards I received an official announcement from the police that my son was exiled to the town of Olekminsk.

In the gloomy conditions of my son's life, this was some comfort. Olekminsk is one of the best places of exile, on the river Lena, 600 versts from Yakutsk and fairly populous. I hastened home to comfort my husband with the news.

The fruits of my intervention were soon apparent. My son was delighted with his place of exile. Knowing nothing of my efforts, he wrote : " I don't know how I have come to be left here, but I am unutterably glad of it, and after the accursed prison, I feel as though I were born again. The mere fact that I am not being watched by sentinels, that I can't see bayonets, nor hear the clank of fetters, makes me feel well off. I cannot enjoy the fresh air enough, I walk by the river and then in the woods and never want to be indoors again."

We were comforted by these letters, and I began to hope that his shattered nerves would regain strength with the healing influence of comparative freedom. But, alas, the Yakutsk region is not a place to restore health. . . . When the winter came, the cruel climate began gradually to sap our son's health. The endless plains of snow stretching as far as the eye could see, the awful cold, forty-eight degrees of frost, the utter impossibility of doing anything for the cold soon reduced him to despair, and he wrote to me :

"Ah ! the cruel, unchanging, indescribable cold ! I sit all day long wrapped up in a fur cloak, in felt overboots and fur gloves, before a glowing stove, and thrust my feet right into the fire. And would you believe it, nothing warms me. My body is as cold inside as outside. Everything is paralysed, I don't want to move, to think, to read. . . . As for work, that's out of the question. What work can one do, when one's breath is freezing and one's fingers are numb? I keep thinking of what Herzen says : 'Annihilation, extinction in the tracts of snow, unheeded, unrecorded . . . that is what is in store for the unhappy exile.' He wrote that fifty years ago. And to-day it is the same as then . . . the government system is unchanged. . . . Thought, independence, protest against violence are punished in just the same way ! And still men have the same insane desire to throw off the yoke and crush the tyranny."

By degrees my son's letters took an even gloomier tone, but what could I do ? Separated some thousands of miles from him, and deprived of all possibility of aiding him, I could only suffer helplessly. Moreover, the unhappy war with Japan had begun, and the means of communication were worse than ever. The post would not take parcels, and was more unreliable than ever with letters ; a telegram took not less than ten days. The exiles were worse off than ever, provisions were dearer, newspapers did not reach them, and they were almost cut off from all connection with their country.

Russia meanwhile was passing through an exciting period. Plehve's death was a turning point in her history, and at once transformed the political conditions of the country. The masses were stirred and were slowly beginning to shake off the lethargy of ages. The blunders of the war too roused the people ; the instincts of self-preservation were awakened, and what had seemed a myth, a dream, promised to come to pass. Every one had visions of freedom ! Even the poor castaways in remote Siberia took heart again ! I too rejoiced. . . . Hoping to cheer my son, I wrote letter upon letter, describing the events of the time. But his replies were despondent. He had suffered so much from cruel and wanton despotism, that he could not believe that the very men, who had with light hearts buried thousands of the young people of Russia in the snowdrifts of Asia would ever really begin to show respect for personal liberty and allow to all men freedom of opinion.

"No, no ! " he wrote to me, " I have no faith in these hangmen ! They won't give up their power of their free-will. What should they give a constitution for, when they don't want it themselves ? To get it we must tear it from them by force."

I was grieved at my son's pessimism, yet time has shown that he was right !

Then came the year 1905, as fatal to my poor family in particular as to our unhappy country in general.

A fresh and unexpected shock completed the ruin of my husband's shattered health.

It happened in March. At two o'clock in the night I waked up to feel that some one was grasping me by the hand. I sat up quickly.

There was a candle alight in the room and my youngest son, a gymnasist in the seventh form, was standing by me.

" What is it ? " I asked in alarm.

" A police search, mother ! Don't be frightened. The house is full of gendarmes. Father is dreadfully upset. Go in to him, mother." I looked in terror at my son. . . . The awful thought occurred to me, that they had come for him, our last one !

Trembling with emotion, I hurriedly dressed. I heard

through the door the sound of footsteps, the jingling of spurs, and my husband's voice speaking strangely loud. I hastened into the study. I found him standing in the middle of the room, very pale, with his eyes straying wildly. He was pressing to his breast the photograph of our second son and repeating over and over again: "I won't give up my boy! I won't give him up!"

The sight of the old man, with his snow-white hair and his eyes full of tears, was so affecting that the police officials all stood round in silence uncertain what to do with him.

Begging their permission to put my distracted husband back to the bed from which they had just roused him, I persuaded him to lie down, on condition that he was allowed to keep the photograph. The inspector remained with him, while I handed over all the keys. . . . The usual proceedings followed. . . . I began to feel sure that it had nothing to do with my youngest son and recovered my self-possession.

What had we to fear? Whatever might be our way of thinking, was it likely with our anxieties and troubles we should have energy for plots?

I calmly conducted the police captain about the house opening drawers and cupboards. At last at ten o'clock in the morning the search was over. Everything had been ransacked and examined and with no result. . . .

I was left completely at a loss to account for the visitation.

On picking up the newspaper the next morning as usual, I was struck dumb! Among the telegrams from St. Petersburg was the announcement that several important political criminals had been arrested, and among the names I read the name of our second son! Everything grew dark before me, the paper fell out of my hand!

So this was the meaning of the police raid! Words cannot describe my state of mind. We were then in the heyday of the period of repression that followed upon the famous " springtime of Sviatopolk Mirsky." Trepoff was reigning supreme. Executions were a daily occurrence. I could have no doubt of the fate that menaced my son! Especially as the telegram contained the terrible words: " Anarchist, bombs, plot."

But all this I must hide from my husband. . . . With a smile I went in to him, and showing him a letter I had written myself summoning me to St. Petersburg on business connected with our pension, I succeeded in persuading him that it was necessary for me to start off at once.

I set off that night.

Leaving my things at an hotel, I went straight on my arrival at eleven o'clock in the morning to the familiar Gendarmerie Department.

Everything was as of old.

Sooner than I had expected, a smart, sleek colonel made his appearance, and asked me what I wanted.

I told him that having read of my son's arrest in the paper, I had come to see him.

The Colonel shook his head regretfully, he was sorry but he must refuse me. Why? Because my son's offence was of so serious and so complicated a nature that absolutely no one was allowed to see him. What was the charge against him? The Colonel was not at liberty to speak of that, but the newspaper report had said: "An anarchist, bombs. . . ."

"But you did well to come," said the Colonel, "as we should have telegraphed for you to give evidence. General Ivanoff wishes to question you himself. . . . He has not yet read all the information, but he will be ready at five o'clock. Wait here!"

This I declined to do. I needed rest. Then it was conceded that I might go away and return at five, on condition that I saw nobody in the interval. "As indeed," added the Colonel, "we shall know if you do." I understood what that meant. Every time I came to St. Petersburg, I was always followed about by spies. I did not mind them, for what had I to hide? . . .

At the hour fixed, I returned to the Gendarmerie Department.

I was met by the same colonel, who again expressed his regret that it was out of the question for me to see my son. Then he asked me to follow him. We walked through passages and up a staircase, and at last came to a halt before a closed door.

Making me pass before him, the Colonel with a sudden movement flung the door wide open. This was the scene that met my eyes: in the middle of the room stood a writing table, on the left of it was standing General Ivanoff, stiffly erect, on the right, a group of officers, and on a chair in front of them sat a young man in an overcoat.

He was perfectly self-possessed, and was smiling and twisting his little moustaches. I noticed that he was very young, and noticed too that he was the only person whose eyes were not fixed on me. I stopped short in the doorway, not knowing what was going on. If they wanted to question me, what was this young man doing here? But the General raised his hand, and pointing to the young man, said with a theatrical flourish, " Well, madam, embrace your son! "

I was thunderstruck. I turned quickly and looked attentively at the sitting figure. He was not my son! I had never seen him before in my life!

For an instant I was struck dumb, then all I had suffered in those two days of anguish, all my hopeless agony at the thought of the fate awaiting my son, all found expression in an hysterical scream. For nothing in the world could I have suppressed it! The words came in a stream from my lips in spite of myself. . . .

The General was angered at the mistake that had been made; evidently some fancied resemblance to the photograph of my son had led them all astray. He looked furious and tried to shout me down. We screamed at each other, regardless of all decorum.

They made me sign a document declaring that I did not recognise the person presented to me as my son, and then there was nothing to do but to let me go.

Shattered and exhausted, but happy in the knowledge that this time the storm had passed us by, I could not leave the same day. I fell on my bed, and, worn out by the two previous sleepless nights, I slept like a log.

Next day I telegraphed that I was returning, and hurried home. All the way back I was worried by the dread that in spite of my precautions my husband might have come across that fatal paragraph. Every newspaper had our name printed in full in the report. What if he should in my absence have read that cruel telegram?

At the station I saw my youngest son, the gymnasist; I was not surprised at his coming to meet me. But I was struck by his face, he looked pale and careworn.

He showed no sign of joy, when I spoke of my good news, and tried to avoid my eyes. My heart misgave me.

"Is anything wrong?" I asked.

Putting his arm round me, he said slowly: "Be brave! There is fresh trouble for you, poor mother!"

"What? what? father?"

He nodded—he could not speak for sobbing.

"Dead?" I cried.

"Worse, mother! Poor father has gone mad."

"No, no! It can't be," I muttered in despair.

Alas! alas! My unhappy husband could bear no more. On his table I found a newspaper with the fatal telegram. This is what the cruel mistake had led to!

When I saw my husband, saw his vacant eyes, heard his hurried whisper: "The gendarmes! A police raid! They are looking for the boys, for the boys!" I felt that all was over. In every face he saw a spy, every ring at the bell reduced him to terror. Sometimes in the night I saw him creep stealthily to the front door, and there he would stand and listen in hiding all night. And when I took him by the hand and tried to bring him back to reality, he would whisper: "Don't you hear them? They are coming . . . for the boys! . . . Don't give them up. . . Who has betrayed them? You, you have betrayed them!"

Though he had lucid intervals which sometimes lasted a few days, the doctors held out no hope of recovery. These moments of sanity were particularly painful, for then he would fret for his absent sons, and all his thoughts were of them. Then I used to read him letters which I pretended came from them, and he would be happy as a child when I read a phrase: "I shall soon be home again," "I have leave to return shortly." But then darkness came again.

What greater suffering could befall us? Yet there was still worse to come.

All this time I was hearing from my son in Siberia, and

the tone of his letters was more and more despondent. In almost every letter he wrote: "I am so lonely, mother, so lonely ! "

In vain I sent him letter upon letter, racking my brains to try to cheer him up, telling him that everything in Russia was moving towards reform, that we were all expecting an amnesty, freedom. His answers were dejected, he did not believe in reform, nor in amnesty, nor in freedom. " Believe me, it will always be as it has been," he wrote, and added : " It's not worth while living."

This postscript drove me almost frantic. And again and again I wrote to him.

Nothing was any use—his melancholy grew more and more hopeless. At last I got two letters, one after the other, from his comrades. They wrote that my son was in an alarming state, that he was suffering from acute melancholia, and that I must try and get permission for him to come home.

Only four months remained before the expiration of my son's sentence. In June he would be free. I felt certain they would let him return before.

I set off in haste to St. Petersburg. But all my efforts were in vain. Lopuhin was there no longer, the new Chief of Police would not see me. I sent in a petition. A week passed, no reply. I made another attempt to see the Chief of Police, and again in vain.

Meanwhile my son's letters were more and more alarming. He wrote : " There is no sense in living on ! Every one is expecting a constitution, every one believes in the amnesty. I alone believe in nothing, and expect nothing. Freedom will never be given by men who would be hindered in their enjoyment of life by it. And if they do give it, it will be such a sort of freedom that it will be more sickening than ever. And I prefer to die rather than to live in the midst of violence, wanton despotism, and oppression ! "

In my despair I wrote to the Chief of Police a private letter, in which I besought him to take into consideration my son's illness. I ended the letter : " Save my son before it is too late ! "

I received no answer.

In the department I was told that inquiries would be made, that is, a month or two would be lost, while every moment was precious!

And returning home I found the awful news. . . . My son had shot himself! And I lived through that!

Alas! I had to live somehow, with my poor husband insane on my hands. What would have become of him without me?

The asylum treatment had done him no good, and he was miserable there. I took him home that he might at least die among familiar surroundings.

I shall never forget how when I read the manifesto of the 17th of October, his poor clouded brain could understand only one thing from it—that now his sons would come back! He begged eagerly to be dressed, and said in a quavering voice:

"I will go to Witte! I will go to Skalon! Now they will give me back my boys! They won't dare to keep them now!"

Alas, our boys!—one was in his grave, the other we knew not where!

Just a month after the famous constitution, my husband was no more. As I closed his eyes, I thought: "Sleep in peace. You are happier than I."

Oh, my Country! I look for Thy renewal! With every nerve of my being I am living in Thy struggle for liberty! In the day when the sun of true freedom dawns on Thee at last—in that day I shall understand why such sacrifices had to be!

S. A. SAVINKOV
Translator, Mrs. Garnett.

*** *It is desirable that no contributions should be sent without previous communication with the Editor, who cannot undertake to return unsolicited MSS.*

Address (for postal communications only), 7 Kennington Terrace, S.E. Stamped envelope for return should be enclosed in all cases.

THE

ALBANY REVIEW

CURRENT EVENTS

WITH the introduction of the English Small Holdings Bill we reach what is, perhaps, the most critical stage in the Government's career. What is the outstanding feature of the present situation? **Government** It is the unpleasant but incontrovertible fact **Policy and the** that, with the exception of the Transvaal **Land Bill** constitution, no great, striking advance, nothing proportionate to the great electoral revolution of last year, has yet been achieved by a Government which has already been in office for sixteen months. The Education Bill, through no fault of the Government, is dead. The Trade Disputes Act merely recovers a position which had been lost. The reform of the Army and the reduction of the National Debt are sound measures, but they will not command the enthusiasm of those who demand, after long years of waiting, some immediate relief of the intolerable burden of the poor. The Budget has disappointed some legitimate expectations. The Irish Council Bill has come to grief. To put the matter in a nutshell, the House of Lords have scored successes all along the line. They have left their mark upon almost every legislative act of the Liberal Party. Unless some definite prospect is held out that a term will be put to this process and that great social reforms will follow, the Upper Chamber will increase its prestige with every month that passes, leaving its supremacy unchallenged. Has the Government sufficiently realised the immense significance of this fact? Of course, provided that a definite programme has been worked out, extending over one or two years and culminating in an appeal to the country, we are perfectly content to wait: and in that case, no doubt, the actual details of the scheme for dealing with the Lords ought to be left until the last stage. What causes anxiety to-day is the fear that the present uncertainty may indicate a rooted timidity and half-heartedness in high quarters. Nothing that has yet been done is plainly incompatible with such an explanation. There is much that distinctly suggests it. The Prime Minister has stated, it is true, that Liberal measures will not in future be whittled down to suit the convenience of the Lords, and that "we have taken our measures for ending this state of things." But the country needs more than this. It needs some practical proof which will assure it that the policy of "getting through what you can" and "looking forward to a long term of office" has been definitely abandoned. The two Small Holdings Bills and the Valuation Bills are thus the crucial points on which the Government's future depends. This session will leave upon all social reformers a distinct impression of barrenness, unless these Bills are not only carried through all their stages, at the cost, if necessary, of a lengthened sitting, but sent up to the House of Lords without being weakened by any concessions whatever. We cannot afford to repeat the experience of the Land Tenure Bill. It is a far more important matter to convince the people that the Government is in earnest than to secure the passing of these Bills by the Upper Chamber. Their ultimate enactment must probably abide the test of another general election. A considerable instalment of housing reform, of income tax graduation, and of old age pensions, must be added to the programme next year; and matters ought then to be brought to a definite issue as between the Upper and the Lower Chambers. It is difficult to see how this issue can be postponed beyond the end of 1908 or the beginning of 1909. If it is to be longer delayed, and if (as is virtually certain) the Lords either reject or emasculate almost every

Liberal measure, the Liberal Party will run the risk of being finally discredited ; and the masses of the people will be tempted to follow the party which holds up Protection as the only means of securing funds for social reform.

The Imperial Conference of 1907 has been more fruitful in its results than any of its predecessors. The

The Results of the Imperial Conference change from the word " Colonial " to the word " Imperial " is in itself a significant event. Taken in conjunction with the opening of the Conference by the Prime Minister, it typifies the changed attitude of the English people towards the colonies. They are no longer to be regarded as subordinate outgrowths of England, but as sister nations, equal in dignity and status with our own. The Conference henceforward is to be a conference between governments, and not a mere advisory committee summoned by the Colonial Secretary. Its efficiency has been increased, and the continuity of its work guaranteed, by the institution of a permanent secretariat. Nor does the advance which has been made relate only to the constitution of the Conference. Practical measures have been discussed, and though the great variety of interests involved requires that the decisions should be of a very general character, yet certain definite principles have been laid down which will tend to prevent misunderstanding and to promote concord in the future. Something in the nature of a General Staff for the whole Empire, coupled with a frequent interchange of officers, has been agreed upon. Further light has been thrown on the naval defence of the Empire, and everything points to a development in years to come of local naval forces, as opposed to a money tribute. Definite approval, again, has been given to the principle of a partnership between the different States of the Empire to secure adequate intercommunication. The question bristles with difficulties, and this country should in no circumstances agree to a system of subsidies which would divert trade from natural to unnatural channels, and would put money into the pockets of particular commercial companies at the expense of less favoured rivals. But the improvement of cable and mail lines—including perhaps a new mail route *via* Canada and New Zealand to Australia—and the encouragement of British trade by reforms in the consular service, which are likely to result from the deliberations of the Conference, are methods which will stimulate imperial trade by improving its machinery, not by crushing foreign commerce at the expense of the consumer. Needless to say, the general effect of the Conference on public opinion has been of even greater importance than its decisions on particular points. What has helped, perhaps, more than anything else to produce that effect, has been the presence of General Botha as Prime Minister of the Transvaal. The policy which brought it about was bitterly opposed by many Englishmen. There are few to-day who do not feel that it was not only the most courageous policy, but the most far-seeing. It has brought home to the people of the Empire, as platform oratory can never do, the meaning of their unique heritage. It has done more to enhance our prestige in the eyes of foreign nations than many years of expansion and war. If the Liberal Government had made no other contribution than this to the success of the Conference of 1907, they would still have deserved the congratulation of every genuine Imperialist.

Even the discussion on Preference has been very far from fruitless. Its immediate result has been, of course, the affirming, subject to a reservation on the part of England, of the resolution of 1902, which " respectfully urges the expediency " of preferential treatment to Colonial goods ; and the defeat of the slightly more dictatorial resolution which Mr. Deakin wished to substitute for it. The position of the Home Government was perfectly well known beforehand, and was stated with dignity, but without the slightest desire to burke discussion, by Mr. Asquith, Mr. Lloyd-George and Mr. Churchill. The people of this country have decided by an overwhelming majority that Preference, to be of any value, must raise the price of the food, and probably also of

Preference

the raw material, which comes to us from over sea, and on which our unique commercial position depends. That statement, coupled with a firm assertion of our right as a partner State to control our own affairs, constitutes, and will certainly constitute for many years to come, the English case against preferential duties. The discussion has thus served to bring home to the popular mind the true nature of our imperial relations. It has also supplied us with fuller information of the various points of view from which the colonies regard this question. Canada, confident in her own resources, carefully abstains from bringing any pressure to bear on any of her partners. Australia, on the other hand, as was revealed in the significant passage at the close of Mr. Deakin's argument, feels that the securing of Preference in our market is of vast importance in her own interest. Free Traders have never denied the existence of such a demand. What they object to is that proposals of this kind should be described as "offers," and nothing else. They sympathise with the difficulties under which Australia labours. But against that sympathy they have to set the interests of the teeming and burdened millions at home.

It is regrettable that a section—and that the most numerous—of the Tariff Reform Party should have seen fit to make this discussion the starting-point of angry controversies. Not content with attacking the mother-country for refusing Preference, they have actually attacked those States which, with a scrupulous regard for the principle of independence, have refused to put a pistol to the mother-country's head. One prominent organ of Tariff Reform speaks, with a sarcasm which is intended to be withering, of the Frenchman, Sir Wilfrid Laurier, and the Dutchman, General Botha, who are indifferent, or worse, to the interests of Imperial unity. Such attacks would be offensive if they were not ridiculous. The majority of the English people, if they cared to prostitute the Conference to such vulgar ends, could make out a case at least as strong as that of the advance guard of Tariff Reform. They might point out

Tariff Reformers and the Conference

that, if a colony blames them for refusing it a preference, they could, with even more justice, blame the colony for refusing them Free Trade. They might point out that, if Mr. Deakin may legitimately appeal to the defeated parties in England against her accredited representatives, England could even more legitimately reply that Mr. Deakin himself is the spokesman only of a minority, maintained in office by the mutual jealousies of two other parties, each larger than his own. The English majority has never indulged, and we believe never will indulge, in barren and futile recriminations which, however much they might flatter the self-esteem of their authors, would lower the dignity and weaken the moral force of the Imperial assembly.

The Protectionists in England are preparing to appeal both to Income Tax payers and to the working classes. **The Protectionist** To the former they will promise further **Movement at** reductions from the intolerable rate of one **Home** shilling (for which Mr. Chamberlain's war was solely responsible) and to the latter they will appeal against their own war tax on sugar. These are the realities underlying that combined policy of Preference and Protection which Mr. Balfour was thought to have endorsed in his speech at the Primrose League, where he demanded that the revenue should be raised from a larger number of articles, so that the burden of particular imposts might be lightened. This interpretation was strengthened in the middle of the month, when Mr. Austen Chamberlain was put up to move the Opposition amendment to the Finance Bill. His speech was Protection pure and simple, relieved by a dash of imperial sentiment. But the amendment itself was colourless, being no more than a demand for broadening the basis of taxation, and to the disgust of Tariff Reformers, Mr. Balfour (who had obviously drafted the amendment *ad hoc*) returned to the fence.

With the best will in the world, we have failed to solve, or even to begin to solve, the Irish problem. It is the price of our great national prejudice against the Irish people. That prejudice prevented the Liberal party—who

Ireland were bound to defer to it on pain of sacrificing a great opportunity of social progress—from giving to Ireland her full measure of justice.

As if this were not misfortune enough, the Liberal Government interpreted their pledges more strictly still. They introduced a measure which, though it went some distance in the right direction, was timid and unimaginative. They proposed to set up a Council with no legislative powers and no means of raising money, with many nominated members, with nominated chairmen for its committees, and subject to the veto of the Lord-Lieutenant, who might even act independently of it, in certain cases, in its own sphere of competence. The Bill may or may not have been "workable." The National Convention in Dublin decided that it was not, and Liberals, who believe that a nation is the best judge of its own affairs, must accept that decision. The rejection of the Bill is a final proof that such compromises will never succeed. They are as bitterly opposed as Home Rule itself. They excite no enthusiasm. They do not set free the time of the Imperial Parliament for social reform. They are not a fair test of the Irish capacity for self-government. They strengthen the hands of the extremist parties, who use them to prove the failure of constitutional methods. There are only two Irish policies. There is the Unionist policy of bestowing benefits from without, while accepting as a permanent condition the hostility of the Irish nation. There is the Liberal policy of trusting that nation to manage its own affairs. There is no other. You cannot combine in one policy all the advantages of courage and faith with all the advantages of caution and suspicion. And the sooner the British public, and the Liberal party, assimilate that hard fact, the better for all concerned.

The article which we print below on the details of the Finance Commission's work in Macedonia only touches on one side of the present situation. A small book recently

published by the Chairman of the Balkan Committee
(*Europe and the Turks*, by Noel Buxton. John Murray), gives
a useful sketch of the question as a whole.
Macedonia The outstanding fact is that the insecurity
of life and property is not diminishing but
increasing ; that in particular the number of murders per
month is actually rising steadily. The improvements, such
as they are, in taxation and expenditure are of much greater
benefit to the Sultan than to the unhappy victims of his
misrule. The significance of the Finance Commission's
work is that it provides a foundation for erecting some
form of international control, if and when the Powers
make up their minds to demand it. Within the last few
weeks the robbing of a British Vice-Consul, and the
abduction of a British subject who has since been ransomed
at the expense of the British taxpayer, should have brought
home to our Foreign Office the indignity to which they are
allowing this country to submit, quite apart from any
question of moral responsibility. The present Foreign
Secretary has not yet put forward any comprehensive
scheme of control for Macedonia. These events provide
an excellent occasion for doing so, and for impressing on
the other Powers how impossible it is for this country to
acquiesce in the anarchy which, in spite of the " reforms,"
still prevails unabated.

In France the prospects of the great social reform programme undertaken by the Clemenceau Ministry—by far
The French the most democratic and advanced Govern-
Government and ment which the Third Republic has yet
its Difficulties seen—continue to be jeopardised by a widening breach between the Ministry and the Socialists. Matters
came to a crisis last month, when M. Jaurès, on behalf of
the United Socialists, interpellated the Cabinet upon the
dismissal of certain teachers and postal servants, who, as
members of trade-unions affiliated to the General Confederation of Labour, had associated themselves with violent
manifestoes issued by the latter body. The various aspects
of the French trade-union movement are discussed by M.

Octave Festy in an article which we print below. The right of French State employés to form trade-unions is subject to a distinction. If they are "workmen" (*e. g.* artisans in the Brest arsenal), they enjoy the right ; if they are "officials," they do not. And the term "officials" includes the two great armies of postal servants and State school-teachers, whose pay is low and who have valid reasons for combining to improve their conditions. The Socialists have long claimed the right for them ; and when M. Briand, the independent Socialist who, as Minister of Education, controls the teachers, first took office in the Sarrien Cabinet in March 1906, he was understood to have insisted strongly on this very point, and only yielded at last to the absolute veto of M. Barthou, the Republican, who at the same time took (and likewise still holds) the Ministry of Posts and Telegraphs. M. Clemenceau has also advocated it. Circumstances, however, and in particular the deplorable violence of the General Confederation of Labour,—a body which ostensibly represents French trade-unionism, but which has largely been captured by a determined handful of Anarchistic Socialists,—have driven both M. Briand and M. Clemenceau into the opposite course. The consequent debate between them and M. Jaurès was unsatisfactory, because on the question of principle they cut a poor figure, while M. Jaurès looked scarcely less incongruous as the champion of the anarchical and anti-Parliamentary Confederation of Labour. M. Briand went strangely far in denouncing all trade-unionism among the teachers as "a breach of discipline" ; M. Clemenceau was much more moderate. Indeed many of his utterances, which were applauded by the Socialists and received in silence by his own supporters, can hardly be reconciled with M. Briand's.

A WILD ROSE

HOVERING soft on a clump of clustering green,
Light as a butterfly,
Pink-white as a sea-shell
Murmuring immemorial runes in an orient estuary,
Sweet wild rose !
The whole round world
Labouring inextricably,
Æon in swallowing æon coil-involved,
Opened out into heaven and earth,
Nebulous hordes and planets blazing alone,
Broke in a rain of creatures,
Huge girths, uncouth bulks,
And a myriad fluttering wings and glittering scales,
That you for a moment there,
Light as a butterfly,
Wild rose, English rose,
Might hover, hover and pass.

G. LOWES DICKINSON

AT THE HAGUE

THE great event of this month is the assembling of the second Hague Congress. It is an event great in itself apart from its results. Towards it all the friends and foes of humanity and civilisation have long been turning in eager or anxious anticipation. The idea of international co-operation as a means of lessening the dangers and mitigating the brutalities of warfare, of improving the laws and customs that regulate international intercourse, and finally of reducing the awful and ever-growing burden of competitive armaments is not new. Dante dreamed of a model emperor under whose wise control all nations would dwell in peace. Marsilio of Padua thought of an universal democratic church, whose ecumenical councils might reflect a republican union of states. Erasmus marvelled how Christians, "members of one body, fed by the same sacraments, attached to the same Head, called to the same immortality, hoping for the same communion with Christ, could allow anything in the world to provoke them to war." Disputes between nations, as between individuals, there must be ; but why should not all parties agree to submit to the old Roman arbitrament of good men ? And might not a general peace be brought about in the Christian world by agreement between the rulers under the hegemony of Pope and Emperor ? The dreadful wars of the Reformation converted at least one calculating statesman into an idealist. The Grand Design of Henry the Fourth sprang, in all probability, from the brain of Sully, in whose Memoirs it stands recorded, an imperishable monument of political sagacity. A treaty "done at the Hague," between Henry of Navarre, Elizabeth and the Dutch Republic, was clearly intended to pave the way for this great League of Peace. Twenty-two years later Hugo Grotius was imprisoned in the Dutch capital, and afterwards taking refuge in France prepared and published his immortal work on the Law of War and Peace.

The book sprang directly from the horrors of the Thirty Years' War. "Holding it to be most certain that there is among nations a common law of rights valid for wars and in wars, I saw," says Grotius, "many and grave reasons for writing on the subject. For I beheld throughout the Christian world a licentiousness in making war that should have put even barbarians to shame. There was recourse to arms on the flimsiest pretexts or for nothing at all, and thereupon all respect for laws human and divine would vanish, as though by a single edict men had been turned mad and licensed to commit every sort of crime." The first object of Grotius, therefore, was to impress on public opinion the idea of a common law binding upon nations, forbidding treachery, unnecessary cruelty and the like. That idea must be accepted or there would be nothing to build upon. Not that the problem of preventing war altogether escaped him. He dwells upon compromise and arbitration, urging that Christian kings and states are especially bound to try this way of avoiding hostilities. And to this end he adds it would be " useful and indeed almost necessary that certain congresses of Christian Powers should be held where the controversies of some might be decided by others who are not interested, and where measures might be taken to compel the disputants to accept peace on equitable terms." Believers in the gradual perfectibility of mankind may quote the immediate success of Grotius and the acceptance of his work as a text-book by rulers and generals as one of the longest forward steps in the tortuous march of Progress.

In the eighteenth century, wrote Sir James Mackintosh at its close, "a slow and silent but very substantial mitigation has taken place in the practice of war ; [1] and in proportion as that mitigated practice has received the sanction of time it is raised from the rank of mere usage and becomes part of the law of nations." It is in a large measure due, he adds, to the labours of Grotius and his disciples that these results have been achieved. They have given us instruments of

[1] Especially in the treatment of captives ; cf. the chapters in Grotius' Third Book on Temperamentum circa Captivos.

reasoning and materials of science; and so the code of war has been enlarged and improved, old questions have been decided to the benefit of all, and new controversies have arisen which will in their turn make for the extension of peace and the improved happiness of mankind. It was not without reason that towards the end of his life Mackintosh, looking back on the period 1630-1830, placed the *De Jure Belli ac Pacis* first among the four books [1] that had most directly influenced the general opinion of Europe.

It would be tempting, if space allowed, to pause and consider in detail how the Grand Design of Sully was elaborated by William Penn and the Abbé de Saint Pierre and Jeremy Bentham; how the system of Grotius was developed by Puffendorf, De Mably, Galiani and other international lawyers; how, while Turgot, Adam Smith and Franklin showed the fatal consequences of war to commerce and industry, Kant destroyed its philosophic basis and justified the thought of perpetual peace as the righteous and probable sequel to the growth of lawful and representative government. Many of the ideas then first thrown out have been adopted in whole or in part. With the nineteenth century the practical movement begins, and the missionaries of peace who should have prepared the way for the Abbé de Saint Pierre began to preach the new gospel of goodwill among nations. In the hands of men like Cobden and Bright " the thing became a trumpet," with the heroes of free trade on her side. Peace could no longer be slighted as the obscure goddess of an almost unknown sect. Scoffers continued to laugh at the movement, but they could not laugh it down. Cobden was far too wise, of course, to expect large changes to come about on a sudden. But he put forward in 1849 a practical programme upon which efforts might be concentrated. I will give the message in his own words:—" Let the Peace Congress, which is spreading its roots and branches far and wide throughout the world, proclaim these four cardinal principles in faith and heart—arbitration instead of war; a simultaneous reduction of armaments; the denunciation of

---

[1] The other three being *The Essay on the Human Understanding*, *The Spirit of the Laws*, and *The Inquiry into the Causes of the Wealth of Nations*.

the right of any nation to interfere by force in the domestic affairs of any other nation ; the repudiation of loans to warlike governments." To these he added the abolition of the right of belligerents to destroy peaceful commerce and merchant shipping in war time. At a great Peace Conference held in Paris in the same year, over which Victor Hugo presided, Cobden proposed a resolution in favour of a simultaneous and proportionate reduction of armaments, illustrating his theme by the history of the rivalry between the British and French Admiralties. Each addition by one led to a proportionate addition by the other, and for a long period of years our Fleet and our Naval Estimates had stood in the relation of about three to two as compared with the French Fleet and the French Naval Estimates. Yet in 13 years of peace the cost of both had risen 50 per cent. :—

> " No sooner is the keel of another line-of-battleship laid down in your dockyards than forthwith fresh hammers begin to resound at Plymouth ; a new forge has hardly begun to work at Cherbourg when immediately the sparks are seen to fly from fresh anvils at Plymouth, and *vice versa.* My first objection to this is its supreme folly—for as both countries increase their naval strength in equal proportions neither party has gained by the change, the only result being a pure waste to the amount of the augmentation. My next objection is the extreme hypocrisy of the system ; for at the very time that all this increase of armament has been going on our respective Governments have been exchanging assurances of mutual feelings of friendship and goodwill. If these professions were made in sincerity and truth where was the necessity for more ships of war and more coast defences ? An individual does not cover himself with armour in the presence of his friends. But my greatest objection to these vast armaments is that they tend to excite dangerous animosities between two nations and to perpetuate fear, hatred and suspicion—passions which find their gratification instinctively in war."

How plain and how simple ! But Cobden quietly warned his audience not to entertain the illusion that they would easily succeed in teaching this little arithmetical lesson to Governments. " I speak from long experience when I say that none are so difficult to teach as professional statesmen. They are so devoted to routine and so fortified in self-sufficiency that they do not easily believe any wisdom exists in the world excepting that which radiates from their bureaux." To-day Englishmen may well be proud that a proposition based upon this simple arithmetical truth will be laid by our Government before the representatives of all the civilised nations in the world. Whatever may be the immediate results of this proposal it will most assuredly bear fruit of inestimable value. It is an achievement not less important than the decision of Mr. Gladstone's Government to submit the Alabama claims to arbitration. In the Temple of Peace, Sir Henry Campbell-Bannerman will stand on a pedestal with Cobden and Gladstone.

We must not be surprised or unduly alarmed because at first sight Germany shrinks from the proposal and refuses to take part in the discussion. It is disappointing no doubt, but the cause is intelligible. Nay, the cause lies in our own policy, and is removable at our own pleasure. Let us look at the facts coolly. Germany has a large and rapidly-growing commercial marine, second—though a very distant second—to our own. In the present state of international law, the whole of this fleet would be exposed to capture and destruction in case of war with any other country. Why has not the law been remedied ? Not through any fault of Germany. It is 122 years since Franklin and Frederick the Great inserted the principle of exemption in a treaty between the United States and Prussia. From that day to the present the opposition of successive British Governments has been the main obstacle to the improvement of the laws of naval warfare. With our support the reform could have been carried by international convention not only at the time of the Declaration of Paris but on several other occasions. It is to be hoped we shall not fail this time when the subject comes before the Hague Conference. The Lord Chancellor is a powerful advocate of the reform, and it is one of the few that our Government can carry without the consent of the House of Lords. Its acceptance would remove the fear of famine from England, and do more to undermine panics and to diminish armaments than any other single measure.

Fortunately in this and other matters time is on our side. Every year that passes increases sea-borne trade and complicates the already complex system of insurances. A modern ship suggests the analogy of a modern shop. Both are probably owned by a company. The fact that the manager or captain is a German does not prove that the shareholders are German. Nor if they were does it follow that the loss or capture of the vessel would injure them. It may be a liner in which British capital is embarked. The cargo may be mainly British or neutral. Both the vessel and cargo may be insured in British or neutral insurance companies. It is all very well for naval and military experts to talk at large about the damage we could do Germany by sending such a ship to the bottom in time of war; but the more one inquires into the complexities of the shipping trade the more uncertain does this theory become. Indeed, the practical dangers and difficulties are already so, great that the system would most likely break down in practice, as the old system did in the Crimean War. If a naval war were to break out between two commercial Powers I think they would probably begin with a reciprocal agreement to let non-contraband private property and shipping severely alone. Besides, is not the occupation of commerce-destruction and prize-hunting on the open seas too odious to be tolerated by civilised opinion ? It is a good while now since piracy was regarded as an honourable calling. Prize law is the last relic of this sport, and it ought to be restricted to contraband-carriers, even at the risk of hurting the feelings of Professor Holland. Another objection to the practice which has been pointed out by a member of the Board of Admiralty is that the modern type of cruiser is not adapted for privateering. She can ill spare men for prize crews. She has no room, of course, for cargo, and the inconvenience of taking the passengers and crew of a large vessel on board is very great, even if the captain is prepared to take the responsibility of sending it to the bottom.

Two or three other subjects in close relation to this larger principle, and of deep interest to us as the greatest maritime Power, will also come before the Hague Congress. Whether the principle of exempting non-combatants at sea from depredation be established or not at the Hague, we may be quite certain that a vigorous attempt will be made to overhaul the present law of contraband, if that can be called a law which is neither fixed nor intelligible nor subject to the decisions of an impartial tribunal, but varies according to time, place, circumstance and interest. To explain the nature of contraband the international lawyer, following Grotius, divides goods into three classes :—

1. Things primarily used for war, such as guns and explosives. These are absolute and unconditional contraband.

2. Things primarily used for peaceful purposes. These are non-contraband goods.

3. Things of an ambiguous character (*ancipitis usus*), equally essential as munitions of war and articles of industry, such as coal, horses or the materials of naval construction.

It requires no special knowledge to perceive that a scheme like this lends itself to endless controversy and friction. With regard to the third class of " occasional " contraband, British authorities have held that in overhauling a neutral vessel mere inspection is insufficient, and the ambiguous goods must be condemned or acquitted according to the circumstances revealed by the inquiry. In the old days we were the only leading Power that placed food in this category. We have seized corn and other eatables merely on the ground that they were on their way to hostile ports where warlike preparations were understood to be going on. More recently when other Powers have done the same thing we have made vehement objections. It is now the custom on the outbreak of war for each belligerent to draw up and publish a list of the articles he proposes to treat as contraband during the war. The lists always differ, and always contain articles of ordinary commerce whose employment in war is merely incidental. Neutral Powers always raise objections in order to protect the legitimate commerce of their subjects with the subjects of belligerents. Diplomatic friction and costly litigation before partial tribunals ensue, and claims for compensation are settled more with reference to fear and convenience than to justice. It is the opinion of those who have given most thought to the subject that the only way to put the law upon a sound basis is for the Powers to sign an international convention containing a list of contraband articles which shall be binding upon all belligerents. Of course such a list could be revised and modified periodically. When contraband is regulated by international convention and the right of belligerents to make law upon the subject in their own interests has been put an end to, a fertile source of international complications will be removed and a danger which perpetually threatens to extend the area of hostilities and has been responsible for many wars in the past will at length disappear. When the two reforms above suggested have been carried, the laws of property and commerce in naval warfare will have been brought into conformity with the following principle :—

All trading vessels, whatever their flag or nationality, should be exempt from capture or destruction unless they carry contraband.

Here is simplicity, common-sense and justice. The present system has none of these virtues. It is complicated, stupid and unfair. With the reform of the law of contraband is closely associated the constitution of Prize Courts. The same international convention which gives a real international character to the law of contraband should also give a real international character to the Courts which administer it. Sir John Macdonell has stated the case with admirable brevity. " The present composition of Prize Courts," writes this eminent authority, " is objectionable, and especially unsatisfactory to neutrals. A Prize Court, as usually constituted, sits in the territory of the belligerent which happens to be the captor; it is composed of the judges of the captor's country ; sometimes it is an administrative body. If there is an appeal it is to a belligerent's Court. In this Court the neutral who seeks restitution of his property is claimant; it is not for the captor to justify what he has done ; the burden of proof lies on the owner." To remedy this state of things the Powers at the Hague might very well agree that in future Prize Courts shall be invested with a truly judicial character, and that an appeal shall lie from their judgements to the Hague Tribunal.

In the whole sphere of politics there is perhaps no study more sublime than that of international law. But there is always the danger of its discussion being confined to experts and of its care being relegated to small-minded officials. To prevent this misfortune and to associate himself with the free discussion of these great concerns should be the object of every good citizen. It is not enough to take a part in local and domestic politics. There is nothing more vital to the security and social progress of his own country than the improvement of its relations with other States, the creation of machinery for the peaceful settlement of disputes, and the adoption of conventions for mitigating the horrors of war. If the Hague Conference did no more than spread the knowledge of international rules and excite interest in proposals for their reform, its existence would be amply justified. As time goes on the work of the Congress and of the Tribunals will become more and more important, and nations will be more and more concerned to see that they are properly represented in the international parliament. But as Mill pointed out in the address I have referred to,[1] nothing can excuse citizens from the duty of aiding in the formation of public opinion on international questions. " Let not any one pacify his conscience by the delusion that he can do no harm if he takes no part and forms no opinion. Bad men need nothing more to compass their ends than that good men should look on and do nothing. He is not a good man who, without a protest, allows wrong to be committed in his name, and with the means which he helps to supply, because he will not trouble himself to use his mind on the subject." In short, it depends on the habit of watching and criticising public transactions and upon the knowledge and solid judgement of them that exist within it whether a nation shall prove itself at home and abroad selfish, corrupt and tyrannical, or rational, enlightened, just and noble.

Francis W. Hirst

---

[1] At St. Andrews, 1867.

FERDINAND BRUNETIÈRE, 1849-1906

IN a nation which has a peculiar fondness for the clash of theories, but loves to see the shafts of logic barbed with disinterested passion, Brunetière might almost have won celebrity without disciples. He was, all through his laborious life, a keen and candid polemist; and with tenacious beliefs, the rare faculty of synthesis, vast learning, abundance both of views and of words, made a brave figure in most of the conflicts which have stirred, tormented or merely amused the French mind in our time; so personal a force, in short, that nobody ever heard or read him with indifference, or without becoming aware of a nature more original than the judgements he delivered, the methods he recommended, and the ideas he fought for. Insulated not by these, but by the aggressive consistency which was the habit of his understanding, he upheld some venerable traditions of the national intellect against the anarchy of the hour with a greater energy than we expect in revolutionaries. " Un orthodoxe audacieux et provocant comme un hérésiarque " is the fine definition of M. Jules Lemaître: it applies to the whole extent of his activity as a critic and historian of literature, a teacher, an orator and a publicist.

I

The paramount business of literary history as Brunetière conceived it is to trace the filiation of ideas and the vicissitudes of form; that of criticism proper, to ascertain and apply sure standards of excellence. On a broad but definite basis he stood as far from the sympathetic curiosity of Sainte-Beuve as from the minute psychology of Taine.

FERDINAND BRUNETIÈRE, 1849-1906

The proverb *de gustibus* exasperated him, for it supposes that like and dislike are essentially irrational, that there are in art no types, no principles, no models. The critic who leaves taste alone and weaves an amiable story out of the sensations his reading has provoked seemed to him the least modest of men, an egoist palming off lyrical confidences for a fruitful appraisal, and so sure that his impressions will interest you that he disdains to justify them upon common grounds. Nor on the other hand did he value the "scientific" impartiality which contents itself with presenting the true image of an author's mind and abstains from judging him. Brunetière never pretended to have no preferences, but he thought it important to find consistent, not casual, reasons for them, and that these reasons mattered more than they. He thought also that the mental processes—not to mention the biographical accidents—of genius are of less interest than the resulting works.

The "social function" of art he held as a dogma, with its consequences—as, notably, that no writer can decline a moral responsibility for what he writes, since a book is an action, and not an indifferent one. In itself, I do not see clearly how that opinion conflicts with this other, that an artist must treat his art as an end, not as a means. There are (in theory) perfect works which it were better for a man's soul if he had never written; it is equally true that the limbo of execrable poets is paved with good intentions. Put the creation of beautiful things for the spirit as low as you like in the hierarchy of human purposes; the great matter is, it is itself a purpose. *L'art pour l'art*, as Brunetière acknowledged, may be variously interpreted. However, it is certain that, like most Frenchmen, he understood the formula in a sense which constrained him to abhor it,—as implying, at once or alternatively, an excuse for lubricity, for misanthropic selfishness and pride, for the invasion of practical life by dilettantism, for that divorce of matter from form which is the negation of art, for the soulless reproduction of insignificant reality! But, rather than discuss the justice of this interpretation, I will quote a few sentences in which he explained his demand for the co-operation of art in the social scheme.

" If we adopt this standpoint, we shall find that the definition of art depends accordingly on that of other social functions to which it bears or should bear a well-ascertained relation; or, as you may prefer to say, it appears that art, like religion, like science, like tradition, is a *Force*, the exercise of which is not to be controlled by itself and by itself alone. In a well-ordered society, these forces should balance one another; and none of them can set up an absolute supremacy without consequent mischief or may be disaster. . . . If art in its turn usurp the whole of life so as to govern it,—well, that might please the fancy of a few *dilettanti* for a little; but we have just looked more closely at the results, and Italy at the Renaissance—I might have added Greece in her decay—are there to show us that the danger is no less. . . . No, the case is the very opposite: the great times in history are just those when these forces found their balance;—and such were in France especially the best years of the seventeenth century, or the first years of our own."

The social, or sociable, virtue in which Brunetière saw the most constant characteristic of French literature shines with a peculiar effulgence in the French Augustans, and beyond all else drew his passionate admiration to a period no longer supreme in the unanimous judgement of cultivated Frenchmen. I do not think he has a more substantial title to respect and gratitude than his conspicuous share in restoring the great poets, preachers and moralists of the seventeenth century to their ancient honour. A revulsion of taste abundantly justified by the mediocrity of the last effete classicists had, as it gathered confidence and hardened into system, tended more and more to disown in a lump, from Malherbe to Delille, the whole succession of writers tainted with the discipline of antiquity. The Romantic generation, with some exceptions, confounded the models in the disgrace of their feeblest imitators, and hardly discriminated between Ducis and Racine or between La Fontaine and Lebrun or Andrieux. For long the golden age could count only upon the superstitious, undiscerning loyalty of pedagogues, though more than once the cry was raised, "Back to the classics." The eclectic drama of Ponsard (hailed as a turn of the wheel about the middle of the last century) had, and deserved, but a momentary vogue; Nisard's careful apologetics were almost ineffective; and the Parnassians, for all their classical properties of order and precision and objectivity, widened the breach in the name of science as well as on the ground of prosody. To Brunetière, if to any one man, belongs the credit of demonstrating completely and persuasively the capital merits of the French classical spirit, of circumscribing more exactly the brief moment of its absolute expression, and of reminding his countrymen that never before or since has so purely national an art blossomed on French soil as then, between the *Provincial Letters* and the last tragedy of Racine. Of the great synthetic work in which he had designed to track the origin and growth, the transformations and decay of the classical French literature, only a precious fragment, covering a part of the Renaissance, has appeared; but his vindication of his masters is spread over a hundred articles and lectures.

Among all those heroes of the French intelligence who charmed him by their unsurpassable lucidity, their masterly composition, their high courtesy and firm, scrupulous expression, their constant appeal to reason, their freedom from the self-assertion of the moderns, their devotion to general truth, but above all by their profound humanity, he preferred Corneille the Christian Stoic, and Bossuet the last father of the Church, the French Chrysostom, the " Theologian of Providence." Bossuet especially was his favourite writer ; he knew him better than any one in our time, and delighted to follow him through all the mazes of controversy, to enter into all the preoccupations of that marvellous activity, and to point out over and over again how the unstudied stateliness of his prose, and the inflexible solidity of his doctrine had overlaid, in the traditional notion of his character, the personal humility and extreme tenderness which the testimony of his coevals attributes to the Eagle of Meaux.

Their complete deficiency in the social quality, the radical inhumanity of their outlook, no doubt provoked

Brunetière's attitude towards the Naturalists of the last generation. That campaign—his first—has lost much of its relish for us since the school is dead ; but we may still enjoy his thorough chastisement of *Le Roman expérimental*. In Zola as a novelist he recognised a rude but vigorous off-shoot of romanticism, a raw colourist incapable of composition, innocent of perspective, an observer whom nothing escaped except the minds of men ; but he dealt more mercifully with the most tiresome scavenger (who was to turn at last into the most tiresome preacher) in all fiction than with the quack philosopher of art whose theories were so much more stupid than his practice was imperfect. In an article written nearly thirty years ago, he exposed the childishness of trying to confuse the sure and cautious methods of a Claude Bernard with that sort of " experiment " which consists in inventing a human case to fit an hypo-thesis ;—and he went on to observe that the adoption of a determinist philosophy, though it may attenuate the human interest of a novel—for " if man is not a free agent, he thinks himself such "—is no excuse for its mediocrity:—

> " If your novel interests me one way or another . . . do not gratify yourself with supposing that I am going to resist my emotions, and that ' the pleasure of fault-finding robs me of the pleasure of being affected by very beautiful things.' Give me your beautiful things first, and then we shall see. Meanwhile, do not let us shift our ground. When we talk to you of fiction, pray, do not answer with metaphysics and physiology."

This was fair war upon an improvised and almost negligible profession of faith. Yet it must be owned that the early studies on naturalism in fiction give a better idea of Brunetière's dialectical vigour than of his notable power to trace principles to their sources and to insinuate a whole poetic into the discussion of one literary phase. Taine should have borne the brunt of so elaborate an attack upon the " human document " cant and the open degradation of the novelist's art to the rank of an ancillary science,—upon that pathological bias, that exclusion of rational motives for conduct, that substitution of temperament for character as the object of inventive psychology, which are the essential vices of the school of Zola. And it was unjust to father naturalism upon so pure and delicate an artist as the author of *Madame Bovary*, whose patient exactitude and scrupulous impartiality imply neither the mischievous confusion of truth with beauty nor the soulless confusion of serenity with indifference, but are strictly and consistently subordinated in all his work to the supreme end of illusion. Indeed it is strange that, valuing his craftsmanship and respecting infinitely his freedom from the posturing and mutinous egoism of the Romantics, the critic should have been upon the whole so little sensible to the immense virtue of Flaubert's work. It is true he came in time to modify somewhat the acerbity of his depreciation ; but the super-ficial arrogance (concealing so much real humility) which appears in the Letters, stirred his bile ; and it is on record that he found *L'Education Sentimentale* unreadable, *Salammbô* pedantic, and that he was unable to discern the human sympathy lying open in *Un Cœur Simple* and latent at least in that heroical episode in the eternal conflict between good purposes and foolish systems which is told in the fragmentary narrative of *Bouvard et Pécuchet*.

Brunetière's critical palate, in fact, had points of insensi-bility, and disabilities that might be called physiological ; while to certain almost unliterary merits he showed him-self it may be excessively responsive. Thus Marot's levity and the occasional prurience of Diderot's *Salons* made him deaf to the homebred charm and delicate malice of the first and blinded him to the vivid and inquisitive talent of the other ; the grace of La Fontaine's *Tales* escaped him ; he saw in Charles Baudelaire nothing more than " un mystifi-cateur, doublé d'un maniaque obscène " ; and, on the other hand, he admired George Eliot beyond any English novelist, and set a fancy price upon the style of George Sand. The love of Bossuet prejudiced him, perhaps, against the Archbishop of Cambrai. He set little store by *l'esprit gaulois*, and hated the spirit of insulation in poets ; and was somewhat easily beguiled by an earnest manner and abundance. Is catholicity of taste ever above suspicion ? In Brunetière at least a manifest want of suppleness is compensated by his extreme candour, which allows the reader to discount as a known quantity his complexional likings and antipathies. The very modesty of his dogmatism clothed his impressions in the form of reasoned judgements, and in how many cases the principle laid down was sound and valuable enough in itself to survive a mistaken application ! Nor were his judgements incorrigible, or the limits of his power to appreciate immutable ; and, for instance, he got to care more deeply for Molière, to throw his defiant secularity of tone and the blemishes of hasty composition more and more into the background, where they should be ; and nobody who knew only his earlier criticisms would have expected so much feeling for the genius of Rabelais, nor so wholehearted an exaltation of *The Human Comedy*, as may be found in the latest writings of Brunetière.

Not the statics but the dynamics of criticism, however, supply the matter which reveals his real superiority. There are living Frenchmen who have brought to the task of dissecting and illuminating great works, of evoking the very features of dead poets, of removing casual obstacles to a just regard, of welcoming and encouraging original appearances, a finer æsthetical sense, a wider curiosity, a warmer intelligence, more humour, more amenity of manner and a more appetising freshness of presentment. Brunetière was a passionate logician, whose constructive but not imaginative brain moved habitually in what Renan called " the category of becoming," concerned above all with the rise and fall of methods, delighted to scent the elusive analogies of style and attitude, and to deduce from them the action and interaction of formulas, and the gravitation of particular minds. Handling masses of corroborative fact with unequalled ease and orderliness, he excelled in the treatment of transitional periods and in bringing out the significance of secondary movements, and obscure or even tedious controversies in the history of letters. He is, perhaps, at his best when dealing with such episodes as the " Quarrel between the Ancients and the Moderns," with the literary echoes of the Jansenist or the Quietist disputes, with the rise of the dogma that man is perfectible ; and no critic was so thoroughly at home in the neglected period of the Regency, when the abortive attempt was made to shake off the yoke of the classical ideals.

Brunetière's name will be long associated with the extension of the evolutionary idea to literary history. His originality in this is easy to exaggerate, for indeed it may be doubted whether the notion be not implicit even in Aristotle ;[1] and its absolute value is of course contestable. It is in such a work as the unfinished History of Classical French Literature that it would have been most adequately tested " by the number and diversity of the facts it reconciles, explains and brings into connexion." But in a volume dealing with the development of French criticism from J. du Bellay to Hippolyte Taine, and in another work which traced the course of lyrical poetry during the greater part of the nineteenth century, he had already shown how the general study of literary history may be illuminated by attending to the obscure and continuous changes which shape and unshape the broader varieties of composition, by observing their interaction, their cross-breeding, the gradual appropriation of a certain range of interest or a certain order of emotion to certain forms, the dissolution of outworn kinds, the generation of new, the irresistible bias imposed by splendid deviations upon the traditional vehicle. The conception may be adventurous, and is certainly restrictive, since it takes no account of works, however illustrious in their loneliness, which neither corroborated nor disturbed an existing tradition. But it has a partial justification in the fact that, of all literatures, the French is that in which the force of example and the contagion of schools have been most constant. Brunetière, moreover, supplied a useful corrective to the material system by which Taine believed it possible to discover the secret of artistic productions. Genius is the unknowable : but

---

[1] As for instance, in such a phrase as this from the Poetics : καὶ πολλὰς μεταβολὰς μεταβολοῦσα ἡ τραγῳδία ἐπαύσατο, ἐπεὶ ἔσχε τὴν αὑτῆς οὐσίαν.

among the ponderable elements in an artist's formation, one which Taine overlooked in his painful preoccupation with circumstances of time and place, with social condition and religious denomination, it seems particularly perverse to eliminate : the influence of predecessors, the dictatorial pressure of approved types. It is upon this element that the evolutionary idea insists, by bringing into relief the play of mind on mind and the authority of older achievement over works in process.

But at any rate such a general view of literary development was peculiarly adapted to the order of Brunetière's own talents ; and perhaps his very idiosyncracies of manner made him the fitter to illustrate it. His writings are conspicuous for continuity, and few have possessed in an equal degree the valuable art of transition. If his style upon the whole wanted variety of movement and was overburdened with abstractions, if the massive architecture of his phrases when stripped of the advantages of oratory has an intimidating effect upon casual readers, and certain archaic formulas and the array of cautious parentheses with which he scrupulously softened his trenchant assertions sometimes provoked his scholars to parody, every paragraph from his pen is indestructible, so severe and certain is the sequence of his thought; and the impression of orderly abundance and lucid arrangement is never absent from his prose.

II

The career of Ferdinand Brunetière was a continual fight, at first for a livelihood and a hearing, later for the efficacy of definite conceptions in face of successive obstacles —an injurious legend of mustiness and ferocity woven about his name, resentful sciolists and theological mistrust, jealous colleagues and official rancour, a capricious public and precarious health.

He was a Vendean by descent, the son of a naval officer; he was bred in seaports, finished a classical education at Louis-le-Grand, and began life dismally by failing to join the teaching profession by the royal road of the Rue d'Ulm. After bearing arms in the great siege, he earned a meagre

FERDINAND BRUNETIÈRE, 1849–1906

subsistence for some years as a visiting master, reading omnivorously in his leisure, so that he was unusually well-equipped with an encyclopædic knowledge of French literature, a relative familiarity with the greatest foreign writers and at least a smattering of science, when his school-fellow, M. Paul Bourget, introduced him, in 1875, to François Buloz. From the date of his first article, on the Naturalists, in the *Revue des Deux Mondes*, hardly a number appeared without his name upon the list of contents. From time to time he collected these contributions; and as he became an accepted champion of a jeopardised tradition, more than one of his books were distinguished by its official guardian, the French Academy.

In 1886 Brunetière was appointed Lecturer on the French language and literature to the Higher Normal School; and the illustrious seminary which had refused him as a student opened its doors to welcome a master coming without pedagogic titles, but accredited by a solid reputation among scholars. There the orator in him found a vent, and a power of words never inferior to his command of his subjects established the formative influence of his strongly personal teaching. Perfectly just, laborious, and kindly under a superficial asperity of manner, he endeared himself to his pupils, several of whom have since done credit to his methods. But his eloquence wanted a wider scope and an audience less special. In 1891 he was asked to lecture at the Odéon, upon the history of the Théâtre Français, and this was the first of many triumphs won from a mixed and not too sympathetic public. Besides his classes at the Normal School, he gave public lectures from time to time at the Sorbonne, on the poets of the nineteenth century, notably, and upon his master, Bossuet. These successes culminated in 1893, when he was elected to the Academy, and shortly afterwards called to succeed Buloz as the editor of the most distinguished periodical in Europe.

From the election to the Academy and an attack upon modern journalism which was the most striking part of his *discours de réception*, Brunetière's career entered upon another stage. His whole view of literature had implied

from the first a protest against its insulation from other
" social functions," and the excursions into various fields of
controversy which almost turned him into a man of action
during the last dozen years of his life were entirely consistent with his intellectual attitude.   Reconciled in middle
age with the Church of his fathers (which indeed his earlier
positivism had always respected and to which his sympathies with the traditional France would at any rate have
leaned) he commenced Christian apologist with a pamphlet
which involved him in a dispute with a venerable chemist
and most of the Paris press.   It was followed by others, and
by a book—*Sur les Chemins de la Croyance*—of which it is
enough to say that, ostensibly applying the evolutionary
theory to a stage in the history of religious ideas, it is at
once a vindication of Catholicism as a social force and a
record of the steps by which his own mind emerged from
Comte's philosophy into the regions of faith.   The book
had the misfortune to incur suspicions of heterodoxy and at
the same time to exasperate a certain sort of rationalists, who
resented as a sacrilege the employment of scientific methods
in other interests than those of science.   Brunetière's sincerity
does not bear disputing ; and, if only as a study in psychology, it is interesting to compare the road he followed
with those different paths which have led the author of *En
Route*, the author of *La Bonne Souffrance* and so many other
intellectual Frenchmen of our time to the same goal.

As a Catholic Brunetière took a rather prominent part
in the unhappy struggle between the Church of France and
recent French governments.   Hopeful of an earlier compromise, he signed along with some other churchmen of
distinction a petition in that sense addressed to the French
Bishops while the Papal decision upon the *associations
cultuelles* was pending.   It need not be added that he was
entirely submissive to the injunctions of the Holy See, and
when they had been given broke silence only to disap-
point the hopes of disunion founded in some quarters upon
rumours of a gallicanism imbibed (it was imagined) from
the study of Bossuet.

In politics Brunetière—though at one time reported to
be ambitious for election to parliament—was not directly

interested, nor did he enroll under any particular banner. But he was a patriot, and his patriotism was not only (like most men's) instinctive, but grounded in a mature and consistent conception of the national civilisation, or, as he called it, *l'âme française*. In a protracted crisis, of which the occasion or the pretext was a highly complicated and technical question of fact, he saw as he thought the historical personality of France attacked, through the institutions and sentiments which most perfectly express it, by centrifugal forces; and he protested loudly and repeatedly, with his voice and with his pen (*Discours de combat*). At the time he was reviled by many organs of opinion, especially by the foreign press, with much ignorance and some indecency, for opinions held in common with other representative French intellects—with Jules Lemaître and Maurice Barrès, Sully-Prudhomme and François Coppée. And he suffered for them later, when in the transformation of the Normal School carried out under the government of M. Combes he found himself all at once without a chair.

A visit to Canada and the United States, where his eloquence drew crowds of students and others, and several courses of lectures given elsewhere abroad—in Belgian cities, in Italy and in French-speaking Switzerland—were the only other events of his last years, besides his books. Deprived of the official place he had so long adorned in the higher education of his countrymen, and soon after afflicted by the partial loss of his once powerful voice, his activity was still further reduced by the progress of a fatal disease. It allowed him however to the last to direct the Review with which his name will always be associated; and he died in harness last December.

It would be rash to forecast the durable influence of Brunetière and impertinent to conjecture his rank among the leaders of French thought in our day. But a word in conclusion of so slight a survey may define the end of his consistent endeavours. He was in several ways a national restorer. In all his writing and speaking he put forward or assumed the notion that there runs through the best productions of the French mind a particular spirit—

sociable, discreet, fraternal—a genius of verbal probity and reasonableness, of economy and of light; that though this is not the foundation of all their qualities, it accounts for most of their especial charm; that there are doubtless artistic virtues within the grasp of French intellects which neglect this spirit and even consciously rebel against it, but that it should be cherished always, and the brief and splendid hour when it was most articulate evoked for guidance whenever alien allurements threaten disaggregation, as a man in danger of losing his moral bearings might appeal to the memory of some illustrious day in his ancestral history on which the best instincts of a race spoke most effectually. *Nosce teipsum* is indeed the point of all his teaching, and as he saw in literature only one—the most subtle—expression of a national civilisation, he extended to practical life upon occasion his effort to interpret the French soul and its essential needs to a generation which seemed to him somewhat unconscious or unmindful. Not that in art or in life he ignored modernity or proposed to treat the lapse of time that separates us from his favourites as an interpolation; not that he tried to buttress a wall of crumbling prejudice and oppose an ideal of stagnation to the eddying curiosity of his coevals. His admonitions were positive, pointing to an anchorage, a centre and a norm. Greater services than his may be conceived as within the power and scope of a similar career. And there are times when above all else the appetite for novelty needs stimulating among the cultivated class, its self-complacency mortified, its liberative adventures encouraged. But a foreigner may suggest without presumption that the generation which Brunetière instructed was not one prone to cling stubbornly to its native models nor to turn aside indifferently from the importunity of strange experiments in letters or in other things; and that therefore with all the limitations I have hinted at, the work he did was salutary in its time and in its kind, and the name of this honest, combative, learned and indefatigable man of letters worthy to be long remembered with gratitude.

F. Y. ECCLES

A PERISHING COUNTRY-SIDE

SOMEWHERE about A.D. 1400, a civilised, cultivated, Christian country known as Greenland passed out of human ken. A couple of hundred years later, Denmark tried to renew relations with her forgotten colony. But the result was not encouraging. Civilisation, agriculture and Christianity had alike been swallowed up in squalid savagery. To quote the words of the chronicler of the long subsequent Moravian mission, " Greenland was so buried in oblivion that no one hardly would believe that there ever had been such a land as a Greenland inhabited by Christians."

So runs the story told by the old Herrnhuter. We do not look for probability in a parable, and analogies proverbially suffer from string halt. Still there is resemblance enough for the purposes of illustration between our own relations with our fields and hedges and those of Denmark with her neglected dependency. To follow up the similitude for a few sentences may help us to see where we are.

Up to fifty or sixty years ago England (the governing classes) had pretty well forgotten the existence of " the country " as entailing any responsibilities or as the possible source of any national danger. It gave little trouble and excited less interest. Then Charles Kingsley chartered a yacht and made Society " grew" for a season or so with the tales of horror he brought back from the low latitudes of rural life. But the stir soon subsided. Just before starvation entered upon its last phase, cannibalism, " there was a man sent from God, whose name was—Joseph." The Agricultural Union made England sit up and rub her eyes.

She had been pricked in the pocket and began to feel the pangs of remorse. Farmers complained of the want of labour. Rent-rolls suffered, and it became clear that the condition of the rural labouring class deserved attention. Expeditions of inquiry were set on foot and these have been dropping back at intervals ever since, with the result that we are now in possession of a really respectable body of evidence as to the actual condition of " the country," of the Green Land of England. We have the comforting assurance that there are still some labourers left, that agriculture, though much reduced in extent, is still carried on, and that an English village is, in some respects, not so completely savage as a Hottentot kraal. The men wear trousers and go to church. Perhaps it may not be too late, even now, to prevent their further degradation and complete disappearance. But the time is short. Let us first try to form an idea of how far things have gone.

The wisdom of owls is said to be ceaselessly directed to the solution of the problem, " Did owls first come from eggs or eggs from owls ? " Do the habits of a class come from their habitations, or *vice versa ?* It is a nice question —in one sense, very much the reverse in another. What country cottages are *materially* is notorious. Delicacy generally declines to consider the conditions of domesticity resultant from such dwellings. Over-crowding is accepted as inevitable. I have been told of a parson who pointed out to the mother of a family of ten her unwisdom in leaving a farmer's cottage of two small bedrooms for an outsider's of three. " More cleaning to do, Mrs. Higgs ! " The Church insists upon the separation of the sexes—in church. Against promiscuity in sleeping-rooms she raises no efficient protest. And what comes of it ? A judge at the Somerset Assizes last year remarked upon the character of the heavy calendar with which he had to deal. Out of twenty-seven cases, twelve were of foul offences upon young girls and children. They came chiefly from the agricultural districts. What particularly struck him was the pitiful precocity of degraded intelligence shown by the children. He suggested as the cause " the imperfect arrangements for the housing of the labouring classes."

Savagery is not too hard a word for a state of things under which the commonest decencies of family life disappear in villages whose morality is watched over by the Church, and whose civilisation ought to advance *pari passu* with that of the lords of the soil of England.

It will of course be said that there are cottages and cottages, that the state of things just described is far from being universal. This misses the point. Farm labourers cannot afford a moral squeamishness which would make existence intolerable under the *ordinary* conditions of village labouring life. Their character adapts itself necessarily, with few exceptions, to the lowest, not to the highest, level of the habitations they may be called upon to occupy. A clergyman of much light and leading two or three years ago declared in the *Commonwealth* that the time had come for England to transfer her hopes from the country and look henceforward solely to the towns for the "red blood and the men of mould" on the supply of which her future as a nation must depend. Give up the villages, he says practically, they have sunk too low for rescue. Let England concentrate her efforts upon the cities. There is something inexpressibly sad in this utterance. Look in half the villages of England and you will find a clergyman passing his life in a more or less strenuous, but always hopeless, attempt to raise, interest, even to amuse a flock crushed into apathetic brutishness by a land-system with which the Church deliberately exchanges support. Whether a higher race, as in Greenland, was swallowed up and lost in a tribe of squalid savages, or whether as with us, it is degraded to the moral and intellectual level of the squalid savage is unimportant. The fact of our rustic population's *being* savage is the thing that matters.

Our explorers report that cultivation is decreasing to an alarming extent. Mr. Rider Haggard "has seen thousands of acres of derelict land within forty miles" of London, and "still further afield more derelict land." Where land has not actually passed out of cultivation its tillage is frequently of a sort scandalous to a populous and civilised country. It is easy to see that every thousand acres "derelict" implies a very much larger area more or less approaching desertion. England has become a country of large farms. One of the reasons is sufficiently obvious. The labour bill for fifteen hundred acres is nothing like a third heavier than that for one thousand. There are proportionately fewer men, fewer horses, less supervision, and less outgo. On the other hand, there is less manure, less weeding, and smaller crops. The great farmer's principle is summed up in the rustic phrase, " A little on a lot is as good as a lot on a little." His pocket profits, his social position rises, and the land suffers with every acre he holds over and above the maximum to which he is able to give adequate attention. " They don't tackle the land as 'em used," the old labourers say. Land can be got in large blocks at a far lower rate than if cut up into small holdings. It is very rare that men with the habit of bodily work have money enough to take even a few acres, the sort of holding that can *only* be cultivated to profit by the personal labour of the occupant. When they do, their credulity makes them fall easy victims to unscrupulous landlords. Here is an instance I heard only the other day from an aged labourer. In the prime of his strength he took seven acres of utterly neglected hill land on a yearly tenancy. He cleared it thoroughly, encouraged by his kind landlord. " Why, John, your land does you *credit !* " As soon as ever it began to repay the dogged labour expended upon it, the kind landlord raised the rent, and refused to grant a lease. " And he'd a gone on wi' ut, too," said the tenant. So he gave up his holding and his ambition and fell back permanently into the position of a hireling. The occupants of small farms are seldom genuine working men. I once asked why a sixty-acre farm was always falling vacant. " The men who have been having it," said my informant, " don't work themselves. They keep a man and a boy. And the land can't carry all of 'em."

Mr. Chaplin, speaking in February 1903, said that England with a population of twenty-eight millions produced sixteen million quarters of corn. Now, with a population of over forty millions, she only produces six million quarters. We are told that foreign competition makes it impossible to grow wheat to profit in England. Posterity will chuckle at our simplicity of belief. The Canadian wheatfield is mostly at an immense distance from the coast. Farms are what we should call impossibly far from a railway. Roads can hardly yet be said to exist. The price of wheat delivered at a railway station is about four shillings a quarter lower than in England, and this difference plus the expense of cartage may be said on land of average fertility fairly to balance the absence of rent. Wages are double what they are here. Food is cheap, but every luxury, almost every comfort of existence, costs far more. Yet the Canadian wheat grower thrives. Why ? Simply because he works. The English farmer practically monopolises the culturable land of England ; the only work he does is that of supervision and market, and he has been strong enough to settle for himself the rate of wage he receives for doing it. This may be put roughly at seven shillings and sixpence per acre per annum. Saddle a Canadian farm of one hundred and sixty acres with a gentleman who does no work beyond doddering about with his hands in his pockets, and attending market ordinaries, and who draws sixty pounds a year from the profit of the crop, and see where Canadian wheat-growing would be. " The land won't carry 'em."

Working men, working for themselves on the land, need no supervision. They supervise themselves and sternly enough. And every acre tilled by the actual labour of the man to whom the crop is to go, means a saving to England, because the cost of supervision so saved goes to the providing of the sort of man England wants, and is no longer wasted on the maintenance of a small class of idlers. Speaking roughly, five labourers could button themselves up comfortably (as the saying goes) in one farmer's coat. Which is worth most ? The coat with the five in it or the one ? Five independent yeomen, men who will work well, and eat enough for health and vigour and breed a race sturdy enough to defy foreign invasion, to do more, to hold its own by co-operation against the invading tyranny of associated capital, or one prize man, too proud for bodily work, too self-indulgent for mental exertion, capable of supervising the unskilled work of others and capable of nothing else ? A hundred years hence it will seem incredible that England should have hesitated. But she has not hitherto had the power of choice. According to M. Taine, the French Revolution was carried out by two or three hundred thousand determined men in the teeth of the French nation. The hands of England are pinioned by a still smaller fraction of her population, the great landowners. She cannot move to help herself.

Within the last twenty years an immense proportion of arable land has been turned into pasture. Two million acres between 1881 and 1901 ! The defence of horse-racing has always been that it improves the breed of a useful animal. The same thing may be said and truly of the rivalry that affords such enjoyable excitement to the magnates of (so called) agriculture throughout England. Cattle and sheep have been greatly improved by the keen competition in pedigree herds and flocks. But the limit of utility appears to have been reached . . . and passed. Prize stock-breeding is " fancy," and the immense sums lavished on it should be debited to " amusement " in our national account-book. The subject is one not to be dwelt on without shame. Throughout the very period during which money and care and thought have been expended without stint on the improvement of sheep and cattle, our breed of labourers has been allowed to sink into savagery. Civilisation can only root itself in the margin between a bare existence and an additional *something*. No margin, no civilisation. Fifteen shillings a week can just feed, clothe and warm an average labouring family. The majority only get from twelve to fourteen. Co-operation might help them. But co-operation is *impossible* among men liable to be turned out of home and village at the pleasure of an employer. The rustic labourer is landless, homeless, hopeless, and his brutalisation is a foregone conclusion.

Two legs of our limping analogy seem to touch the ground. Civilisation and cultivation are disappearing. Our rural labouring population is on the way to savagery, and of the main staple of human food we produce less and less every year. The importance that her Greenland still possesses for England is no longer that it is a nursery for men or a source of food supply. She is indifferent to the quality of her population and she can get her corn from abroad. But it is the playground of the rich. The arts of social life are perishing among our Greenlanders. They can no longer make their own clothes, or brew their own beer, or bake their own bread. Their cookery goes as far as boiling bacon and potatoes and cabbage together in a net. As far as their own initiative is concerned, sports and pastimes are dead among them. They are beyond amusing *themselves*. If they are to be amused, somebody must do it for them. But " Sport " flourishes wherever wealthy men are to be found. It is the focus of the life of England, and the class of men it calls into existence are her disgrace.

For a layman to speak of heathenism as the established religion in the very headquarters of clerical influence—the country villages—almost savours of blasphemy. Let a clergyman speak. Listen to the Rev. C. L. Marson, whose experience as a country incumbent entitles his opinion on the subject to respect. Villagers, he says in effect, have left off believing in " Our Father in Heaven, in Law, in Order, and the Body Social." They have " got as far as the gospel of the Encyclopædia and the Mountain." They " want no God but their own bellies, and no master but their own appetites. They crave for independence and emancipation, a competitive scramble and a repeal of the Commandments." It is unhappily not far from the truth. And it is (still more unhappily) perfectly natural that it should be so.

Somewhere in Charles Reade's great book (*Never Too Late To Mend*) a state of things is described not very unlike what is going on around us at this moment. The scene is a jail. The prisoners are crushed into despair and idiocy by a cruel system carried out by a merciless jailer. The justices who should protect them twaddle and do nothing ; the chaplain exhorts to patience and washes his hands of responsibility. The State is torpid and the Church is timid. The natural consequence is that the prison is hell upon earth. By and by another chaplain comes upon the stage. He is incarnate Right, and he hurls himself at the throat of Wrong because to do battle with Wrong is the very purpose for which God has put upon him the armour of Righteousness. And he wins. Half dead himself, he deals the blow that sends Apollyon to the ground. But there is a moment when the issue seems uncertain. Proofs fail him. The very sufferers whom he is risking everything to save are cowed into turning against him. They are treated, they say, like the farmer's—excuse the slip of the pen—like the *Jailer's* own children. " Well, sir," says the authority who holds the scales in which men's lives are trembling, " what do you say to that ?"

" I say, use your eyes."

That is enough. When Mr. Wyndham introduced the Irish Land Bill, he referred to certain Irish tenants as "living under conditions which you would not find among the Kaffirs of South Africa." What else can be said of the English labourer ? Let England use her eyes. As a nation, she values Religion more than any other possession. But she is unhappily content with the outward signs so exultingly referred to by the rural clergy in general. Villagers go much to church, more perhaps than they used. There is more " circus " about it, and their eyes and ears love to be tickled. But to outside observers it is obvious that Religion and Conduct have come to move upon different planes. They do not interfere with one another, they never indeed seem to meet. The Church, the official representative of religion, has stood unprotestingly by during the long process of brutalisation to which the labourer has been subjected in the interest of his " betters," and the labourer has consequently come to the conviction that religion is rubbish. He is perfectly civil about it, he does not profess atheism or agnosticism, he goes on touching his cap to the parson, and is not to be stirred up to indignation on the subject of religious teaching in the school. But Belief has died out of his soul. The husk of Christianity has choked the vital germ it was meant to protect.

All this makes up a gloomy picture enough. Is nothing ever going to be done for our Greenland and for its inhabitants whom our wicked neglect has brought so low ? The Green *Isle* receives attention and to spare. Her entire land system has been revolutionised in order to raise the condition of the Irish tenant. Is the English labourer less deserving of England's sympathy? Men are beginning to say significant things. They say that the moral of making a gigantic concession to Ireland in order to obtain "some lasting basis of agrarian peace," is that our suffering toilers of the land have been unwise in allowing "agrarian peace" to remain so long undisturbed. They are paying for their possession of the virtues that distinguish the Saxon from the Celt. They have gone on in law-abiding beyond the point where resistance becomes a duty. To those who have eyes to see, rural disturbances would have been far less impressive than the silent protest of departure which has been going on for years. But they would have been far more effectual in procuring redress.

Where is redress to come from? To whom are we to look for legislation that will fix the labourer in comfort and independence upon the land? In the present House of Commons the party of reform are in a vast majority. They have power and to spare. What they want is courage to encounter "the contempt of families." Let them draw it from the great mass of the English people. They are town-dwellers. Their interests are at stake. The supply of men to the towns is even more important than the supply of water. The man-springs their conduits tap are tainted and choked by the small class who claim rights around them. The traditional safeguards, existing Law, and Religion as represented by the Church, have proved themselves powerless to deal with this all-important abuse. Our urban populations have an interest in the good management of our rural districts far superior to that of the present managers, the handful of squires and farmers and parsons who conjointly control them. Let them agitate now, let them *insist* at the next General Election on our greatest National possession being put under National management. It is a worthy issue for the inevitably approaching struggle between Peers and People.

The Land Bill comes at a moment when Hope has reached its extreme point of tension. It is welcome to England, as an instalment. But if it is to satisfy England, it must give valid guarantees for the future extinction of the debt.   D. C. PEDDER

THE STORY OF *THE TIMES*

EXACTLY a hundred and nineteen years after its first appearance by that title (1788) as a daily paper, on the 1st of April, 1907, a new phase of its existence was entered upon by the great journal whose genesis, or rather whose composite ownership by " widows and gentlemen " supplied A. W. Kinglake with one of the most humorous episodes in his *Invasion of the Crimea*. The mechanical improvements, gradually and tentatively effected, that fill the earlier chapters of the Printing House Square chronicle have been told too often to bear recapitulation here. The new joint-stock company into which the famous broad-sheet has been turned leaves the paper, as it found it, the possession of the Walters to whom the smaller owners had from the first been willing wisely, as Kinglake says, to confide everything to do with the management. Incidentally indeed the recent decision in Mr. Justice Parker's department in the High Court of Justice shows Kinglake's humorous account of the newspaper's diminutive proprietary to have been not burlesque but truth. It may be that the host of small and nameless holders of an interest in *The Times* had increased rather than diminished. The will of John Walter the First had bequeathed his interest to his posterity, and had provided that those who for the time controlled the undertaking should have absolute power. Only six years less than a century after the death of the real founder of *The Times*, the multiplication of small proprietors made it convenient to adopt legal formalities which in the first instance gave rise to an absurd report of the Walter dynasty having been dethroned. Its early accurate information of commercial

282

movements, and its quickness in detecting frauds, were chief among the reasons for *The Times* being called " the organ of the City." That was in the era of J. T. Delane, with Mowbray Morris for his manager and Marmaduke Blake Sampson (1848–73) as City editor. Next, by its general support of the administration of the day and its consequent receipt of political news, its utterances were invested with a sort of official importance on the Continent. Then came the era of mistakes and ineptitudes, closed, one may hope, by the new company formed.

Just a generation since, in 1877, Delane's retirement and Chenery's succession were the subject of a characteristically caustic comment by Lord Beaconsfield. " But Mr. Chenery is a professor, he has a chair ; and as for John Walter, he is a most admirable John Bull sort of man, but quite without the tact for a great newspaper's social diplomacy." Still in the prime of life, a little more than thirty years after his father, the second John Walter died in 1847. The third, so genially pooh-poohed by Lord Beaconsfield, departed in the year in which Mr. Gladstone gave up office. The second member of the Walter dynasty was not only a ruling king but a titular editor. To whomever his immediate successors may have entrusted the control, the Walters have been, as they will now continue, the real masters and directors. In their hands and largely as a result of their good business brains it is that, to a degree in which no other newspaper has been, *The Times* became a real moulder of popular notions, if not of public opinion. In University common-rooms, in episcopal palaces, in rural rectories, at country house dinner-tables, as well as at military messes, in drawing-rooms and at clubs, persons from the middle of the nineteenth century to its close, not only took their ideas from *The Times;* they actually reproduced its articles in their small-talk. In this way the newspaper wove itself into the warp and woof of the intellectual texture affected by the respectable and well-to-do classes.

What were the processes which, conducted in the interior of Printing House Square, established these relations between the newspaper and the public ? *The Times* never posed as a journal with a particular mission, political, social, moral or intellectual. During its best days it confined itself to the objects natural and proper for a great commercial undertaking ; as a purveyor of news it kept well ahead not only of all its competitors; it generally contrived to distance the government of the day. It thus made itself the pioneer and exemplar of journalistic enterprise for later generations. Even the most dashing feats of Archibald Forbes for the newspaper he served so well in South Africa did but reproduce what even in the pre-Crimean or W. H. Russell period had been done by the officers of the Walter dynasty. In other ways than these *The Times* has served as the pattern and the originator of the best newspaper methods. The second John Walter, in addition to being the owner and manager, was the first, if not the only one, of his house to be the titular editor also ; he instituted for all time the newspaper precedent which makes it an editor's sole duty to keep his hand on the pulse of public opinion, to prescribe a line for his writers, but himself to write no more than proof-correcting implies. The earliest specimens of the latter day leading article were those written by Dr. Stoddart at the second John Walter's inspiration. Harmony between popular thought and the newspaper's leading columns was secured by the reconnaissances of the Rev. Peter Fraser, himself in his turn an article manufacturer. Gradually the "slashers" of Stoddart were superseded by the more measured essays of Thomas Mozley and Frederick Rogers. In this respect as in others, the example set was soon universally followed. To be in hot water with authorities of State and Cabinet Ministers had become one of the newspaper's traditions. The second John Walter's differences with the Duke of York caused him to spend some time inside a prison. Between *The Times* chiefs who followed Walter and the more masterful ministers of the day, relations were often, to say the least of it, strained.

With the advent of Thomas Barnes to Blackfriars, *The Times* introduced the earliest of the literary potentates called by Carlyle "able editors." The most notable and interesting chapter in the story of *The Times* under the Barnes dispensation would be that relating the quarrel between the editor and the Lord Chancellor, Henry Brougham. The beginning and the cause of the feud was William IV.'s coronation. Brougham had taken offence at the comments of the newspaper on the Duchess of Kent's absence from the ceremony. The authority for its information was not divulged by Barnes, but proved to be Brougham's *bête noire*, Lord de Ros. The mutual dislike of Barnes and Brougham was embittered by some particularly stinging attacks on Lord Grey of the first Reform Bill, from, as some thought, the pen of the young Benjamin Disraeli. Suspicion next fell on Lord Durham. The matter soon passed out of every mind except that of Brougham, whose *amour propre* had been mortally hurt by the newspaper. Two years later *The Times* was, on its first introduction, violently opposed to the new Poor Law Bill. The details of this measure had been prematurely and surreptitiously sent to Printing House Square by one of Brougham's subordinates. The Chancellor's threats did not induce Barnes to give up the traitor's name. During a whole session and season, the Chancellor's many enemies both in club and cabinet were amused every morning by finding him transfixed by some fresh shaft of literary ridicule. Barnes himself, before his promotion to the great editorship, had been a literary Bohemian, turning out good stuff at short notice on any subject, a real man of letters, and inspired by some personal animosities against the State for not paying due honour to literature. " There is," he once said, " no living with these bigwigs and their confounded airs ; well, let us live against them, then." And so he did. The original idea of the family, in which the chief ownership of the newspaper descended from father to son, was to employ the cleverest pens available for filling its columns, but to keep the actual management as a domestic heirloom. For some time this arrangement proved more or less practicable. In the palmiest period of *The Times* the arrangements with article-writers and correspondents were made directly by a Walter and his able manager, Mowbray Morris.

The most powerful recommendations often proved to be those of the Tennant family or of the Rothschilds, who first introduced R. C. Jebb to Delane. The writers who were the backbone of the paper had either been born into

it or had gone through the whole journalistic mill. Stoddar·
and Barnes had both started as Parliamentary reporters
before his succession to Barnes in 1841, J. T. Delan;
himself, the son of a *Times* manager, had acquired the
technique of journalism in the sub-editor's room.

With J. T. Delane opened an entirely new era in the
annals, not only of Printing House Square, but of the
English newspaper system. His social position was so
remarkable, his editorial methods in the example they set
and the influence they exercised are still so widely and
deeply felt, that a few words must be given to the man
and his work ; he made no pretence to learning ; unlike
some of his successors he paraded no particular literary
sympathies or prejudices ; he was a shrewd, genial, open-
minded man of the world, whom natural aptitudes and
exceptional opportunities had endowed with great experience of human affairs and character, of statesmen belonging
to every school of thought and rank of life, Continental as
well as English. His intellect more nearly resembled that
of Palmerston than of any other member of his own craft ;
generally indeed he had been run into the Palmerstonian
mould, and had contracted not a little of the Palmerstonian
manner. Some aspects of his administration were, as will
presently be seen, entirely his own. Others he had inherited
from some of his Walter predecessors. The very title which
had superseded the journal's older and periphrastic description of itself implied the desire of its directors to associate it
with the best brains and the most representative pens of
the period. The archives of Printing House Square used
to include a memorandum from S. T. Coleridge in 1805,
offering his services and specifying his terms ; he would
attend at the office six hours a day, write as many articles a
week as required, provided first that the paper showed itself
independent of the Administration, secondly that it advocated " the due proportion of political power to property,
the removal of all obstacles to the free transfer of property
and of everything that might artificially promote the accumulation of property in large and growing masses." This
amounted to a demand for a large share in controlling the
paper's policy. Neither the Walters nor their editors

would have divided their prerogative with a contributor even so illustrious as S. T. C. Moreover, apart from the personal irregularities of the poet-philosopher, his recent performances in journalism elsewhere were of a kind not likely to have recommended him to Printing House Square. He had written in *The Courier* an article against the Duke of York. While the number in which it was to appear was going through the press, the Treasury got wind of Coleridge's contribution, and intervened so effectively that the two thousand copies which had already been printed off were suppressed and the offending article never obtained full publicity. Barnes anticipated Delane's disinclination to trust too much to the shining of any bright, particular stars, of whatever magnitude, for the illumination of his columns. His work was to organise the best literary staff in London, including as it did Sterling, who had invented a "thunder" all his own for which he owed nothing to the bolts forged by Stoddart against Napoleon.

Though Barnes had not seen his way to employ S. T. Coleridge, he anticipated Delane in making the paper a platform for communications on subjects of the day from influential or interesting writers. In this way were first attracted to the paper Stanley, Bishop of Norwich, as well as, under the *nom de guerre* of "Anglicanus," the Bishop's more famous son, the Dean of Westminster; Jones Loyd, afterwards Lord Overstone, George Grote, the historian of Greece, whose occasional communications, signed "Senex," continued through part of the reign of Barnes into that of his successor. The most sensational of occasional stars in the Barnes constellation was Benjamin Disraeli, whose "Runnymede" letters (1836) were in effect modernised parodies of *Junius*. The future Lord Beaconsfield never forgot the good turn done him in his struggling days by the great newspaper's investiture of his pungent paragraphs with the honours of big type. Throughout all the changes and chances of his career he gave *The Times* the preference when he had any information to bestow. As for other politicians associated with the paper, it may be recorded here, on the testimony of Sir William Harcourt himself, that he only wrote occasionally as a personal friend of Delane. "I never," were Sir William Harcourt's words to me, "took *The Times* shilling, received a penny for my work, nor did I at any time write a leading article, nothing, in fact, whatever beyond the letters signed 'Historicus,' supporting Lord John Russell in 1856, and ·a few shorter letters, signed simply 'H.,' some time afterwards." Delane, he added, was a delightful companion, without, it may be, what is called the charm of strong personal magnetism, but a tolerant, easy-going British cosmopolitan, who was welcomed in every house, and who knew how to cull his honey from every flower. The distinguishing feature of his temper and of his editorial methods was his dislike of what he called plunging. No man appreciated more a literary composition of the sort styled "slashing," provided it were well done, but he would have nothing to do with a writer whose subject ran away with him. He gave his men their heads, but on condition of their showing they knew when to stop. This habit of mind explains, no doubt, Delane's disposition at first to doubt the practicableness of the total repeal of the Corn Laws. In much the same temper, Barnes, fourteen years earlier, hesitated a good deal before he finally committed himself to the Grey Reform Bill. With reference to what happened in 1846, I may take this opportunity of correcting a certain very widely spread but entirely misleading impression concerning the attitude of the newspaper upon Sir Robert Peel's conversion to Free Trade. The late Lord Dufferin conclusively disposed of the fiction that Mrs. Norton gave Delane the earliest information of what the Cabinet proposed to do. According to *The Times'* statement on the 4th of December, 1845, Sir Robert Peel and his colleagues had decided to meet Parliament in the first week of the following January with a recommendation for considering the Corn Laws, preparatory to their total repeal. It has been reserved for Sir Spencer Walpole, in his admirable history,[1] to point out that, so far from such a decision having been adopted, ministers had made up their minds to resign. They did so; the Queen sent for Lord John Russell; jealousies between Grey and Palmerston prevented a Liberal administration being formed. On the

[1] *History of England from* 1815, in six volumes, vol. v. p. 133.

20th of December, 1845, Peel consented to resume the seals. Thus, instead of petticoat inspiration enabling *The Times* to divulge a State secret, the newspaper had shown itself hopelessly wrong at every turn in the matter. Sir Spencer Walpole, as I have said, alone of latter-day chroniclers has reminded us of the true facts. Kinglake's detection of the mistake at the time brought him and his writings into the newspaper's black books. *The Times* had begun with laughing at Cobdenism as a kind of midsummer madness. The anti-Corn Law demonstrations had no sooner been held in Manchester than it discovered the lead to be a great fact.

The secret of Delane's excellence as an editor was his skill in getting their best and their most characteristic work out of his men. He pointed the gun, but if a slight change of position were suggested, he was always ready to consider it. In other words, he acted on the principle that a capable writer will turn out a better article the less his presentation of the case is interfered with by outside agencies. What may be called the secret history of a particular leader on a *cause célèbre* during the first half of the last century illustrates what I now mean. The article itself was strongly condemned in certain quarters at the time; both editor and paper, it was said, were actuated by unworthy motives. What really occurred was as follows. The leader in question was the work of the late George C. Brodrick, afterwards Warden of Merton, who is my authority for the details. "I had," he told me, "no bias on the subject either way; I wrote only from the published evidence. While I was doing it, something told me I had better consult my chief before summing it up in black and white. On my doing so, Delane frankly told me that my view was not his own. 'If, however,' he added, 'you think justice requires it, by all means take it.'" To pass to the handling by *The Times* of other burning questions of our own time. As regards the American Civil War of the 'sixties, Lincoln himself had expressly disclaimed the idea of its being a crusade for the abolition of slavery. Gladstone also had described Jefferson Davis as having created a nation. No one denied how much might be said in favour of the principle of State-right being more sacred than that of federal union. By at first espousing the Southern cause, *The Times* only erred in company with, not, as has sometimes been said, the music halls, but philosophers and statesmen.

Sir W. H. Russell's recent death has recalled the national services, too well known to be re-told now, rendered by the newspaper through his pen in our struggle with Russia. These services were not seriously diminished by those disclosures of the English movements and conditions which, appearing in *The Times* during the December of 1854, were known in St. Petersburg as soon as in Pall Mall, and did the enemy so good a turn. The earliest years of Delane's editorship had been marked by the detection of the frauds on bankers, which founded the paper's power east of Temple Bar. The Crimean episode formed a fit sequel to such a beginning. If one excepts the appeals to Bismarck, neither very dignified nor politic, to act as European mediator in 1877, *The Times*, under Delane, made no great mistakes. Directly the consummate business sagacity of Mowbray Morris and the statesmanship of Delane were both withdrawn, the restless innovations and the irritating interference of their successors introduced the era of blunders and absurdities that would have overthrown any paper whose roots had struck less deeply into the national life. Among the compositors and in the business department, improvements, brought from beyond the Tweed, set every one by the ears. The writers only echoed the shibboleths of a clique, being altogether above the common-sense of the nation. What Delane would have called the plunging epoch only came in as the last of the old hands went out. It began with the puerile bolting of the Piggott bait. The merest tyro in his craft might have detected the forgeries before he had read six lines of the first letter ; he would have known that C. S. Parnell never put pen to paper except upon compulsion. " My crabbed calligraphy involves an effort so painful to me that I write about three letters a year ; "—such were Parnell's words at a club dinner, numbering among the company two well-known *Times* persons, in 1886. After the Piggott imposture came the Jameson raid. Co-operating with ambitious capitalism, a feminine pen had completed the nobbling of *The Times* by the South African plutocracy. This was at least a practical way of asserting its claim to a revival of a long-forgotten or disused style. "The organ of the City!": Yes, diamond monarchs one day, nitrate-kings the next, something in fact that might be mistaken for a trade-circular up-to-date.

Since then Printing House Square has missed no occasion for emphasising its rupture with the *régime* of its greatest rulers in other days. Formerly a restraining force and a moderator of popular passion, it has become the ringleader of any or every experiment conceived in a spirit of political adventure, if concealed by a patriotic and fine-sounding name. The experiences thus acquired by *The Times*, if rather undignified, are not without modern precedents or parallels in our newspaper system. *The Standard* had been in a bad way before the clear-headed commercial Scot to whom it then belonged, James Johnstone, entrusted its plenary control to W. H. Mudford. The Printing House Square company is to-day a fact. Its formation may be followed by the discovery of some newspaper man, capable of reviving the credit and power even of *The Times*. Its prestige still survives. Independence of fashionable coteries and modish drawing-rooms, can make it again a force. To regain its position it has simply to retrace its steps. Thus will the greatest newspaper the world ever saw re-clothe itself with its former authority and honour. The resources necessary are there ; prudent administration is the one thing wanted. At present *The Times* is among newspapers what the House of Lords is in the constitution, not a check upon ill-considered policy, but the permanent supporter of the Conservative mode in favour, for the moment, with Mayfair or Pall Mall on the one hand and Capel Court on the other.

T. H. S. Escott

THE LIFE AND WORKS OF
'FATHER IGNATIUS' [1]

"THIS work," says the intrepid chronicler, "has been compiled at the very gates of the Abbey and within reach of no other sounds than the voices of Nature and the Monastery Bell"; where apparently neither the whisper of criticism nor the blended many-voiced roar of contemporary opinion have penetrated to disturb her mind with thoughts concerning the effect of her words on those beyond that radius. Fortunately indeed, for had any such considerations influenced her, the book had been unreadable, or more probably unwritten. But since these influences have not touched her, the reading public is the richer for 600 pages, compactly printed, upon " Father Ignatius."

Who would have believed such a book could be readable? Who could have made it so but a chronicler whose good faith was impenetrable, whose mind on this subject was inhibited from discrimination? The black-robed theatrical figure of the revivalist recluse had to be seen against a blazing background of enthusiasm kindled by himself to deserve contemplation. In such a book as this we catch the very breath of the Ignatian inspiration, and we can judge of it as competently as though a masterly writer had handled the story. Indeed, there are only three kinds of biography for the reader preoccupied with human nature : those written by able, clear-sighted men whose knowledge of the world and of history enables them to estimate what was useful and effective in a particular life, those written by men who care more for truth than for their hero, and those which are the work of infatuation.

[1] *The Life of Father Ignatius.* By the Baroness de Bertouch. Methuen & Co.

The first kind of biographer speaks with an authority of his own ; the last two are the only biographers who are not tempted to reserve or alter facts. If we cannot have impartiality, so rarely combined with imaginative sympathy, then give us blind enthusiasm which tells us everything, since it cannot conceive of anything being interpreted or estimated in a manner unfavourable to its object. If the piety of the chronicler had in this case been blended with discretion the picture would have been toned down for the benefit of unsympathetic eyes, and the result would have been unprofitable and left the detached spectator unmoved and uninterested. The biography of a man whose widest and most permanent appeal to his fellow-men lies in his never having hedged to avoid the charge of folly, would have been worthless if written by one, who feeling the pertinence of such a charge, had hedged himself in consequence. But a biography of " The Monk of Llan-thony " written under his own eye, in a style which as the author would express it comes "straight from the shoulder," bearing in every line the whiff and wind of missionary oratory, is well worth examination.

There are other features of the story besides the fascination of its events which make it interesting. In the first place it is a thread in the history of the Anglican Church during a critical period. Father Ignatius acted as a kind of lightning rod on the rising edifice of Ritualism during the " No Popery " storms of the sixties. At first, no doubt, his vagaries increased Protestant animosity ; but afterwards the contrast between his ell and the inch which the majority of the High Church demanded, must have worked in their favour. The juxtaposition of an extremist tends to make an ordinary reformer seem a mild, reasonable person, and once the cries of "thin end of the wedge," "half-way house" have died down (it is noticeable such cries never succeed in wresting back an advantage gained), the extremist becomes a protection to his party. When the popular imagination had become familiar with such a portent as a self-dedicated Benedictine Monk in Anglican orders, purple stoles and unlighted, or even lighted, altar

candles ceased to seem objects of great import. There
is also another feature of greater general interest, namely,
the miraculous element. The career of " Father Ignatius "
has been as full of miracles, wonders, and divine
interpositions as the life of any mediæval saint. He
has apparently raised one man and one woman from
the dead ; he has revived a dying woman and a dying
horse to normal vigour ; he has apparently taken poison
himself with impunity ; many who have mocked and
opposed him have been visited by swift supernatural retribution ; the figure on a crucifix has turned its head to
regard him ; he has extinguished flames of hell by sprink-
ling holy water ; he has been comforted by the visits of
angels, and vexed by those of demons ; the crucial
moments of his career have been marked by apparitions,
visions and signs ; the virgin has visited his monastery,
and has turned by her presence a bush into a source of
miraculous healing power, so that a leaf from it has been
known to heal in a few minutes a case of chronic hip-
disease. These wonders and miracles are apparently as
well attested, in most cases, as any recorded in the lives of
the Saints or of the Apostles ; but—and here is the significant fact—nobody now heeds them. Such stories of living
people are repugnant to those who wish to believe similar
stories true in the case of men and women who died long
ago. Modern miracles are often a source of embarrassment to believers instead of rejoicing ; the only difference
between this life of a modern miracle-worker and a
mediæval chronicle (allowing for the fact that the former is
told in glaring journalese) is that the friends and admirers of
Father Ignatius clearly did not welcome these supernatural
manifestations. Under cover of warning him against the
danger of spiritual pride they urged him to keep them as
dark as possible, while at an earlier date all such sympathisers
would have triumphantly pointed to them as evidences of
a genuine mission. This is a significant contrast. But
now to the story itself, which even abridgment cannot rob
of its power to astound and entertain, nor a sceptical
reviewer of its final appeal to sympathies of one kind or
another.

In London, on November 23, 1837, Joseph Leycester Lyne was born to a well-to-do couple of good family. The chronicler is anxious to persuade us that although his bearing was such as to earn him the name of " Saintly Lyne " at school, and his character exceptionally sensitive, he was not without some of the failings of small boys. It appears that he certainly stole on one occasion a fourpenny-bit to buy sweets ; a fact which his extraordinary father attempted in after years to use as a weapon with which to publicly blast his reputation. A portrait of the elder Mr. Lyne tempts the pen ; but he must be constructed from this incident. Three facts connected with the future monk's boyhood are of sufficient significance to be mentioned : he saw a ghost ; he became strangely enthusiastic about the Jews as the sacred race, baring his head whenever he met one, asking everybody when they thought they would return to Palestine, and invariably praying for them ; and when about fourteen years old he suffered a very serious nervous breakdown. The illness was brought on incidentally through this very enthusiasm. He received at the hands of a master, exasperated by it, a severe flogging, which he bore pluckily until he fell down unconscious. Recovery was slow and uncertain; from this time forward for many years his dreams and solitary reflections were often made terrible to him by the dread of hell. While under the care of a clergyman at Spalding he received the first of those mysterious communications which were always in future to decide his course of conduct. He was fond of music, and therefore of attending choir practices; while sitting on the altar-steps one afternoon, listening to the organ, a strange sensation crept over him of another presence, and he heard a soft, persistent whisper say, " Why do you turn your back upon My altar, where I am so often present in the sacrament of My Blood and Body?" Thenceforward he held and taught the doctrine these words imply with the confidence of one who has received a revelation. During the time of Confirmation he suffered much from a sense of worthlessness; for to him this was a period of final dedication. He was prepared (against parental wishes) for ordination at Glenalmond Seminary, where as a student he was remarkable for surprising aptitudes in some directions and for a complete inability to understand mathematics, or to follow a train of reasoning.

One evening, as the students were making their way in straggling procession across the quadrangle to the College Chapel, one of them chanced to remark that they looked like a lot of monks on their way to vespers. The words struck his imagination. As a sudden shake may precipitate the crystallisation of fluid in a vessel, so his vague dreams changed to determination, and he knew what life he longed for. He was then working hard under rather Spartan conditions, and perseverance ended in a second nervous collapse, which was accompanied this time by blindness and general paralysis. He recovered rapidly, and quarrelled with his father over doctrine, who turned him out on the world. As a catechist in Inverness he got into the hottest of water for teaching in the Free Kirk schools the Eucharistic Presence and the veneration of the Virgin; and being afterwards given charge of a deserted mountain church in Glen Urquart, he at once made its services symbolise his own beliefs. The Presbyterians did not stand this long; his licence was withdrawn, but not before he had made a permanent impression on some parishioners, and proved that opposition was not likely at any time to stop him. After his ordination he took a curacy under a High Church vicar in Plymouth, a step which, as the chronicler expresses it, " was destined to be a marble pillar in the Colosseum of ecclesiastical phenomena."

There he became the friend of Dr. Pusey, who remained till death his advisor and administrator of the Sacrament of Penance ; there, according to the chronicler, he gave the first proof of his power of healing. In his parish one woman had persistently refused his ministrations ; after having literally shaken off the dust from his feet in consequence, " her daughter, a fourteen-year-old girl, was suddenly stricken with abject idiocy, and her whole body broke out from head to foot with loathsome sores." On the mother's appeal he went straight to the bedside, and, in answer to his prayer, " intelligence flashed back, not in a glimmer but a flood; and in the sight of all present, the disfigured flesh resumed its natural childish fairness and purity."

At the end of nine months he instituted a community of Brothers. There were but two others beside himself, and their first night in the house was marked by a strange occurrence. One Brother, woken by a sensation of light, got out of bed and, peeping over the bannisters, saw " standing erect, without candlestick, one of the large altar tapers in full blaze." He called his fellow-Brother, and, after a space of amazement, one of them raised it in trembling hands and bore it back to the chapel. " Dr. Pusey interpreted the manifestation as a Heaven-sent sign of Divine approval, and the lighted taper as an emblem of the illuminating influence which monasticism was to shed upon the Church. At the same time, he urged the Brothers and their Superior to treasure those marks of power in the silence of their own spirits, and as things too sacred to be desecrated by the touch of public curiosity."

This first attempt to form a monastic brotherhood was frustrated by a severe fever, and during delirium he suffered the excruciating torments of imaginary damnation. A breath of comfort came to him at last on a message from Dr. Pusey, and he rallied into sufficient composure to continue an active life. Nevertheless it is important to remember that during the years of ecstatic preaching which followed, ceaseless activity and consistent severity of life were within him but a hollow vaulting above a flaming frenzy of terror.

After a journey in Belgium, where the goings to and fro of processions and of monks and nuns in streets made a deep impression on his mind, he became an East End missioner and worked among the population of the Docks with zeal and surprising effect. He penetrated into disreputable haunts, and exhibited a composure in front of threatening circumstances which, aided by the dramatic instinct, dispelled animosity and conquered contempt. Through the agency of a Relic of the Cross he raised a girl, Lizzie Meek, from death in the presence of her mother, three neighbours, and two young children. He persuaded the resuscitated girl to accept dedication to the religious life ; but on the return of an old lover she married, and, both dying within a month of marriage, he regarded this event as a retribution fulfilling a last warning he had given her.

At this time he consecrated himself as "Brother Ignatius" of the Benedictine rule of the Pre-reformation Church, and put on the black robe with which he is henceforward associated in the popular imagination. In consequence he was obliged to leave the mission, and at Clayton, in the Diocese of Norwich, he established his first monastic community in a wing of the compliant rector's house. His services in the church and the sight of the black robes excited the neighbourhood into a condition of chronic riot. He was pelted and abused, and the curious and the converted who attended his services had to run a gauntlet hardly less severe. Stones were thrown through his window at night, so that on retiring he always took the precaution of putting a candle between himself and the blind, for fear his shadow on it might offer a mark. His life was constantly threatened, and on one occasion a bonfire was prepared for him in the fields, from the flames of which he was hardly rescued by the efforts of an old woman armed with a pewter tea-pot. His health began to fail, and with it his confidence in his mission; but all hesitation vanished on seeing, one night, the elevated Host turn to a globe of fire in the hands of the officiating rector, from which a single ray "flashed like a meteor across the silent sanctuary" and struck his heart. He now started on his first preaching itinerary; and returning with £300, the fruit of offertories, he took an old dilapidated building near Norwich. The Community moved in solemn procession to their new abode, when the Father set to work with such energy that the windowless, windy old house became quickly habitable, while all the time the observances of the Rule were carried out with absolute strictness. Midnight and early dawn services were never omitted, and at their first recital of Matins the bell tolled without the aid of human hands. It was during the singing of the Credo in this church that the Rev. Mr. Moultrie observed the figure on the crucifix turn and look at Father Ignatius.

There were still some funds in hand, but the monks

were largely dependent on offerings in kind and in money for their support. The opposition and hatred they aroused almost equalled the scenes at Clayton ; but they seem here to have had also a stronger backing. "Father Ignatius" showed that he could face and even manage angry crowds. On one occasion of his return the chronicler describes a triumphant entry into Norwich, during which men and women laid their coats and cloaks in front of his feet. She records also that a woman was struck dead in her own doorway on, uttering " an abominable malediction " against him, and another instance of a slighter offence being visited with a curious retribution. A woman had screamed " Curse your bald head " after him ; the same day her little boy became bald. " By miraculous dispensation and before her own eyes, the entire mass of the child's hair literally fell from his head at her feet, leaving his skull a bald counterpart of the Monk's tonsure." His power over those he attracted was so great at this time, that when some members of his congregation transgressed a solemn prohibition to attend a dance, held in a building which had long ago been consecrated, the majority of the men chose the exacted penance of being flogged publicly by him in church and the women of lying on ashes during the service, rather than have the doors closed against them in consequence of their disobedience. No wonder the feeling against him ran to dangerous heights ! On one occasion a crowd set out to break into the church, which they were only prevented from accomplishing, says the chronicler, by a storm which broke over them in a terrific rattle of thunder and a downpour of threshing rain. Once during his absence some of the monks mutinied, partly owing to an imposed penance for a breach of silence by which each offender had been compelled to trace 12 crosses in the dust with his tongue. These incidents, however, coming close together in this abridgment of the chronicle give an exaggerated impression of his domineering force. In physique he was exceptionally frail, and he seems to have appealed to feminine interest by rousing an emotion of protecting pity. Though the boys in the school called him " The Blazer," the impression he seems oftener to have created was one of mildness, at least when not on the platform or in the pulpit. He often, too, appeared worked out and almost lifeless.

Absent on a missionary journey, the news reached him of a scandal connected with one of the Brothers, which was to prove a whip in the hands of his enemies. The offence was of that kind which detesters of the monkish life have sometimes used unscrupulously as a general accusation. In describing his bearing during the storm of execration the chronicler is surest of meeting with wider sympathy. He never lay low till a storm blew over, nor did he cease to urge the claims of a life which he believed in before audiences which were ready to mob him. The next blow was the discovery that he had under a misapprehension signed a legal document which gave away his right to the priory buildings. The Brothers, always a few, were now finally disbanded, and after spending his small private fortune in vain litigation, he was obliged to accept money from his friends to recruit his broken health abroad.

The second crisis of his life occurred about this time. Left alone while staying in the Isle of Wight, he experienced the strange emotion of conversion. Walking on the beach after days of deep despondency and "a prey to that morbid horror which had haunted his soul from childhood," he began to recall past scenes. "My own physical sensation was one of complete obliteration, a sudden cessation of all outer sight and sound." He felt himself standing in the court of the Temple of Jerusalem. In the vision which followed, the Virgin placed for a moment her Child in his arms. "I dare not dwell," he says, "on the rapture of the Divine contact." Henceforward he was possessed by a constant happy confidence in his religion, and the note of "salvation" dominated his appeals. He drew large audiences in London, and the contributions of the converted enabled him to build the Abbey of Llanthony among the Welsh mountains. The spot was lonely and remote ; the roads were steep and bad, and the six monks and their Abbot were first housed in a barn and a single room. If the reader would take away a penultimate picture of this enterprise, let him imagine the coming on of winter and the monks round a stick fire, shivering in their cowls, the blankets hung across the gaping windows waving in the draught, the broken tiles above admitting sparks of moonshine or drips of rain, while one reads out, in reverential monotone, some homily or the life of some by-gone saint. Two absconded, one fell ill ; but the Abbot, with the clink of the mason's chisel upon the stones of the rising monastery in his ears, showed more than his usual resolution of heart. After many difficulties were overcome, the aim of his years was completed. There is no space to tell of the restoration to life, through the aspersion of Lourdes water, of a builder crushed to " a distorted mass of pulp " by a falling crate of stones ; nor of the miraculous passing of the reserved Sacrament through an iron door, nor of " the highest note in this biography," the apparition of the Virgin on two occasions, accompanied by celestial lights and music, in corroboration of all which events are mustered a number of witnesses. The chronicler after the manner of chroniclers leaves us with these marvels on our hands. It is strange to read of them in a book, illustrated with rather theatrical photographs of the principal actor, who in some cases presents a pathetic spectacle, as though playing at being an Abbot with a very small cast. The good faith of all concerned is convincing ; the testimony is as sound as that on which our ancestors accepted such stories, but we—the benefit that we get from the book, is the sensation of living in two different periods of the world's history, at the same time. In reading of ages very different from our own it is easier to believe anything may have happened ; the remoteness of events tends to prevent many from applying the same tests of credibility. The degree of involuntary scepticism, therefore, with which readers, willing to accept ancient miracles, follow the story of " Father Ignatius," may be some test of the extent to which they are under this historical illusion.

Desmond MacCarthy

THE BIRTH OF VIRGIL

(Dante, *Inferno* I. 70)

Nacqui *sub Julio*, ancorchè fosse tardi,
e vissi a Roma sotto il buono Augusto,
al tempo dei Dei falsi e bugiardi.

"I WAS born *under Julius*, though it was late ; and lived at Rome under the good Augustus, at the time of the false and lying gods."—With these words the shade of the great Mantuan poet, the founder of the Roman Imperial literature, introduces himself to Dante, at the out-set of his journey through Hell, Purgatory, and Paradise, as the guide destined to accompany and direct him through so much of his journey as was terrestrial, and lay within or upon this earth. For the first two stages, for the passage through the Underworld, and for the ascent of the Mount of Purgatory at the Antipodes, Virgil, as he announces, will be a sufficient and authorised director ; but for Heaven another and worthier guide will be provided ; "for that Emperor, who reigns above, because I was rebellious to His law, wills not that entrance into His city should be made by means of me."

The symbolic purpose of this distinction, between the present and the promised guide, is transparent and universally recognised ; and equally transparent is the propriety, from Dante's point of view, of the function assigned to Virgil. Truth is attained partly by human intelligence, but the highest truth only by divine grace and revelation. Virgil, the inheritor and consummator of the intellectual efforts which preceded the Christian revelation—Virgil, who gave a final form and a new beginning to that language and poetry of the Roman Empire, which was for Dante the eternal language and poetry of the world—Virgil, who fore-felt, indeed, and foreshowed (as Dante believed) the coming of Christ, yet was himself the first and most powerful preacher not of Christ but of Anti-Christ, the first to salute effectively that new deity of the Roman Cæsar, which, embodied in the successors of Julius and Augustus, fought successfully for three centuries against the accession of the Messiah to His rightful sovereignty upon earth—Virgil, both by his achievements and his limits, represented exactly, for Dante, the culmination and the defects of Man not yet enlightened by the self-revelation of God.

The brief biographical particulars, by which Virgil is made to disclose his identity, have, in all respects but one, that close and precise relevance to the purpose, which is perhaps the most remarkable feature of Dante's style and way of thinking. We are told, *first*, that he was an Italian, a full-born native of the Imperial state ; *secondly*, that he celebrated the " coming of Æneas," that is to say, the foundation of Rome, and more particularly, the foundation of Rome as a spiritual state, the seat prepared for the Vicar of Christ. This significance of Æneas' enterprise, though not here stated by Virgil, is expressly and fully set forth by Dante, in the following discourse between the two poets; and we are correctly referred for it to the *Sixth Æneid* in particular, the account of Æneas' journey to the Underworld, and the revelations there made to him, " the causes of his victory and of the Papal Mantle." [1] We are thus shown precisely in what respect the *Divina Commedia* depends historically and poetically upon the *Æneid*, and why Virgil, and no other, should hold in the later poem, in the *Æneid* of a better Rome, that large but limited place which he actually does. *Thirdly*, we are told that the life of Virgil coincided with " the time of the false and lying gods," that is to say, with the establishment under Augustus of the Imperial pretensions to deity. And *lastly*, Virgil informs us that he was himself a rebel against the true and heavenly " Emperor ", that is to say, he recognised, acclaimed, and promoted those false pretensions of deified

---

[1] *Inf.*, ii. 13–27.

men, by which the spiritual Governor of the World, the veritable God-Man, and his appointed representatives, the Pontiffs, were unlawfully debarred from their terrestrial throne. All this is perfectly true and exactly appropriate ; the biographical statement could not possibly be improved, with regard to its intention, by any omission or addition whatsoever.

But with these statements Dante, to the amazement of his expositors from earliest to latest, combines one assertion which, taken in the *prima facie* sense, is not only false, but would, if it were true, destroy the very basis of all the rest. " I was born," says Virgil, " *under Julius*, although it was late," " Nacqui *sub Julio*, ancorchè fosse tardi." This is held, not unnaturally, if we take the sentence alone, to mean that Virgil was born when Julius Cæsar was monarch (48–44 B.C.), but very near the end of his life and reign, that is to say, in or not earlier than the year 45 B.C.

Now in the first place, this date is enormously wrong, too late by twenty-five years or something near a generation, the true date being 70 B.C. And further, if the alleged date were right, the rest of the biography, though it might be in some sort true, manifestly could not bear the significance which Dante here and elsewhere assigns to it. On both grounds, error and incongruity, the statement would be surprising if found in Dante anywhere, and is especially surprising in this place.

On the mere question of error, the probability or improbability that Dante should be wrong by twenty-five years respecting one of the chief dates in the first century before Christ, we need not dwell at any length. Among his expositors, one of the most positive in pronouncing the error, merely as an error, impossible, is one of the nearest to the poet's own time, and the best qualified, so far, to estimate his general equipment. Nor is it easy to refute Benvenuto upon this point. The age which witnessed the establishment of the Roman Empire was more interesting to Dante than any except (if we should except) his own. He possessed, and claims and proves himself to have deeply studied, books which gave a general outline of that age, sufficient to exclude utterly a statement so absurd as that the birth of Virgil nearly coincided with the death of Julius Cæsar. Nor, so far as I am aware, has any error of his, comparable in matter and gravity, ever been cited by way of illustration. It would require us, for instance, to suppose that Dante had not got the faintest notion, even at second-hand, of the contents and historical bearing of Virgil's *Fifth Eclogue*. The supposition is perhaps not disprovable by chapter and verse, but few readers of Dante will venture to call it likely. And even if we assume the possibility of the error, there would still remain the incongruity, the irrelevance, and worse than irrelevance, of the statement in this particular place. The whole account of Virgil here given comes briefly to this, that he was the originator, the founder, of Roman Imperial literature, the leader in the production of poetry framed and governed by the conception of the Roman Empire as a sacred world-state,—the first of the Augustans. This is fact; and all that Dante here says of Virgil, and the whole propriety of the place assigned to Virgil in the *Divina Commedia*, depends upon the fact. "Art thou then that Virgil, and that *fountain*, which pours abroad so rich a stream of speech? O glory *and light* of other poets! . . ." Such is the salutation with which Dante, blushing with humility and delight, receives the Great Leader's description of his career. What is signified by these figures of *fountain* and *light* is plain enough here, in their context, and is made still plainer in the *Fourth Canto*. There we see Virgil (and Dante with him) rejoining his compeers, the group of Roman and Imperial poets, with whom, in the Limbo of the Underworld, is his eternal abode. Homer is included in the group, to represent the preparatory work of Greece; Dante himself is adopted into it, to represent heirs and successors. The rest are the *Augustan* poets in the large and political meaning of the word, the Latin poets of the Empire—arranged, we may note, correctly in order of date—Horace, Ovid, and Lucan. Approaching these, Virgil is none the less saluted as *the highest Poet (l'altissimo Poeta)*.[1] He is the chief, the leader, the prince of human language and thought, as estimated by the standard of a Christian Imperialist, by Dante, a true and loyal subject

[1] *Inf.*, iv. 80.

of the Holy Roman Empire. All this is intelligible and true, if we assume the true date of Virgil and his work, its true relation in time to that cardinal change of Roman ideas and of the Latin language, which bears the name of Augustus. It is not true, unless we assume, as the fact is, that the decisive operation of Virgil *preceded* the whole Imperialist movement in literature, and set the pattern of it; that all the work of Ovid, and all the vitally significant work of Horace, is subsequent to the decisive entrance of Virgil ; that all the body of Augustan poetry is later than the *Bucolics* and *Georgics*, most of it later than the *Æneid ;* that it is all in various ways not only Augustan but Virgilian, and could not have been what it is, if Virgil, first and long before, had not sounded his new and inaugurating note.

But how is this conceivable, if, as Dante is understood to say, Virgil was but just born when Julius Cæsar fell, if Virgil was an infant at the time when Augustus achieved power ? If this was so, then one of two things—either Virgil, as a poet, instead of being the leader of the Augustan age, must have been one of its latest products ; or else, if the Augustan movement in thought and language really began with Virgil, then all the Augustans were junior by a generation to Augustus himself, and some of them, Ovid for instance, would be junior by two generations.

Such is the palpable absurdity, the plain contradiction, of which Dante is guilty at the very outset and foundation of his systematic poem, if, when he made Virgil say—

Nacqui *sub Julio*, ancorchè rosse tardi,

he meant that the birth of Virgil preceded indeed, but barely preceded, the death of the first Roman Emperor. The offence would be aggravated, we may remark, by the ostentation of exactness. We are particularly asked to note, as if it were not only true but specially important, that though the birth of the poet *did* precede the death of the sovereign, it was not by much—and this although what follows cannot be properly appreciated, unless we know and realise that Virgil, as an adult and accomplished poet, was *the first* who proclaimed effectively to the world the deity of the deceased Julius, and asserted the devolution of that sacred character to the inheritor of his name and power.

To call this hypothesis impossible would be perhaps too much. In the way of human error, nothing perhaps is strictly impossible. But more improbable no hypothesis could be, and as a basis of interpretation it is inadmissible. Any supposition must be preferable, or in default of any, none—the abandonment of the verse as hopelessly obscure. And to try first the positive and more comfortable way, we should consider exhaustively, what are the conditions to be satisfied by an interpretation really acceptable.

Three things such an interpretation must do, none of which the primary interpretation does. *First*, it must show some significant and interesting connexion between the birth of Virgil and the person of the first Emperor, in his character as a pretended god. For this, and this only, is the aspect in which Julius is here introduced; he was one, and the first, of the " false and lying gods." We have hitherto assumed, without remark, that this description signifies the Roman Emperors, and especially the two who are mentioned, the founders of the cult, Julius and Augustus. But as commentaries on Dante seem to be generally silent about this, it should perhaps be further explained. There is nothing, except the Roman Emperors, to which the description, " false and lying gods," can be here referred, if we duly regard the context and the opinions of Dante. He could not so describe, for instance, the gods of Roman mythology, Jupiter and the other Olympians. Milton might have so described Jupiter, and indeed does use very similar language about him; because Milton held the view that the pagan gods were really devils, who deceived their worshippers into accepting them for deities. But Dante held the view, totally different and at least equally defensible, that the figure of Jupiter was an imperfect adumbration, a human and partly erroneous conception, of the true Deity, God Himself. He actually speaks of Christ as the *crucified Jove* (*Giove crocifisso*); and this way of looking at the matter is not only well-founded in history, but absolutely necessary to Roman Catholicism as apprehended by Dante. Moreover, even if Jupiter and the rest had been, for Dante, "lying gods," it would still be pointless to distinguish the time of Virgil as the time of those gods— who were worshipped for centuries after Virgil exactly as they had been for ages before. The worship of the Augustus, on the other hand, was the essential and characteristic novelty of Virgil's time. To this therefore clearly Dante here refers, borrowing his sarcasm upon the Imperial pretensions from such authors as his favourite Lucan, who, in his treatment of the subject, fluctuates between pompous flattery and scathing contempt. Lucan's "dead gods of Rome" (*Romanorum manes deorum*) signifies the same thing as Dante's *bugiardi Dei*, and puts it much more strongly. Moral distinctions between different Emperors may of course be admitted—and Dante does admit them by making Virgil call his patron "the *good* Augustus"—without prejudice to the condemnation of all the Emperors, in respect of their claim to deity, as liars. As a deity then, a pretended deity, Julius is here brought in ; and the first problem for our interpretation is to find some real and interesting connexion between Julius, in this character, and the date of the birth of Virgil.

Further, a satisfactory explanation of the words " I was born *sub Julio*" must show why "under Julius" should be expressed not in Italian but in Latin. Latin is little used by Dante in his Italian poetry, and when it is, there is commonly an obvious reason or necessity for the licence. A Latin psalm, hymn, prayer must of course be indicated by its proper words—*Te Deum, Veni Creator, In exitu Israel;* and a poetical quotation, if sufficiently important, may be similarly distinguished—*manibus date lilia plenis.* But no literary offence is more displeasing to a delicate taste than gratuitous polyglot, an alien idiom inserted arbitrarily or to save the trouble of speaking correctly. If, then, Dante means no more than that Virgil was born in the reign of Julius, why does he not say it in the vernacular ?

Lastly, and above all, we should require some real justification for the strange and enigmatical words *ancorchè fosse tardi*, "though it was late." " I was born *sub Julio*, though it was late," is no proper way to express the sense hitherto assumed, " I was born late in the time of Julius."

So clumsy and pointless a periphrasis is not fairly attributable to the composer of the *Divina Commedia*.

Let us, then, start again without prejudice; and since the supposition of Dante's ignorance or carelessness has proved so unfruitful, let us start by supposing on the contrary his complete knowledge and profound study of the subject. For really this is, in the present matter, the more natural supposition. All the material which we have for the life of Virgil, with insignificant exceptions, was extant in the time of Dante, and might naturally be open to his investigation. What historical documents he had, he studied, and so did his contemporaries, with a passionate and scrupulous thoroughness which no age has surpassed. Let us suppose, then, that he knew, and had considered, all that there is to know about the birth of Virgil ; that the learned readers, whom he desired to satisfy,[1] knew it all too ; that he assumes their knowledge, and might naturally write whatever such readers could interpret. And let us, then, ask, what is known or knowable about the date of the birth of Virgil ?

Tradition places it in the year 684 of Rome (70 B.C. by our era), in the month of October, and on the Ides or 15th day of the month. From the year we can deduce nothing (as has been only too completely ascertained) which throws any light upon Dante. The year had no special association whatever with the name or the fortunes of the first Emperor. Let us, then, next try the month. At first sight this looks equally unpromising : the Emperor is not, and never was, associated with the month of October. He has, indeed, a month of his own—a month which, bearing his name, has eternalised (so far as it is possible for man) the memory of his unique and almost superhuman greatness. But it is the month of *July*. And it is scarcely too much to say that, if any event is to be associated through its date with the name of Julius, it is through the month of Quintilis, converted into *Julius* in honour of his deity, that the link of association must be sought.

In this embarrassment we go back then to Dante ; and

---

[1] This should always be carefully borne in mind in considering a problem in Dante. He assumes learning in his readers, all the learning of his time, and makes no attempt to meet the popular intelligence.

we may now observe, not without hope, that he appends to his *sub Julio* the exception or qualification, "although it was late." What was late? We have assumed hitherto that the subject of this remark is the birth of Virgil. But Dante does not say so ; he says that *something* was late, and, so far as the words go, may perfectly well mean that it was the date, that is to say, the month, and not the infant that was belated. And this, as a matter of fact, it certainly was. In 70 B.C. all the true months—the months of the natural year—were, and long had been, in consequence of accumulating error, behind the nominal calendar. The accumulated error amounted to almost exactly three months, and persisted, as all the world knows, until Julius Cæsar, in 46 B.C., rectified it by inserting ninety days (three months) in a single year, and took means to prevent the error in future, whereby it came to pass that his name, as that of a deity, was given to the month in which he was born.

Consequently, a child whose birth was recorded, in the year 684 of Rome, as occurring in the middle of October, was really born in the seventh (not the tenth) month of the true year, in the height of summer, not in the autumn ; and if the birth had been properly recorded, according to the true calendar as afterwards established by the Emperor, would have been described, and should now properly be described, as born *sub Julio*, in the month and under the auspices of Julius. But the true and proper name of the month was then "late," "lagging," "behindhand," by a whole quarter; *Quintilis*, or *Julius*, which should have been present, lay nominally three months in arrear; and Virgil therefore figures in history, though falsely, as born in the middle of October.

This, then, I venture to think, is what Dante means by his terse, but correct observation. Deeply interested as he was in astronomical and calendric studies, and in the history of the age which witnessed the foundation of Imperial Rome, he might very naturally have observed the error respecting the season and true character of the time, which presumably lies in the statement that Virgil was born on the Ides of October. Nor would he think it pedantic, or irrelevant, as perhaps we might, to introduce a notice of this error, and of the fact as corrected, into his poetical biography of the

Augustan poet. It is irrelevant only upon the assumption that there cannot be any real significance in the true fact, the birth of the first Imperial poet in that portion of the year which was to bear the name of the first Emperor. But Dante of course would not have admitted this. As a sound astrologer, he would have maintained, on the contrary, that the fact was, or probably might be, a sign of destiny, and more than a sign, an actual element in the natural and spiritual influences, which contributed to mould the nascent soul of the Imperial poet and prophet, and to fit him for his appointed work of revealing and worthily celebrating the evolution of the Roman world-state, from the beginning by Æneas to the new beginning by Julius and Augustus, the building of Imperial Rome, of a throne for the Vicar of Christ.

It is true, as Dante sadly acknowledges, that Virgil did not perceive (and perhaps, when we consider how much was revealed to him in his *Fourth Eclogue*, was guilty of rebellion in refusing to perceive), that the throne of Rome, the spiritual throne, was not really destined, and could not lawfully be given, to the head of the political Empire. In making Julius and Augustus into gods, in annexing the spiritual headship to the political, the poet did the very same wrong, which was done reversely by those of the Popes who strove to annex the political supremacy to the spiritual—the error and crime against which the whole *Divina Commedia* is designed to protest. But it was none the less true, that Virgil, by the will and providence of the Almighty, powerfully aided to build the throne. For this reason chiefly he holds his place in the story and symbolism of Dante; and for this reason Dante thought fit to introduce him with the statement that he "was born *sub Julio*"—Italian could not give the point—"*sub Julio* (though *Julius* was belated), and lived at Rome under the good Augustus, at the time of the false and lying gods."

A. W. VERRALL

THE LABOUR MOVEMENT IN FRANCE

IN the course of the lively discussions which have recently taken place in the Chamber, the continued existence of the General Confederation of Labour has been seriously threatened. To judge from most of the speeches for or against it, the deputies appear to have had no very precise idea of its nature and functions. The truth is that there are distinctions to be made between the elements which compose the general organisation of the French trade unions ; and the tendencies which inspire it are subject to certain counter-currents, much more powerful than is generally supposed. The present study aims at explaining these distinctions, and bringing to light these conflicting currents.

I

It is tolerably well known that trade combinations in France have for long, and definitely since 1879, been in the hands of the Socialist parties, which subordinated their economic action to their own political aims. After a number of years the unions awoke to the inconvenience of such a state of things, and when internal disagreement caused the formation of new groups among the Socialists, the associations found it more and more intolerable to be involved in their dissensions. In the course of a Labour Congress held at Nantes in 1894 open war broke out between the principal unions pledged to political action and those which had gradually become convinced of the paramount importance of economic action. The latter having obtained the upper hand proceeded at the Congress held in the following year at Limoges to found the

General Confederation of Labour to unite together, "without reference to any political school," the greatest possible number of Trade Unions.

The formation, thus inspired, of the General Confederation of Labour, did not, as was to be expected, put an end at once to the political leanings of many of the unions: leanings which, it may be remarked in passing, were noticeable, though in a somewhat modified form, at the Amiens Congress. Nevertheless, it is indubitable that the years 1894-5 mark the growth of a breach between the unionists and their former Socialist leaders: a breach still further widened by the policy of the Waldeck-Rousseau Ministry. When M. Millerand brought Socialism into the government, half of the Socialist party ranged itself on the side of the Minister of Commerce, while the other half repudiated him and his action. And this state of affairs was reflected within the Trade Union movement, for while a majority of the labour organisations, in sympathy with revolutionary tactics, violently denounced governmental Socialism, some, more inclined to regard political action with favour, received M. Millerand's accession to office with acclamation, and a still smaller section, considering corporate action as the essential thing, remained more or less indifferent. The existence of the General Confederation of Labour had not, so far, been characterised by any brilliance: the shock of these events placed it under the control of a coalition formed on the one hand of independents (*libertaires*), who had recently joined the Trade Union movement in the hope of finding in it a field for their ideas, and on the other of Socialists of the revolutionary type, more or less imbued with the doctrines of Anarchism and more or less opposed, like the independents, to any sort of parliamentary action.

The men who thus acquired control over the Confederation, men shortly to be designated as "revolutionary unionists," represented, in 1901-2, certainly not more than a very insignificant proportion of the organised proletariate in France: at the same time, however, the rapid spread of their ideas and the success of their propaganda is incontestable. The political tendencies still existing in some of the local unions were weakened by their attacks. The Socialist party, then in gradual process of acquiring that unity which it ultimately attained, was not long in realising that it was losing control of the Labour movement and rapidly getting out of touch with the Trade Unions. Before long, except in isolated localities, especially in the north, there was no longer any common action, or any agreement, official or unofficial, between the Socialists and the associations.

The power of the revolutionaries who controlled the Confederation grew with the increased area over which their sway was exercised, until their virtual supremacy over the movement became as rigid and intolerable as that of the Socialist cliques which it had replaced. They were lynx-eyed in keeping politics out of the Confederation: they waged war on any federation or union that violated the political neutrality which was the first clause in the Confederate statutes. In their furious proscription of all political faith they created a creed of negations by which all law, all government was condemned as useless, even as accursed: whose dogmas were anti-parliamentarianism, anti-stateism, anti-militarism, anti-patriotism. Members of Parliament or of any elected body were stigmatised as " vile politicians " or worse. Pending the proclamation of a universal revolutionary strike, their one idea was to force upon the Trade Unions what they called *l'action directe*, *i. e.* the use of violence or at least of threats of violence against public authorities and against employers, with whom they would allow no negotiation either before or after a strike. Theories or actions contrary to this creed were severely condemned.

Certainly, the Trade Unions did not always practise the revolutionary doctrines that they preached : but excuses were found for them, as long as they adhered to their doctrine. The case of the Typographical Union (composed almost entirely of compositors) was different. This union, after shaking off the Socialist yoke in 1894, had stood alone, or almost alone, in adopting a line of action analogous in many ways to that of the English and German unions. It now refused to swallow the principles of revolutionary Trade Unionism. At various meetings held in Paris and the provinces, exception was taken to the action of the union by delegates of the Central Committee of the Confederation. They denounced its co-operation with employers, its negotiations during strikes, its recourse to wages boards of mixed composition for determination of the hours and remuneration of labour, and its using the parliamentary machine, where, however, the union had avoided committing itself to alliance with any party. In reply to these attacks the Typographical Union defended itself vigorously, and entered a protest, in common with the unions affiliated to it, against the tyranny of the officials of the Confederation, and the injury caused to the Union by the persistent campaign to which it had been subjected. Feeling in the world of organised labour ran high over the dispute, which lasted through the spring and summer of 1904 between the Union and the Executive of the Confederation, and in its course the views of the two parties became more clearly defined. In opposition to the Revolutionaries stood the Reformists—a term vague enough to include both such associations as the Typographical, which relied on legal economic methods, and those which once more ranged themselves on the side of parliamentary Socialism.

The Typographical Union seized the opportunity afforded it by the Report of the Committee of the Confederation to lay its grievances before the Congress that met at Bourges in September ; but in spite of the contention of its delegates, the Report was adopted by 825 votes to 369. The Typographical and one or two other unions then made various proposals for the adoption at the coming election of the principle of proportional representation on the Central Committee, one representative having hitherto elected from each association, irrespective of its membership. Their idea was by this means to transfer the direction of the Confederation out of the hands of a coalition formed of organisations which were, for the most part, so weak as to be practically non-existent, full of radical ideas, and in no sense representative of the majority of the confederated unions, into the hands of the big unions which were, on the whole, less revolutionary in their tendencies. The attempt, however, failed : the principle of proportional representation was rejected by 822 votes to 388. These two votes, both of course taken on the basis of one member for each union, were followed by another success for the revolutionary section in the adoption, after a hasty and superficial discussion, of a proposal authorising the Central Committee to organise an agitation, " that on May 1, 1906, all workmen do on their own initiative cease to work more than eight hours a day."

The Congress of Bourges was thus a triumph for the Revolutionists : but it revealed for the first time the existence among the Trade Unionists of a party which, while quite independent of any political sect, was opposed to extreme or violent measures. The Unions of Lithographers, Clerks, Engineers, and Tobacco Workers ranged themselves on the side of the Typographical. The definite gain from their attempted revolt was the recognition of their autonomy by the radical leaders, who, however, continued their policy unchanged.

Shortly after the Bourges Congress they made the eight hours' resolution, thus light-heartedly agreed upon, part of their platform : and for the next eighteen months an increasingly active campaign, in the course of which no method of agitation was neglected, was carried on by the Central Committee of the Confederation. The Federatives followed its lead, but most of them contented themselves with preaching the eight hours' day without committing themselves, on the part of their members, to cessation of work at the end of the eighth hour. Every possible cry was revived in order to attract men to the movement ; the seventh day holiday, the abolition of piece-work, etc. As the fatal day approached, it became increasingly evident that the mass of the federated unions were going to refrain from action. As early as June 1905 the typographers had decided to try to obtain, as far as possible, by means of an agreement with the masters, a nine hours' day : an eight hours' day they regarded for the present as impracticable. On April 5 and 6, 1906, a meeting of delegates of the federated unions was held, in view of the action to be taken on May 1, but in no case could the delegates declare their union ready for the fight, and the Conference had to content itself with the conclusion that on May 1 several courses of action would lie before the workers: they could leave work after eight hours, go on strike, or agree to do no work at all that day.

Nevertheless the May movement had its serious side. There was, as a matter of fact, very little stoppage of work after the eighth hour, and the strikes that did take place were mostly explicable by the circumstances of the moment, the great mining strike that followed the Courrières disaster, the political events that marked the elections and, last but not least, the absurd panic by which, since the end of April, the leisured classes and even the Government itself had been possessed. As a matter of fact, the workmen failed almost everywhere in their demand for an eight hours' day : at best they obtained either some slight advance in wages or some reduction of the working day. The net result was a decided check to the revolutionary section of the unionists.

The discredit accruing to the promoters of the May movement was certainly less than it would have been in any other country ; but there was a fairly strong feeling against them in some of the unions. Towards the end of July, the Union of Textile Workers, whose headquarters is at Lille, and which had always maintained a close connection with parliamentary Socialism, declared their intention of bringing forward, at the Congress to be held at Amiens in October—first, the advantage of legislative action as a means of realising the demands of labour; and second, the necessity for an agreement between the General Confederation of Labour and the united Socialist party : that is to say, they proposed a unification of the economic and political agitation by the proletariate. Their first proposition was tantamount to an attack on the *libertaires ;* the second questioned, if indirectly, the political neutrality of the unions embodied in the statutes of the Confederation. For two months the Labour press discussed the motives of the Textile Union. When the Congress of Amiens was opened on October 8th, it was common knowledge that there would be a lively contest over them. Moreover, the

Socialist Associations of the north, sympathising with the Textile Union, had given notice of their intention to lay a similar motion before the Socialist Congress to be held at Limoges in the beginning of November.

II

Exact statistics of the Amiens Congress are not easy to obtain. Some 300 delegates represented 991 associations: but it is impossible to estimate even approximately the number of unionists which this total represents, since the mode of voting continued to be based on the system of one vote for each association, irrespective of its numerical strength. It may here be remarked that this defective method affected less than might have been expected the importance attached by the working class to the Congress' decisions.

The first business of the Congress was to discuss the report of the Central Committee ; and here the failure of the 1st of May could not be slurred over. An attempt at explanation however, was sought in the ill-will or even open opposition to the movement displayed by some of the reformist unions, especially by the engineers. Their delegates entered an energetic protest against such allegations and finally compelled the secretary to retract them. The principal delegate of the Typographical, as a proof of the injustice of the attacks to which this association had been subjected at the time of the Congress at Bourges, laid before the meeting the highly satisfactory results which they had obtained in the course of their nine hours' day campaign by a mode of procedure entirely different from that of the so-called *action directe*. Several delegates blamed the officials of the Confederation for the fiasco of May 1st. Others criticised the capture of the Organ of the Confederation, the *Voix du Peuple*, by the revolutionary unionists. The replies of the Executive were feeble : their explanations halting : in fact throughout the Congress they occupied the stool of repentance, a quite unaccustomed position.

On one important issue, however, their action was

approved by the Congress. In 1905 the Central Committee had broken up all connection with the International, whose headquarters is Berlin, because of its refusal to enter on the minutes of its prospective Conference at Amsterdam the three following questions : Anti-militarism, the General Strike and the Eight Hours' Day ; of this the Congress approved : at the same time urging the Committee to demand once more that the three questions be incorporated in the minutes of the Conference.

On the other hand, it showed no sort of inclination to accept the proposal of certain radicals on the committee, that the tactics of May 1 be renewed and a new date fixed for the commencement of a new Eight Hours' Movement. For appearance' sake, they resolved to continue the work of propaganda, but they left the date to be fixed after consultation with the unions concerned—a decision practically equivalent to annulling the resolutions of the Congress of Bourges.

These points settled, the Congress turned to the central question—the attitude of the Confederation to politics generally, and more especially to the united Socialist party. The debate lasted for two days. The Congress decided, after several hours' discussion, and in the presence of nearly fifty speakers whose names were on the paper, that three speakers should be chosen to represent each of the three main views—i. e. revolutionary, reformist, and what might be called Socialist trade unionism : taking this last to mean the view of that section that desired to enter into relations with the Socialist party, and was thus favourable to the proposals of the Textile Federation. The protracted debates that ensued showed clearly enough the points of contact and of difference between the various parties. Socialist and reformist Unionism agreed in vigorous denunciation of the intolerance of the revolutionaries, who, while furiously attacking all political methods, yet had a political method of their own, which they would like to force upon every one, the method of anti-parliamentarianism, anti-militarism, and abstention from voting at elections; while the Socialists and Unionists bent all their energies to showing the inadequacy of Trade Union action alone to effect any complete or final emancipation of the working classes, and to proving the advantages which they had obtained in the past, and would obtain in the future, from labour legislation. But while the Socialistic Trade Unionists looked to the Socialist party as alone capable of securing such legislation, and consequently regarded union with it as indispensable to the Confederation, the reformists and revolutionists were here at one in opposition : the former because, although they approved of labour legislation, they were unwilling to owe allegiance to any political party; the latter. because they rejected, on theoretic grounds, all recourse to legislation and regarded action by the unions themselves, in the form of a general strike and of *l'action directe*, as all-sufficient. The reformists, again, found themselves in sympathy with the revolutionary criticism of the warfare waged, under various circumstances, on the delegates of the Confederation by the Socialist groups of the north and their friends among the unionists.

Bearing in mind, then, the heads of the proposals of the Textile Association: (1) need for labour legislation and the participation of organised labour in obtaining such legislation, and (2) agreement with the united Socialist party, it is easy to understand the tactics employed at this juncture by the revolutionary and Socialist unionists in Congress. The former endeavoured to get a vote on the proposals as a whole, by which means they could· count on securing the support of the reformists who shrank from union with the Socialists : while the latter, on the contrary, wanted the voting to be by sections ; for, seeing that on the first clause they would have the help of the reformists, and then inflict a blow on the radicals, they were ready to risk a defeat on the second. The proposal that the voting be by sections was lost, amid great uproar, by show of hands ; the proposals were then rejected *en bloc* by 774 votes to 34, there being 183 blank returns and abstentions.

In the hope of securing a different decision, another motion was brought forward by the Executive of the Confederation itself. After recapitulating the statutory political neutrality of the Confederation, and stating that the aim of the movement was, over and above the defence of its corporate interests, to carry on the class war by means of general strikes, this motion recognised that the members possessed "full right of free participation, outside the corporate group, in any form of warfare that corresponded to their political or philosophical conceptions," and accorded the same liberty to the Confederated associations "which are not bound, as associated unions, to trouble themselves about any party or section freely pursuing the end of social transformation in its own way." The part of this motion that referred to the class war and the general strike gave satisfaction to the revolutionaries ; the rest pleased the reformists, and, in a lesser degree the Socialists, since it left them latitude for legislative activity. Finally, only eight votes were recorded against a motion which contained something for everybody.

This vote, exploited as a great victory by the revolutionary Socialists, was really in the nature of a check to their tactics. Certainly, the Congress might have been called almost unanimous on the class war and the general strike ; but now-a-days these are so little more than platonic formulas, in whose practical application hardly any one believes, that even the reformists had no hesitation in subscribing to them. Far more important was the liberty left to the unions and their members, on the proposal of the Executive and with the sanction of the Congress, freedom, to quote from the reply to a question, "to enter into whatever relations they might find desirable" with political parties, with the sole proviso that, by the statutes of the Confederation, such relations should only be "accidental" in character. Up till now they had always refused to recognise such liberty.

Little need be said of the hasty and confused debate held at the close of the Congress on the question of Anti-militarism. Two motions were before the meeting : one anti-militarism pure and simple, the other anti-militarism plus anti-patriotism. Put to the vote, the second motion was carried by a majority of 488 of the voters, not of the delegates. An extraordinary number of revolutionary unionists refrained from voting, preferring the first motion, which was not put up. Anyhow the result was far from being a success for the pure independents (*libertaires*).

If the course of development thus traced has been made clear no lengthy summing-up is needed. At the Amiens Congress several points were gained by the revolutionary or *libertaire* unionists : for example, their reports were passed by considerable majorities, while the decision of the Congress in the conflict between the Committee and the International was a triumph for them. The formulas of the class war and the general strike were accepted with practical unanimity. But, on the Eight Hours' Day question, and to a lesser degree on Anti-militarism they were defeated. Moreover, whereas two years previously, at the Congress of Bourges, their supremacy had been absolute, their authority had now to be justified : again and again were they forced to promise toleration, to recognise rights they had denied, more especially the right of free recourse, outside of party, to political action. The reformist organisations, on the other hand, to which such severe treatment had been meted out at Bourges, had won recognition from their adversaries : their watchword " Neither war nor alliance " was the watchword of the Amiens Congress in the determination of relations between the Confederation and the Socialist party. They appeared as a force to be reckoned with. One more point must be noticed. The debates, though animated, had none of the aggressive character that marked them at the Bourges Congress ; the impression conveyed is that of the growth of a certain cohesion between the hitherto discordant elements of organised labour, an impression which entitles one to the hope that, in a more or less distant future, the reformist unions and federations, which unite the tendencies and methods of English Trade Unionism, will leaven the French Trade Union world.

OCTAVE FESTY

THE PROTECTIVE COLORATION OF
BIRDS

EIGHT years of bird-watching in India have convinced me that, so far as the struggle for existence is concerned, it matters not to a bird whether it be conspicuously or inconspicuously coloured, that it is not the necessity for protection against raptorial foes which determines the colouring of a species, in short, that the theory of protective coloration has but little application to the fowls of the air.

The bird most abundant in India is a crow (*Corvus splendens*), not unlike a jackdaw in appearance. This creature is found all over the country, and is so bold and impudent, so great a nuisance to the human inhabitants, that it has won for itself the name of the Indian House Crow.

It is certainly not protectively coloured, nor is it immune from the attacks of the larger birds of prey. Indian crows are social birds, which roost in trees in companies numbering many thousands. To each roosting-place all the crows that live within a radius of twenty miles repair at bedtime. These arboreal dormitories are well known to the larger birds of prey. All the peregrine falcons of the vicinity that have not managed to secure a duck for dinner, all the hungry Bonelli's eagles and goshawks, betake themselves at sunset to the nearest local dormitory, and each secures a crow for its supper amid an uproar that baffles description. Yet, notwithstanding its conspicuous colouring, and the ease with which birds of prey are able to capture it, the crow is the most thriving bird in the East.

If a naturalist be asked to cite a perfect example of protective colouring he will, as likely as not, name the sand grouse (*Pteroclurus exustus*). This species dwells in open, dry, sandy country, and its dull brownish-buff plumage with its soft dark bars assimilates so closely to the sandy environment as to make the bird, when at rest, practically invisible, at any rate to the human eye. Unfortunately for the theory, this bird stands less in need of protective coloration than any other, for it has wonderful powers of flight. Even a trained falcon is unable to catch it, for it can fly upwards in a straight line as though it were ascending an inclined plane, with the result that the pursuing hawk is never able to get above it to strike.

So keen is the sight of raptorial birds that none but the most perfect examples of protective coloration can possibly baffle it. A disguise which may deceive nine men out of ten will not suffice to delude an eagle. This being so, there is no room for variation as regards colour in a protectively-coloured organism. Yet we find that in almost every species of bird there is much variation in colour, even among the individuals that live in the same locality.

Again, the young of many species differ greatly from the adult birds. Of this the sea-gulls afford a familiar example. A still better example is furnished by the beautiful Indian paradise flycatcher (*Terpsiphone paradisi*). For the first two years of his life the cock is a beautiful chestnut bird, but at his third autumnal moult he turns as white as snow. No change of habits accompanies this transformation. The hen retains her chestnut plumage throughout life. Obviously both the white and the chestnut forms, which often occur in the same wood, cannot be protectively coloured.

The phenomenon of sexual colour dimorphism affords further evidence of the comparative unimportance of protective coloration in bird life, but of this more anon.

Equally inimical to the theory of protective coloration is the existence, side by side, of species which obtain their living in the same manner. On almost any Indian lake three different species of kingfisher pursue their profession cheek by jowl; one of these—*Ceryle rudis*—is speckled black and white, like a Hamburg fowl, the second is the kingfisher we know in England, and the third is the magnificent white-breasted species—*Halcyon smyrnensis*—a bright-blue bird with a reddish head and a white wing-bar. It seems incredible that each of these three species is protectively coloured.

Every observer must have noticed how birds love to sit and bask in exposed situations. The Indian oriole (*Oriolus kundoo*), the green parakeet (*Palæornis torquatus*), the roller (*Coracias indica*), and the king crow (*Dicrurus ater*) are among the most conspicuously-coloured birds in India. Nevertheless, they always perch by preference on a bare branch, a telegraph wire, or other exposed place; and India literally teems with birds of prey. When thus perched they are distinctly visible from a distance of several hundred yards. Hunting birds of prey have eyes only for moving objects. They take their quarry on the wing, and, as they sail through the air, look out for flying things. All stationary objects, no matter how showily coloured, seem to be ignored. This explains how it is that so conspicuous a bird as the red-wattled lapwing (*Sarcogrammus indicus*), which lays its eggs in the open, on dry stony ground, flourishes in India.

The theory of protective mimicry forms part of the larger theory of protective coloration. An Indian cuckoo, *Surniculus lugubris*, is so like the king crow, mentioned above, that it is a matter of the utmost difficulty to distinguish between the two birds. Both are jet black and slenderly built, and have a long, forked tail. The cuckoo is parasitic on the drongo. The latter is very pugnacious at the breeding season, and will not let another species so much as approach its nest, but it is deceived by the extraordinary likeness of the cuckoo. There is no denying that the cuckoo profits by the so-called mimicry. This fact, how-ever, is no proof that the disguise is the result of natural selection. We must remember that the cuckoo cannot profit by the likeness until this is nearly perfect. I regard it as purely fortuitous. Organisms are so plastic that it would be surprising if sometimes one species did not resemble another in no way related to it. As Messrs. Beddard and Finn have shown, this does sometimes happen. There is a New Zealand cuckoo which closely resembles an American hawk, but is not like any of the local hawks. It is impossible to maintain that the similarity of two birds separated by half the globe is of any advantage to either.

The phenomena of sexual dimorphism are supposed to lend support to the theory of protective coloration. When the sexes differ in colour it is nearly always the cock that is more showily dressed. This Darwin sought to explain by his well-known theory of sexual selection, or, as it should be called, feminine selection. The famous naturalist was at great pains to demonstrate that hens select their mates. They certainly do so. There are in the Zoological Gardens at Lahore a number of peafowl. Some of the cocks are pure albinos. Now, no hen will so much as look at a coloured cock when there is an albino in the same enclosure with her. Where Darwin went wrong was in thinking that the cock does not exercise a similar selection. His idea seems to have been that any old hen was good enough for a cock ! This is, I submit, opposed both to common sense and observation. I have seen a cock Indian oriole, who is more brightly coloured than the hen, sitting in a tree and watching complacently a duel between two hens. Each lady was trying to drive away her rival in order that she might secure the cock for herself, for the oriole is a monogamist. On another occasion, when I was watching a cock and a hen paradise flycatcher hawking flies in a shady grove, a second hen appeared suddenly upon the scene. The newcomer was at once attacked so savagely by the hen already " in possession " that she was glad to make herself scarce.

Darwin further assumed that the hen selects the most handsome of her suitors. Is this assumption correct ? If so, does she select the most beautiful suitor on account of his appearance, or on account of his vigour, of which his beauty is but an outward expression ?

Wallace's explanation of the comparative dulness of the hen is her greater need of protection, since, according to him, it is she alone who incubates. In support of this hypothesis he alleges that in those species which nest in holes or which build domed nests the hen is quite as conspicuous as the cock. There are, unfortunately for Wallace, some exceptions to this rule. The honeysuckers build covered-in nests, yet the cock is a bird of gay attire, and the hen is dull brown. There are many other objections to this theory. Birds of prey rarely, if ever, attack an incubating bird ; it is therefore doubtful whether a sitting bird is exposed to unusual danger.

The white cock paradise flycatcher incubates the eggs turn about with the chestnut hen. The nest is an open cup, and the cock, when sitting on this, is a very conspicuous object ; his long white tail feathers hang over the edge like satin streamers. Similarly the showily-coloured cock minivet (*Pericrocotus peregrinus*) incubates equally with the dull hen in an open nest.

In some species which build open nests, the amount of sexual dimorphism is so small as to make it impossible to say whether the cock or the hen is the more protectively coloured.

It seems to me that we must have recourse to the physiologist for the explanation of the phenomena of sexual dimorphism.

W. DEWAR

THE MORMON INVESTIGATION

FOR " rapid-fire legislation " the Senate of the United States holds the world's record. Its recent achievement in passing 991 pension bills in an hour and six minutes shows that there is at least one Upper House that is able to "hustle" upon occasion. The history of the Mormon investigation, however, suggests that in dealing with some matters the American Senate affords little ground for the charge of undue precipitancy. Mr. Reed Smoot, a Mormon apostle, was elected Federal Senator by the Utah Legislature on January 20, 1903. The validity of his election having been challenged, the Standing Committee on Privileges and Elections began an investigation on March 2. Two days later Mr. Smoot took his seat. The last witness was heard on March 27, 1906, when the new Senator had already served half his term. On June 1, 1906, the Committee decided by seven votes to five to report against his claim. The majority and minority reports of the Committee were presented to the Senate on June 11, 1906. That body began its discussion of them on December 11 following. It was not until February 20, 1907, that the case was settled by a vote of forty-two to twenty-eight in Mr. Smoot's favour.

If the investigation conducted by the Senate Committee had been concerned merely with the status of Mr. Smoot it would have had little interest for English readers. It ranged, however, over the whole question of Mormon doctrine and practice, and collected material of first-rate importance for the student of curious religious and social developments. In the INDEPENDENT REVIEW for August 1904 an outline was given of the general situation and of the evidence presented during the earlier stages of the inquiry. That account may now be completed by a summary of the later testimony and of the conclusions of the Committee. First, as to the continuance of polygamy within the Mormon Church. Nothing made known afterwards eclipsed the sensation caused by the confession of Mr. Joseph F. Smith, the Mormon President, that, although he had not taken any additional wives since the doctrine of polygamy had been formally abrogated by the manifesto of his predecessor in 1890, he had continued to live with the five wives he had previously married, and they had since that date borne him eleven of his forty-two children. It will be remembered that he defended himself by explaining that polygamous cohabitation was not the same as polygamy. Abundant evidence was given to prove that Mr. Smith's example had been widely followed. In the words of the Committee's report, " A majority of those who give the law to the Mormon Church are now, and have been for years, living in open, notorious, and shameless polygamous cohabitation." The report also finds that the Mormon leaders have not been as careful as their President implied to distinguish between the continuance of previous polygamous relationships and the contracting of new ones. " Since the admission of Utah into the Union as a State the authorities of the Mormon Church have countenanced and encouraged the commission of the crime of polygamy, instead of preventing it, as they could easily have done." Since the manifesto several polygamous marriages have been contracted even among the apostolate. The most remarkable instance was that of Apostle A. H. Cannon, performed in 1896 on the high seas off Los Angeles by Mr. Smith himself. Five other Mormon apostles and bishops are mentioned by name in the report as having taken plural wives in recent years. And it is stated as beyond doubt that " under the established law of the Church no person could secure a plural wife except by consent of the President of the Church." The Committee further charges the Mormon leaders with a deliberate conspiracy to suppress testimony to these damaging facts. Several of the most important witnesses subpœnaed, including the officials accused of such practices, left the country to avoid appearing at the investigation, and the Committee has no hesitation in attributing their absence to instructions received from the highest Mormon authorities. The conclusions of the majority report on the general questions of polygamy and polygamous cohabitation are not impugned by the minority report, which contents itself with discussing how far Mr. Smoot can be charged with connivance at the conditions disclosed by the evidence.

The Committee pronounces no less confidently on the question of the political authority of the Mormon Church. It asserts that "the said first presidency and twelve apostles do now control, and for a long time past have controlled, the political affairs of the State of Utah, and have thus brought about in the said State a union of Church and State contrary to the Constitution of said State of Utah, and contrary to the Constitution of the United States, and the said Reed Smoot comes here, not as the accredited representative of the State of Utah in the Senate of the United States, but as the choice of the hierarchy which controls the Church and has usurped the functions of the State in said State of Utah." "Domination" is the word used elsewhere in this report to express the political relation of the Mormon authorities to their followers. In the opinion of the majority members, the "consent" to his candidature obtained by Mr. Smoot from the hierarchy was regarded by the people of Utah as equivalent to an endorsement, and "made it impossible for any one else to become an aspirant for the same position with any hope of success." On this point there was considerable conflict of testimony. In America, as elsewhere, the successful and the defeated candidate at an election do not always agree in their analysis of the causes of the result, and an exact computation is likely to be especially difficult when the direct or indirect influence of a religious organisation is one of the factors. Quite possibly some of the charges brought against the Salt Lake authorities are exaggerated. In Utah and other States in which Mormons form a large proportion of the population it is only natural that an apostle, without exercising undue pressure, should profit politically from his ecclesiastical position, just as in an English County Council election a popular Anglican clergyman or Nonconformist minister may be expected to appeal more successfully to certain sections of the electorate than a candidate of no definite church connections. But there is good reason to believe that an influence of a more authoritative type has been brought to bear upon elections in these States. It came out on the evidence of creditable witnesses, including in one instance a former Judge of the Supreme Court of Utah, that candidates for political office had been selected by the Church leaders ; that at an election in Idaho the people had been told by Mormon apostles that there had been " a revelation " that they should vote the Republican ticket ; that refusal to support the approved candidates involved a risk of business ruin ; and that opponents of this political dictatorship had been formally excommunicated. In the course of this testimony reference was made more than once to a class of the community known as " Jack-Mormons," *i. e.* persons who were " Gentiles " in religion, but found it expedient to agree politically with their Mormon neighbours.

In its discussion of the political phase of the question the Committee's report lays great stress upon the terms of the oath administered in the ceremony known as "taking the endowments," a ceremony which usually accompanies the performance of a marriage. It has been proved, says the Committee, that the oath is taken substantially in this form : " You and each of you do covenant and promise that you will pray and never cease to pray Almighty God to avenge the blood of the prophets upon this nation, and that you will teach the same to your children and to your children's children unto the third and fourth generations." In the opinion of the Committee such an obligation is " wholly incompatible " with the duty which a United States Senator owes to the nation. " It is difficult to conceive how one could discharge the obligation which rests upon every Senator so to perform his official duties as to promote the welfare of the people of the United States, and at the same time be calling down the vengeance of Heaven on this nation because of the killing of the founders of the Mormon Church sixty years ago." The questions relating to this endowment ceremony brought into the investigation an atmosphere of tragic mystery which one immediately recognises as appropriate to the traditions of this strange sect. The silence of the witnesses was no less significant than their answers. Several of them, when pressed for an account of the ceremony, " could not remember." In one case a man who had been separated from the Mormon Church for thirty years still felt so keenly the obligations he had contracted that he refused to divulge them. While another witness, a woman, was making her disclosures she was so seriously affected that she trembled continuously and spoke with great difficulty. Only one person who appeared before the Committee declared that he had always considered the endowment oath obligations in the light of a joke. As he was so light-hearted over the whole business he had no hesitation in testifying that the Mormons who took this oath bound themselves to secrecy on penalty of the following mutilations : " That the throat be cut from ear to ear and the tongue torn out; that the breast be cut asunder and the heart and vitals be torn from the body; that the body be cut asunder at the middle and the bowels cut out." It was further stated that during the ceremony the priest wore robes bearing the marks of the compass and the square on the left and right breasts, a rent like a button-hole over the abdomen, and another over the knee. These marks were for the purpose of impressing the penalties upon the minds of those present. Another piece of symbolism was the anointing of the right arm of the person initiated that it might be made strong to avenge the blood of the prophets.

These revelations should prove a valuable source to any novelist who wishes to repeat the success of " A Study in Scarlet " and other popular representations of Mormon terrorism. If, however, we find them too gruesome for acceptance, we may excuse our unbelief by appealing to the minority report, which dismisses altogether the evidence as to the obligations contracted in the endowment oath, asserting that it is " limited in amount, vague and indefinite in character, and utterly unreliable because of the disreputable and untrustworthy character of the witnesses." On the other hand, it is at least equally open to us to accept as trust-worthy the evidence thus impugned, for it is so accepted—at any rate as far as the oath of vengeance is concerned—by the majority members. It may also be worth while to mention an incident to which the attention of the Committee was called during the inquiry. At a meeting held at Eureka, Utah, Bishop Daniel Connolly, commenting on the proceedings at Washington, denounced as "traitors" those who had revealed the endowment oaths, and said he "had known traitors to be shot." When taken to task for the violence of his language the Bishop explained that he was indignant at the witnesses who had violated their oath, but that if he had known there was a reporter present he would have been more guarded. It is surely not without significance that a Mormon bishop, speaking without a view to publication, should have accused these witnesses not of lying but of breaking faith. It may be added that this evidence, even in some of its most sensational features, agrees with that taken before a Judge of the United States Court in Utah in 1889 in the case of certain Mormon aliens who applied for admission to American citizenship.

Much interesting information was supplied respecting the business concerns of the Mormon Church. This section of the evidence may appear to have little connection with the main subject of inquiry, but it was probably admitted as bearing upon the general question of the power exercised by the hierarchy, and no doubt contributed to the finding of the Committee that the Mormon leaders "claim divine authority to control the members of said Church in all things, temporal as well as spiritual." How political and commercial activities may work together was shown by a witness from Idaho, who attributed to the authority of the Mormon Church the passing in that State of a bill placing a bounty of one cent a pound on all sugar manufactured within its borders in 1903, and half-a-cent a pound on that manufactured in 1904. It was estimated that the bounty amounted to $76,000 in 1903 and to $150,000 in 1904. There are four sugar refineries in Idaho, and the Mormon president is at the head of three of them. Another witness, Mr. C. A. Smurthwaite, who had lived in Ogden,

Utah, for more than twenty years, and had contributed largely to the Mormon funds, told a remarkable story. In 1904 he was establishing independent salt works. President Smith regarded this enterprise as competing with the salt works run by the Church, and commanded Mr. Smurthwaite to desist on pain of being ruined by the cutting of rates. This command was not obeyed, and in consequence Mr. Smurthwaite was summarily excommunicated. The Church salt company at once reduced the price of crude salt from eight to two dollars a ton. This not only rendered it impossible for the independent company to make any profit, but destroyed its credit with the banks. The same witness estimated that President Smith was receiving from $1,500,000 to $2,000,000 a year in tithes, and added that no accounting had ever been made for income from this source. It is only fair to state that in May of last year an announcement appeared in the press of the United States to the effect that the Mormon Church had decided to withdraw from all its business enterprises. The reason given for this change of policy was that the converts and newcomers whom the Church thought it expedient to protect years ago were now able to maintain their commercial standing without its assistance. Journalistic opinion, however, is inclined to regard this reform as not unconnected with the publicity given to the Senate investigation.

I have now outlined the most prominent features of the evidence and of the Committee's report. It remains to summarise the net results of the whole investigation. In the first place, the attack upon the Senator from Utah has proved a fiasco. The fact that Mr. Smoot himself is not a polygamist distinguishes his case at once from that of the Mormon official who was excluded from the House of Representatives in 1900 for the reason that he had broken the law against plural marriage. The argument drawn by the Committee from the possibility of conflict between his obligations to the United States Government and to the Mormon Church was obviously a doubtful ground for rejection. The extent to which a Senator may justifiably go in promoting or safeguarding non-political causes—business interests, for example—is a delicate problem of casuistry, and not a few Senators would be made personally anxious by any judgment which seriously restricted their freedom in this respect. And the alleged responsibility of Mr. Smoot for the sins of omission and commission that can be laid at the door of the Mormon hierarchy is discounted by the evidence that, in the words of the minority report, "he has never at any time, and particularly he has not since the manifesto of 1890, countenanced or encouraged plural marriages," but that, on the contrary, he has exerted his influence "to effect a complete discontinuance of such marriages." It is true that he has "silently acquiesced" in the polygamous cohabitation continued from the earlier period, but, as the minority report is careful to point out, even Congress itself might reasonably be charged with sharing this indifference.

But while the promoters of the anti-Smoot agitation have failed in their immediate purpose they have at least succeeded in impressing the country with the gravity of the problem. The investigation has entirely dispelled the comfortable belief that polygamous practices had been brought to an end, and that the Mormon Church had been loyal to the agreement with the United States Government in virtue of which Utah was admitted to Statehood. It is not merely a question of the continuance of the polygamous relationships entered into before the 1890 manifesto, though even in that matter the Mormon distinction between polygamy and polygamous cohabitation has not hitherto been adequately appreciated by the outside world. The majority report, as already noted, deliberately accuses the Church of countenancing and encouraging not only the continuance of previous relationships, but also the contracting of new plural marriages. It also shows, by quotations from official publications, that the Mormons are instructed to believe that the revelation approving polygamy is of higher authority than the manifesto forbidding it.

While the exposure of these conditions is sufficient to arouse anxiety respecting the social welfare of the region dominated by Mormonism, a no less serious political situation is brought to light by the deliberate pronouncement of the Senate Committee that there exists in that region an *imperium in imperio.* If, as is by no means unlikely, the Democratic party should gain considerable accessions during the next few years and thus threaten the present Republican supremacy, the Mormon vote might easily turn the scale in national politics. It is generally recognised that in Utah the Mormon leaders control all the political offices, that in Idaho and Wyoming no one can be elected to any such office without their consent, and that their authority is considerable and is increasing in Montana, Nevada, Oregon, and Colorado, to say nothing of the Territories of Arizona and New Mexico. It must be remembered that in the composition of the Federal Senate every State in the Union, irrespective of its population, is represented by two members, so that the combined vote of Utah and Idaho, representing a total population of 438,521, counts for just as much as that of New York and Pennsylvania, representing 13,571,009. As long as the Mormon vote is worth so much at Washington it is almost hopeless to expect any action to be taken for the enforcement of the law in the face of the opposition of the Mormon Church. The history of this very investigation casts a strong light upon the zeal of the politicians. If the Senate Committee had wished, it might easily have completed its inquiry in the spring or summer of 1904, so that the Senate might have settled the case before the end of the long session. But there was to be a Presidential election in November, and it was expedient that the situation should not be complicated by any decision on this disturbing question. "Careful handling of the Smoot case," said the *New York Evening Post,*[1] "becomes more necessary as the campaign advances. The staunch Republicans of the Senate Committee have a difficult course to steer. If at any time before November 8 Smoot's unseating appears probable, Utah and her three neighbours are more likely than not to appear in the Democratic column. On the other hand, the least intimation that the Mormon apostle may retain his seat may cost the support of a host of high-minded people in the close [2] States of the East and Middle West." The League of Women's Societies sent an anti-polygamy "plank"

[1] May 3, 1904.
[2] A "close" State is one in which the two parties are closely matched.

to both parties previous to the National Conventions of that year, with an appeal for its incorporation in the " platform." The Democratic Convention accepted this suggestion, but the Republicans were too adroit to risk the loss of the Mormon States by any such pronouncement. By the summer of 1906 the reports of the Committée had been presented. Why did not the Senate come to the vote before adjourning? Again the *Evening Post*[1] supplies an answer. " The Republicans unquestionably fear that Smoot's unseating will cause the loss of the group of Rocky Mountain States where the Mormon vote holds the balance of power. . . . There is not any doubt that the Republican managers want the case to rest until another election is over." It was not a Presidential election this time, but an election of the State Legislatures which would have the duty of choosing Federal Senators. The stiffest fight was in Idaho, where the retiring Senator, Mr. F. T. Dubois, was a candidate for re-election. During the last few years Mr. Dubois has done more than any other man to open the eyes of the American public to the Mormon peril, and has come to be regarded as the protagonist of the opposition to the Mormon power. The whole authority of the Church was consequently brought to bear against him. Those who cherish the fond belief that Mr. Roosevelt is not a " party man " will probably be surprised to hear that this authority was seconded by the influence of the President of the United States, who sent a leading member of his cabinet, Secretary Taft, all the way to Idaho to speak against Mr. Dubois. The ostensible reason of this Presidential interference was the need of assisting the forces of " law and order " to cope with certain labour troubles which had arisen in the State. The strength of this plea may be estimated from the fact that any such issue was entirely ignored in the " platform " of the Idaho Republican Convention. Mr. Dubois, in protesting to the President that the only question before the electorate was that of Mormonism, invited him to test that statement by obtaining the opinion of the United States district judges, marshals, attorneys, or any other federal officers in the State. However, the net result of

[1] June 12, 1906.

the election was the defeat of Mr. Dubois, and the establishment in Idaho of the "law and order" of which the polygamous band at Salt Lake City are such admirable defenders and exponents.

To-day the power of Mormonism in American politics is more firmly set than when Mr. Smoot was elected. Its present beneficiary is the Republican party, because that party alone can reciprocate its services. Should the Democrats gain control at Washington, there can be little doubt that there would be a modification of the instructions sent to Mormon voters from head-quarters. The hierarchy would show as great versatility as the Erie Railway in Jay Gould's time in adapting itself to contemporary political conditions. Nor is it likely that the Democrats would be any more scrupulous than the Republicans in their attitude to Mormon support, especially as it would be so easy to justify a policy of non-interference on the ground of the favourite Democratic principle of State Rights. The only hope is in the growth of a national sentiment powerful enough to punish with certain defeat any party that ventured to purchase Mormon votes by complicity with Mormon lawlessness.

HERBERT W. HORWILL

THE FINANCE COMMISSION IN MACEDONIA

THERE is a general impression in England that the reforms introduced in Macedonia by the Powers as a result of the last revolt are a fraud and an imposture. It is perfectly true that the Porte was able to contract their scope and impair their efficacy by playing upon the jealousies of the Powers and the reluctance of Austria and Russia to co-operate with the English, French and Italian Governments in the imposition of drastic changes. Nevertheless something has been done, a beginning has been made, which might, if developed under favourable conditions, result in a real amelioration of life in Macedonia. But time presses. Can the pace of Macedonian reform be accelerated sufficiently to anticipate the day of a foreign war or of a general insurrection? That will depend upon the support given to the men who compose the Financial Commission. The operations of this international body are indeed severely restricted; but let us avoid the error of supposing that its control over the three vilayets of Macedonia is purely nominal. Its influence, though small, is real. Its first function is to examine the budget. Unfortunately army expenditure (about two-thirds of the total) is excluded from its purview at present, and the Commission has to confine itself to the items of civil administration, including, however, the police and rural gendarmerie.

As a matter of fact this year's budget has been severely criticised both as regards expenditure and taxation. Though the Commissioners are supposed to be incompetent to deal with military expenditure, they can and do use their influence and authority to correct and amend fiscal abuses throughout the three vilayets of Macedonia. Their difficulties are enormous. One member of the Commission belongs to a country whose system of administration and finance stands only second to that of Turkey in the European black list. Another is accredited to a government which openly proclaims its adherence to the *status quo* in Turkey, and another adopts the same attitude in the hope of obtaining for his clients valuable concessions and commercial privileges from the sublime Porte. Even if some of the reformers were not half-hearted, reforms would be difficult enough for two reasons. First, the Sultan will fight hard against any measure excepting Macedonia from the general system. In a certain sense it is true that when you break up the fiscal and administrative uniformity of the Ottoman Empire you break up the Empire itself. Again, no real reform can be *executed* in Turkey until the Turkish officials are removed or placed in subordination to independent European authority. Turkish officials are more than the instruments of a bad system. They are themselves an abuse of the first order. If the Turkish system were administered by honest, well-paid and competent men, it would no longer be the Turkish system. If any one doubt this let him consider how Egypt was made prosperous by Lord Cromer.

But let us see what has been done. In each vilayet there is now an inspector who acts under the Commission and reports upon abuses. Some tax-gatherers have already been convicted and punished, and some irregular taxation has been put an end to.

On the initiative of Mr. Harvey, the British Representative on the Commission, several important steps have been taken. The heads of the villages have received lists in French, Turkish, Bulgarian, Servian and Greek, of the taxes they are legally bound to pay, and the villagers have been made to understand that these taxes and these alone can legally be enforced. This simple measure will undoubtedly put a stop to many cruel exactions, and is in itself a revolution ; for, incredible as it may seem, there is no record of such a thing having ever before been published in Turkey. Happily there is also some machinery for redress. All complaints made in the localities are examined by the Commission through its inspectors, and the tax-gatherers are under their supervision. All the local registers and accounts are now being examined, and leakages are being stopped. The Commission, indeed, is protector of the fisc as well as of the taxpayer, and perhaps it is a shrewd perception of this fact that has made the impecunious Government of Turkey a little more yielding at times than might have been expected.

A considerable sum of money nominally assigned to agriculture under the head of the Agricultural Bank attracted the attention of our Commissioner, who suspected that the sums passed into the bank for the encouragement of agriculture were not being applied to that purpose. By persistent pressure an Imperial irade has been obtained which orders that the revenue earmarked for agriculture (about £50,000) shall henceforth be properly employed. This is a real-advance ; but it must not blind our eyes to what is the real obstacle to agriculture in Macedonia— namely, the insecurity of life and property, due to a combination of Moslem misrule with racial and religious animosities. Nor can this security, which is the basis of all improvement, be established without justice and police. In Macedonia justice consists of wrongful sentences tempered by Consular redress and protest. The police is not only weak and inefficient, but so ill-paid that it cannot be other than corrupt. At the present time, owing to the murderous activity of Greek and Servian bands whose attacks upon Bulgarian and Vlach villages are tolerated, if not encouraged, by the Turkish authorities, the state of Macedonia is actually more wretched and more perilous to the peace of Europe than for some time past.

A report has been prepared by Mr. Harvey upon the taxes in the three vilayets, from which it appears that many are small, vexatious and unproductive. It is to be hoped that in the course of time the criticisms based on this report, and the study which the Commission is giving, will lead to important and beneficial results. The system of taxation seems to press unduly and disproportionately on agriculturists, while the towns get off with comparatively small contributions. Thus the taxes on sheep, pigs and horses are peculiarly vexatious and unpopular. Their actual yield is quite disproportionate to the amount entered in the books, and is said to be diminishing year by year. The personal tax has produced so much unrest throughout the Ottoman Empire that it has just been abolished by an irade and at the same time the tax on domestic animals has been repealed. Thus the work of the Finance Commission in Macedonia has contributed to relieve agriculturists throughout the Turkish dominions. An attempt is also being made to amend the collection of the tithe, another tax very unequal in its incidence. But here again the difficulty of reform is enormous, because the tithe, like so many other Turkish taxes, has been mortgaged for the service of debt. The Empire has so long been on the verge of bankruptcy and financial ruin that one hesitates to prophesy; but in the opinion of shrewd observers in Macedonia and Turkey, a collapse is imminent if the double strain of extraordinary military expenditure in the Yemen and in Macedonia should last much longer. The raising of customs duties is the last desperate measure sanctioned by the Powers; but no power on earth can prevent the misapplication and absorption of revenues in the bureaux of Constantinople so long as Turkey continues to be administered by the Turks.

But what is perhaps an even greater grievance than the taxes themselves is the fact that the people of Macedonia derive practically no benefit from them. The army, which eats up the lion's share of the revenue, gives no security to the villagers, but only keeps before them the grim spectre of massacre. Up to the present time practically the only expenditure from which any economic benefit is derived is the annual sum (about £330,000) that is applied to sustain the railways built under the system of "kilometric guarantees." Nor has the wit of man ever devised a more wasteful system of creating and maintaining railways than this. Until the last two or three years almost nothing had been spent on the repair of roads or bridges ; in fact, there are hardly any roads to repair. Many of the so-called roads are only tracks, and many of the bridges which once existed have disappeared under Turkish rule. Apart from the railways, which serve strips of Macedonia, the means of transport are far worse than they were at the time when St.

Paul wrote his epistles to the Thessalonians, or when the Emperor Galerius constructed his *porta triumphalis* over the main street of Thessalonica.   It is only during the last three or four years that the magnificent Roman bridge at Uskub, which spanned three-quarters of the river (the last arch having been destroyed long ago in military operations), was restored by a local Bulgarian.   Uskub, the second town of Macedonia, has 30,000 inhabitants and a garrison of 10,000 Turkish troops.   There is not a single macadamised road, not a single decently paved street, nor any system of drainage.   Yet the Turkish municipality has lately spent £4,000 on the erection of a local theatre—a grim joke to perpetrate in a place where laughter is unknown and where every one lives in daily fear of being robbed or murdered !   Nor is there any respect for persons.   A few weeks ago the Acting British Vice-Consul was seized not far from the town, and stripped of all his valuables by a couple of armed brigands.   If our Foreign Office is really competent and willing, this incident, and the kidnapping of Mr. Abbott in Salonica, should serve as a powerful lever for real reform.   We ought to insist upon the establishment of an effective European police in every considerable town of Macedonia.   Then at last a start would have been made, the people would begin to hope, and the work of the Financial Commission would bear fruit.

A Recent Traveller in the Balkans

WHAT DOES LORD AVEBURY WANT ? [1]

I HAVE heard that a Moderate candidate in the late L.C.C. election was very nearly induced to withdraw and join the Progressives by a perusal of Lord Avebury *On Municipal and National Trading.* I can well believe the story. The body of the work consists of snippets from such authorities as Mr. Holt Schooling's magazine articles, Mr. G. R. Sims' bitter cry in the *Tribune,* and the observations of an American professor who has been very roughly handled by another American professor of the same surname. What can be done with an author who quotes Mr. Holt Schooling's egregious calculation that municipalities make a loss of five and a half millions because they do not put by annually five per cent. on the outstanding capital of their reproductive undertakings in addition to providing one and one-third per cent. for repayment of capital, and then says :

> " I do not pretend to be an authority as to what percentage ought to be written off for depreciation, but Mr. Schooling has had a long experience in such matters, and is well qualified to judge " ?

It is almost incredible that it should never have struck Lord Avebury to ask himself whether British railway companies, for which he has the highest admiration, British water, gas, and tramway companies, and all the other companies working such classes of business, are in the habit of

---

[1] *On Municipal and National Trading.* By the Right Hon. Lord Avebury, P.C. Macmillan and Co. 1906.

putting by even one and a third per cent., to say nothing of six and a third per cent., annually for depreciation. If Mr. Schooling is right, nine-tenths of the commercial institutions and individuals in the country are on the high road to bankruptcy, and it is difficult to see how the banks which confidingly lend them money can escape sharing their fate.

To examine such a work as this in detail would be unworthy of a serious periodical. But something of value may be got out of the book if we can discover from it what Lord Avebury really wants. If we can do that, we shall know what the ordinary average ill-informed and prejudiced anti-municipalist really wants. When Lord Avebury quotes Mr. Schooling and Mr. Sims as authorities and tells us what an American said about our tramway system, and what a friend who happens to be a gas-company director, and therefore must know, said about municipal gas, we seem to be listening to the man on the 'bus.

What then does Lord Avebury want, with regard to the institutions commonly associated in our minds with municipal trading, of which the supply of water, gas, electricity and tramways are the principal? It is easy enough to say what the company promoter wants: it is that the first person who asks should be given all the requisite powers, and should be allowed to take possession of the subsoil, or the surface of the public streets, and to inconvenience the wayfarer by continual repairs and alterations to his property, without paying a penny for his privileges and without incurring any obligations. But this is too preposterous to be openly claimed. A water company in possession of the only source of supply and with unrestricted powers of charging would be able to appropriate to itself nearly the whole ground value of a town. It is easier to find substitutes for gas, electricity, and trams than for water, and consequently the results of unrestricted powers in these cases would not be quite so striking, as is shown, for example, by the fact that the Gas Light and Coke Company has recently been selling gas at a penny below what it is entitled to charge under its sliding scale. But they would be the same in principle, and the unrestricted "franchise," as the Americans call it, would in most considerable places sell for a large sum, if put up to a fair auction. Lord Avebury admits this at any rate of tramways when he complains that London (and by implication other towns) were enabled by the "unfortunate" Tramway Act of 1870 to become possessed of the tramway property "for a sum far below its real value" (p. 74). The "real value" in Lord Avebury's mind is obviously the value of the concession of exclusive rights to run railways in the streets in perpetuity, as opposed to the value actually paid for under the Tramways Act in pursuance of a bargain which historical documents show to have been perfectly well-understood at the time it was made, namely, the value of the plant and other material objects taken as parts of a working tramway.

Outside London, which sometimes seems to a mere "provincial" to be outgrowing sentient capacity, nobody interested as ratepayer or owner in a particular town has the least wish to make a present of a valuable "franchise" or concession to the first person who asks for it, or to the first person or set of persons who commands enough "influence" either with the local or the central authority. If Lord Avebury and his friends, or such of them as have a real desire to benefit the public, would only take this obvious fact to heart, they would see that in order to diminish municipal trading without introducing or rather increasing corrupt influences, they must discover and popularise alternative means of retaining the whole or most of the value of the perpetual franchise for the ratepayers, and ultimately for the owners, or, what comes in the end to much the same thing, to the consumers.

In the water and gas period of the nineteenth century it was hoped to reserve the value to the consumers by the plan of prescribing maximum charges and maximum dividends. The result is thus described by Lord Avebury on p. 87, when he asks us to "look at the West Middlesex Company," which, as he says, "was paying its maximum dividend. The shareholders are (*sic*) entitled to no more. If the profits increased, the directors were bound to reduce the price of water. Indeed, they had already done so to some extent. In fact, therefore, the so-called shareholders were preference shareholders. The ratepayers had a valuable property in the company." Lord Avebury seems incapable of seeing that if the so-called shareholders were preference shareholders, the [water-] ratepayers must have been the ordinary shareholders, and that he is a municipal trader *malgré lui*. Can anything be much more grotesque than this recommendation, by an ardent individualist, of a system which resulted in putting the management of a business capable of paying its preference dividend and more, in the hands of the preference shareholders? What becomes of the appeal to the efficiency of self-interest? Lord Avebury unconsciously answers himself on this head when he commends the gas sliding-scale system because the plan "not only gives the consumer a share in increased profits, but also gives the companies a motive for economy." In other words, the "so-called shareholders" who were really "preference shareholders" had to be bribed with offers of dividend beyond the prescribed maximum in order to induce them to give the unrepresented consumers the advantage of diminishing cost of production. The remedy, such as it is, has been adopted not only, as Lord Avebury tells us twice on two consecutive pages, "in London and several other" places, but in over two hundred, as is well known to those who think it necessary to look at obvious sources of information such as the Board of Trade Gas-Company Return before attempting to instruct the public on municipal trade. The sliding-scale system, whatever its merits in regard to gas, does not seem easy to apply to other services, and no one seems to have suggested that it can well be applied to water or tramways. Certainly Lord Avebury does not.

By the time street railroads, as the Americans, with their eye for the reality of things, call tramways, began to be introduced, the maximum dividend plan was discredited, and after consideration it was decided not to apply it to the new invention, but to adopt instead the plan of allowing local authorities either to construct tramways themselves and lease the working to companies, or to give companies concessions to construct and work, terminable at the end of twenty-one years if the local authority should then determine to pay for the plant valued not as old iron, but as plant used in a going concern. The terms of this second alternative were carefully discussed at the time, and it is on record in the minutes of evidence taken before select committees and elsewhere that they were perfectly well understood by every one concerned, and that the actual wording of the important clause was the result of suggestions made on behalf of the corporations by the Town Clerk of Manchester with the view of preventing good-will being " edged in." Now, strange as it may appear, Lord Avebury seems to have no objection to the first alternative offered by the Tramways Act, nor even, perhaps, to its extension to other enterprises. On p. 92 he says :—" I question whether any man of business will doubt for a moment that if our municipalities would lease their gas-works, tramways, and electric lighting concerns, and (sic) without any increase of charges, it would be a substantial boon to the ratepayers, and do much to reduce our rates." This, perhaps, is not conclusive, as Lord Avebury may have in his mind " of course it would be better still to sell the concerns outright, and still better never to have touched them." But three pages earlier he says, " the amount received from the tramway lines which are leased must, of course, be deducted from any estimate of profit on municipal trading," so that in his opinion to own a tramway is not municipal trading, and the general trend of the book is to show that everything which is municipal trading is wrong, and everything which is not is right. We may take it then that in Lord Avebury's opinion Glasgow and Manchester were quite right, and gave a " substantial boon to the ratepayers " as well as did " much to reduce the rates " when they constructed the old horse lines, and leased them to companies, and that towns which have adopted the same policy with regard to the modern electric lines have equally done well. But if this is so, if there is no harm in municipal ownership, what becomes of all the clamour about the ruinous increase of municipal debt ? According to Lord Avebury " the United Kingdom has practically the same urban population as the United States ; therefore it should have about the same urban street railway track mileage, namely, 14,000 miles," or about four times as much as it has. Imagination boggles at the thought of what Lord Avebury and his friends would say if the local authorities borrowed enough to make up this alleged deficiency.

It is difficult, therefore, to feel quite satisfied that Lord Avebury's solution of the tramway question is to be found in the first alternative offered by the "deadly" or "unfortunate" Tramways Act. What then is his real desire? In one place (p. 101) he seems to agree with his American authority for British matters, Mr. Meyer, that Dublin did very well to get $70,000 a year as wayleave from the Dublin tramway company; but generally in the scattered pages which deal with tramways in his most disorderly book any attempt on the part of a local authority to make any sort of bargain with tramway promoters is regarded as the height of wickedness, and it is mere levying of "blackmail" for a local authority even to insist on a street being widened before a portion of it is partly withdrawn from ordinary use by a tramline! So abominably wicked is this last action that even the fact that it obstructs the L.C.C. in its municipal trading and accumulation of debt does not condone the offence. There is therefore some ground for believing that Lord Avebury agrees with the permanent officers of the two Houses of Parliament who really govern this country in all matters for which private bill legislation is required. Although the right to run tramways is obviously of enormously different value in different districts, these gentlemen have held that it ought to be granted on the same terms in all districts, and have therefore refused even to allow proposals for wayleaves to be put before the committees of the Houses which fondly imagine that they determine the fate of legislation. If it had not been for this hindrance to the arrangement of reasonable terms, many more municipalities would have made arrangements with companies instead of doing the work themselves. Lord Avebury and his friends are simply kicking against the pricks of common-sense when they propose that concessions should be given away for less than they are worth. They have some dim consciousness of the fact, and hence arises the extraordinary confusion and contradiction which is characteristic of their writings, and of their proposals for a policy, when they are rash enough to make any. What can be done with a writer who

complains that " the municipal tramways on the other hand "
(*i. e.* as contrasted with railways), " have been constructed
without any payment for the roads along which they run ;
they have even been carried outside the district of the
authority which operates them," and yet desires company
tramways to be constructed without any payment or any
equivalent for payment ?   Perhaps to be perfectly fair, we
should say any equivalent beyond the cost of maintaining
the road between the rails and eighteen inches outside the
rails, since there is nothing to show that Lord Avebury
disapproves of that blackmailing provision of the deadly
Tramways Act.   On the other hand, however, there is
nothing to show that he approves of that provision or even
of the companies being obliged to maintain their rails.

EDWIN CANNAN

CROSS CURRENTS IN PHILANTHROPY[1]

W E are apt to be puzzled by the war of contend-
ing factions in the cause of industrial betterment.
Why should they fight at all ?   They have the
same aim ; progress and reform are the watchwords of each,
and their efforts appear to be disinterested.   Yet they are at
war, and the fighting is not less fierce because the causes of
it are obscure.   Could anything seem more reasonable than
a policy which aims at securing industrial peace by profit-
sharing and co-operation, industrial welfare by thrift and
small investments, industrial efficiency by skilled training
and apprenticeship ?   It is something of a shock to the
onlooker to find that, in the eyes of the leaders from a

---

[1] LIST OF BOOKS REVIEWED

Glimpses into the Abyss. By Mary Higgs. P. S. King and Son. 3*s*. 6*d*. net.
The Children of the Nation. By Sir John Gorst. Methuen. 7*s*. 6*d*. net.
The Next Street but One. By M. Loane. Arnold. 6*s*.
Report on the Physical Condition of Fourteen Hundred School Children. By
the Edinburgh Charity Organisation Society. P. S. King and Son. 5*s*. net.
Women's Work and Wages. By E. Cadbury, Cecile Matheson and George
Shann. Fisher Unwin. 6*s*.

350

different camp, profit-sharing is but an insidious dodge of the capitalist, thrift and saving a senseless if not actively dangerous habit, and apprenticeship a misunderstood relic of a dead system. We think we can safely applaud the model factory and the garden city,—until we are startled by the proclamation from the other side that the one is a degrading sop, and the other a gilded gage for deluded labourers. What does it all mean? In the familiar field of national politics we are accustomed to the party warfare, and may be content to explain it by a reference to inherited prejudices and instincts based upon unconscious self-interest. In the newer politics of industry a similar explanation may perhaps serve. The aim of the rival factions is only nominally the same; actually both end and means are determined for each by subtle undercurrents of thought and feeling, due sometimes to position and possessions, or the want of them, sometimes to hidden prejudices inherited from feudal days, or quite opposite prejudices due to an experience which dissociates the present from the past and links it to an ideal future.

In the field of philanthropy, however, and of general social reform, where the same oppositions are painfully evident, a different explanation is needed. The advocates of rival policies are here disinterested, not apparently but really. All alike aim at the betterment of lives less fortunate than their own, and, more often than not, they are united by identity of class and a similar experience of life. Yet they too split into hostile camps. Do but mention the free provision of food for unfed children, of pensions for the old, of work for the workless, of shelter for the homeless, and you will be applauded with enthusiasm or crushed with chilling disapproval according to the camp in which you happen to be. Clearly in these cases we must go behind the causes of class prejudice or self-interest. These do not explain why Sir John Gorst and Dr. Macnamara are on one side, and Sir Arthur Clay and Mr. C. S. Loch on the other, nor why Mrs. Higgs faces one way, and Miss Loane and Mrs. Bosanquet the exactly opposite way. It is not a question of Socialism *versus* Individualism; still less of Want *versus* Wealth. What then?

At bottom, the cause seems to lie in the difference of view-point, due to a difference of analysis of the problems and a concentration upon different aspects of the lives which all alike are anxious to raise. The opposing factions do not see the same problems; the remedies they offer are aimed at different evils. Their proposals conflict with one another, we say: it would be truer to say that they do not meet at all, for they are worked out upon different planes of thought, with premises drawn from different elements in the lives considered. And then the question arises whether they may not after all be complementary rather than contradictory, and whether a fusion of the premises may not lead to a reconciliation of the conclusions.

This difference of view-point, leading to very divergent estimates of social problems and remedies, is well illustrated by some of the books which have recently attracted attention. These may be divided roughly into two classes, according to the method of inquiry adopted, in turn depending upon the attitude and line of approach on the part of the inquirers. In the one class, the inquirer stands outside his subject matter, his eyes fixed upon the conditions, the structure, the circumstances, and the material setting of the evil examined, not upon the lives themselves in which the evil is manifested. In the other class, the view is essentially internal and intimate. Penetrating beneath the structure, the inquirer attempts to present the evil in terms of life and character; to depict it, not as a mass of suffering but as a medley of light and shade, of good and ill; the sufferings of the people being sometimes self-caused rather than superimposed, the want always relative to *their* needs and capacities, not to ours, and the whole to be judged from within as well as from without. The remedies demanded are then seen to be not simple but very complex,— innumerable indeed, and all depending upon growth of character and function, not upon change of circumstance and structure.

We are far from assuming that the one view is right, the other wrong; still less that the two are incompatible. The work of Mr. Charles Booth has shown that both can be combined, to some extent at least. But it is certainly true that in all social inquiries, even as in his, one characteristic or the other tends to predominate, and determines the result. And, as a consequence, the literature of practical sociology is marked increasingly by a one-sidedness amounting to more or less bitter partisanship.

As an example of the external view-point we may take first Mrs. Higgs' *Glimpses into the Abyss.* The title suggests the impressionist of the style of Mr. Jack London; and though the comparison is not a fair one, since Mrs. Higgs has given much more than six weeks to the study of the vagrant, it is fair to say that where Mr. London erred there too she errs, as all do err who make a short and sudden plunge into a preconceived inferno. Their estimate can never be a true one, any more than Dr. Johnson's estimate of the Highlands was a true one. Alien eyes are as incapable of seeing the truth as Fleet Street spectacles. So, when we read the book to discover what are the sufferings of the tramp, we learn instead what were the sufferings of Mrs. Higgs herself when subjected to the conditions of a tramp's life. That is of value, doubtless; it is an index to the evil nature of the conditions and the treatment. But that is not enough; we must know more of the nature of the tramp before we can condemn the treatment of him as utterly inhuman or senselessly repressive. What *is* he or she? How comes he to be an outcast? What degree of repression is made necessary, what amount of encouragement is made possible, by the evil and the good in him or in her? Mrs. Higgs does not really tell us. The remedies she suggests may be excellent: her plea for a change in our three-century-old treatment of the vagrant is in accordance with the recommendations of the Vagrancy Committee. But, setting aside the male tramps, we have a right to ask for more information about the female vagrant whom Mrs. Higgs has made her special concern. A few statistics, a few descriptions of filthy lodging-houses, may take us half-way to a decision as to remedies. But what is the nature of the homeless woman, and how comes she to be on the road? We are given a theoretical account of the manufacture of derelict womanhood. We are told that women " on the road " are almost forced to become women "on the street."

We read of one or two instances of girls left stranded and temporarily homeless. We also read much about the disintegration of the home. With all the emphasis of italics it is urged that " the home must be made the centre of all our thought, the focus of national consciousness." We are told to attack the causes of the nomad life, and so on. But the outstanding feature of the book—its plea for a shelter and a common lodging–house for women in every town in the kingdom—hangs in the air, out of connection with the evidence, apparently at variance with the writer's own sentiments, and supported only by the discovery that the existing conditions of the vagrant's life are execrably bad. Mrs. Higgs rather strengthens than upsets the conviction that the shelter life and the common lodging-house life are anti-social, and that the true line of reform lies, not in the indefinite multiplication of municipal shelters and lodging-houses, but in the expansion of her own principle that " it belongs to womanhood to befriend womanhood." A woman friend in every town, by all means—with all which that implies; but not a permanent abode for the nomads. Mrs. Higgs succeeds in enlisting our sympathy, but fails to convince us by her arguments, just because her analysis is not carried deep enough. The conditions of the tramp-life are only one side of it, and that the external side.

A very different book may be taken as an illustration of a similar failure. Sir John Gorst's *Children of the Nation* is an eloquent plea for the State care of the children of the poor. It is full of trenchant criticism of existing conditions, of which the very existence is taken as evidence of our national neglect. The criticisms are doubtless valid, and the conclusions follow from the premises. But both premises and conclusions are conditional, in the sense that they apply only so long as we consider the external conditions by themselves. Of course a system of State feeding and medical care, (with strict punishment of neglect,) is better, *as a system*, than the *status quo*, whereby every young life is left to the mercy of haphazard combinations of neglect and care. But that is not enough: the system has value only as it fits the whole social life to which it is relative; and the best systematisation of conditions may fail horribly if it is in disharmony with the life-motives upon which it is imposed. Like Mrs. Higgs, Sir John Gorst may be right. But the statistics of physical defects, used to build up a dark picture of social waste, do not, by themselves, prove his point.

We may turn now to illustrations of the opposite point of view, which we have described as internal and intimate. Nothing could be more marked than the contrast between the two books already referred to and Miss M. Loane's *The Next Street but One*, or the *Report* on the children of a single school in Edinburgh compiled by the Charity Organisation Society of that city. In both of these, widely as they differ from one another, there appears the characteristic of close observation of individual lives ; and the picture presented is therefore an extraordinarily complex one. Miss Loane's book is a series of pictures of the actual and many-sided lives of poor people, drawn with an appreciation and knowledge only possessed by one who has really entered into those lives, and lived close to them for years. She finds nothing " abysmal : " to hint such a thing would be to insult the poor. There is much to pity ; still more to admire ; much to condemn, too, though not nearly as much as in the stupid and insolent " charity " of many of the rich. The lives in mean streets are seen to be as other lives are— only harder, and therefore often braver ; never necessarily hopeless ; usually full of the germs of good, the development of which may be checked for a while, but not inevitably stifled, by the conditions of the life. Remedies ? There is only one remedy for imperfect life—to grow better ; but that means a many-sided growth in which every element of character, and *therefore* of circumstance, is involved.

Now, of such a book only one criticism is possible. It is too optimistic, and just a little blind to the big issues. In watching the life, the observer has lost sight of the " oppression of circumstance," even as the observer of the external class loses sight of the buoyancy of life. From one extreme—too much attention to structure—we have passed to the other—too much neglect of the influence of structure. Undue concentration of view upon the outside is met by equally undue concentration upon the inside. Miss Loane certainly sees the life of the poor from within and at close quarters. She sees the vast potentiality of independence and interdependence, compared with which the power of improved mechanism is mere impotence. She sees the absurdity of the " benevolist," and despises his institutions, which, after all, are intended to fit people to live outside them, not inside. But in the very closeness of her view of the life, she almost fails to realise the power of its external setting. Too low a wage spells immorality, she says ; an intermittent wage spells thriftlessness, we may add. But what then of the conditions of industry which so largely determine the lowness and irregularity of the wage ? What of the anæmia traceable to intermittent service, and the consumption due to home-work ? After all, the life is sometimes at the mercy of a system not always visible to the close observer.

Optimism, however, is not always a result of the close scrutiny. The Report on the Edinburgh School children is the reverse of optimistic. It is a cold and matter-of-fact presentment of the physical, mental, and moral condition of 1400 children from a poor school, based on a systematic investigation worthy of the reputation for thoroughness which the Charity Organisation Society has earned. Every family—781 in all—was visited carefully ; case-papers were compiled for each, with not less than fifty questions asked and answered, and verified by reference to employers, police, clergy and others. And the picture is even gloomier than any sketch of an abyss, and very much more telling. But there is this big difference : we are taken behind the scenes and shown the omnipresent character-causes of the evils. External conditions are not neglected ; bad housing and poor wages are allowed due influence. Yet they are made to seem insignificant by the side of internal conditions— drink, carelessness, laziness and neglect. The picture is thus the complement to that of Sir John Gorst, and points to a different conclusion. What that conclusion is we are not told, but are left to judge for ourselves. Stunted growth, deformities, disease, hunger and dirt, are all admitted and scheduled—a terrible list. But behind them—what ? Take one fact alone : of the 781 families examined only 293 can be called sober ; 425 are found definitely to be drunken, and the remaining 63 suspected of drink. What are we to say now of Sir John Gorst's remedies ? Is this evil to be met by free meals from the State, or any other device of paternal government ? The question almost answers itself. The deeper defects call for subtler cures than any legislative contrivances intended to stop up the obvious holes of want and hunger. Shall we then contentedly leave the matter in the hands of churches and charities ? The Report gives us the answer in the form of one of the most striking commentaries on the futility of voluntary effort which we have ever read. There is no lack of relief ; from church or chapel or charitable funds help is given to 449 families, of whom 135 are sober ! Here are some random samples from a long and monotonous list : " Lots of charitable aid ; both parents drunken." " Food and clothes from school and churches ; parents drunken and lazy." " Church, school, and ladies' help ; father a drunkard and malingerer." " School food for children ; two churches look after them ; both parents drunken ; mother keeps brothels." " C.O.S. and church give help ; both parents drink, children neglected, father in gaol." We are not told whether these are to be taken as statements of cause and effect, or examples of palliatives which do not touch the real evils. In either case the inference is obvious : voluntary philanthropic effort is as impotent as State-aid is mistaken. And so the non-possumus attitude of the C.O.S. becomes intelligible. What on earth *can* be done till drunkenness and fecklessness are changed to sobriety and common prudence ?

It would be easy to multiply instances illustrative of the way in which differences in the line of approach lead to differences in the result of the inquiry. But it would be unfair to imply that the opposing attitudes are never combined. They are sometimes harmonised, especially in books in which two or more people collaborate ; and one example of such combination may be mentioned.

In the excellent account of Women's Work and Wages in Birmingham, the authors have given a very fairly complete picture of the conditions of work and wage in women's industry, together with a really admirable analysis of the life-motives which affect these conditions—the weaknesses and shortcomings, the limitation of outlook, the lack of ambition, the carelessness and instability, to which—in part only—women owe their underpayment. And, as the picture is a fair one, so too the remedies proposed are fairly balanced. If there is a little bias in favour of mechanical devices such as wages-boards and the institution of a national minimum, it is slight ; there is no neglect of the internal improvements which must accompany and vitalise the external remedies.

Now these examples of recent estimates of social problems, and of recommendations for the treatment of them, point to a conclusion which goes some way towards a reconciliation of the rival parties in the cause of social betterment. We are exposed always to two dangers : that of failing to see the trees for the wood, and that of losing sight of the wood for the trees. We fall into one or the other according to the point of view with which we start, and the method of approach we adopt. And once started on this line or on that, we travel on towards something perilously near bigotry. The dangers are sometimes avoided, though not often ; seldom by any single inquirer, especially when general poverty and its attendant evils form the subject of inquiry. And the tendency to over-emphasise one view and neglect the other is increased the further we travel along the road chosen, till at last we end in the definitely hostile camps of Character *versus* Circumstance or Individualism *versus* Socialism. Should the inquirer take the external view, then the more he gazes the more is he impressed by the great patches of black darkness, by the groups, masses, or percentages of lives dragged on in an impossible setting, submerged by the sheer physical disabilities of a too poor existence. No remedies except big ones seem worth considering ; no others can appreciably affect the problem. How far he will go—at what point he will stop along the line that stretches from legal and institutional reform to upheaval and revolution of the social structure—this is a question dependent upon his own idiosyncracy. If he sees an abyss from the view-point of a different world of comfort, cleanliness, and ease, then his sentiment, untempered by reason, is likely to clamour for revolution ; if he succeeds in examining the structure of the evils more dispassionately, he will be content with reform. But a definite change in the conditions of life he will demand in any case. But now suppose the inquirer starts, through the influence of example or accident or some inherited bias, along the other line of approach, which leads below the structure to the complex life within. For him too the terms of the problem and the remedy become more and more surely defined. Daily and hourly accumulations of impressions gathered from constant observation of subtle causes leading to momentous results, in which circumstance seems to play an insignificant part, lead him on to a fixed belief that it is character, and character always, which calls for change. *His* experience is of strong will and courage making a good life out of poverty, of weak will and flabbiness drifting to failure in spite of quite reasonable opportunities. Evils there are everywhere, of course, and of every kind ; vice, drink, thriftlessness, stupidity—*these* are the real evils. And what legislative besom can sweep these away ? What use in free meals or a minimum wage, or even a decent cottage to the 54 per cent. who drink, shirk work, and spoil their lives just as much as circumstances let them ? You may get rid of nits in the hair by your system of washing and inspection, of adenoids by medical attention, or of hunger by meals. But neglect and the drunkard's home ? Or the brothel-keeping mother ? And so the opposite camp is formed, and the fight of warring social principles grows more bitter.

There is a story of a working woman, of poor and very low class, whose standard of life fluctuated with the vicissitudes of a hyacinth in a pot. This " external accident " came into her life quite accidentally, without will or purpose on her part ; but it interested her, appealed to her, turned her from a slut into a good and careful wife ; and her character changed for its sake. But, at the moment of its blooming, it was broken and destroyed ; and with its fall she too fell, back into the ways of the slattern and the drunkard. True, the cause of its fall, and therefore also of hers, was her husband's temper ; character and not mere accident lay behind the change of external circumstance. But, none the less, it was this latter change, and not any change of character, which was the secret of her moral growth and decay. The application of the story is very obvious. We may, and indeed must, separate causes into the two classes, the external and the internal ; we may dwell, and indeed can hardly help dwelling, upon one set to the partial exclusion of the other. But in life there is no such separation ; character and circumstance are inter-twined as the warp and woof of every motive. And the analysis of a social problem and the proposal of a remedy can only be true to life in proportion as they harmonise and bring together the elements which, separable in idea, are in reality inseparable.

E. J. URWICK

₊ It is desirable that no contributions should be sent without previous communication with the Editor, who cannot undertake to return unsolicited MSS.

Address (for postal communications only), 7 Kennington Terrace, S.E. Stamped envelope for return should be enclosed in all cases.

Lightning Source UK Ltd.
Milton Keynes UK
UKHW02f2042060418

320655UK00006B/145/P